MW01168702

Yield Curve Dynamics

State-of-the-Art Techniques for Modeling, Trading, and Hedging

RONALD J. RYAN, Editor

Glenlake Publishing Company, Ltd.
Chicago • London • New Delhi

Fitzroy Dearborn Publishers
Chicago and London

ISBN: 1-888998-06-7

Library edition: Fitzroy Dearborn Publishers, Chicago and London
ISBN: 1-884964-74-5

Printed in the United States of America

1261 West Glenlake
Chicago, Illinois 60660
glenlake@ix.netcom.com

This book is dedicated to the large team of people who have believed in and helped build the many index innovations that make Ryan Labs the finest index design and advisory system in the world. It is also dedicated to the many scholars and practioners who have had the vision and fortitude to pursue index innovations and applications, as represented by the authors of this book.

CONTENTS

PREFACE

The global economy is extremely sensitive to interest rates. Due to decades of borrowing, America and other nations have become debt-laden societies. You would be hard-pressed to find 50 companies in the U.S. Fortune 500 that have more equity than debt on their balance sheets, and these are the United States' largest and best enterprises. Obviously, you cannot buy stock in America, but you can buy our bonds, since debt is the way that we finance our country. It is hard to believe that this young economy is now the largest debtor nation in the world.

All U.S. bonds (debt), and many non-U.S. issues, are priced off of the U.S. Treasury yield curve, which provides the base rates. As a result, these bonds move similarly to the Treasury issues that they are derived or priced from. The Treasury yield curve represents only eight auction issues that are continually refreshed with new issues weekly, monthly, or quarterly. What is amazing is that these eight Treasury auction issues control the yield destiny of all bonds. In fact, most debt is priced from the Treasury yield curve, which forms the cost base. Most mortgage loans, commercial loans, and personal loans are priced as a yield spread off of some maturity-spot on the Treasury yield curve. Indeed, the Treasury yield curve controls the risk/reward behavior of most debt in America, and has a significant impact on the global debt markets as well.

To understand the American economy's past, present, and future, one must study the Treasury yield curve. The future of the American economy—and thus, given the interdependence of world markets, of the global economy—may well rest on the success of how we finance this curve. God bless the Treasury Yield Curve!

Ronald Ryan

CONTRIBUTORS

Y. K. Chan

Dr. Yuen Kwok Chan is a director in the mortgage research group of Salomon Brothers. His current responsibilities include the development of pricing and hedging strategies for mortgage derivatives, factoring in the interacting of interest-rate and prepayment risks. Dr. Chan taught at the University of Washington and worked for Boeing before joining the fixed-income strategies group at Bear Stearns. He has published numerous papers on probability and stochastic processes, and holds two patents on synthetic aperture radars. The two factor term-structure model that he developed has been widely used for mortgage and CMO trading.

D. James Daras

Mr. Daras is an executive vice president and treasurer of the Dime Savings Bank and its parent company Dime Bancorp. In addition, he is the chairman of the bank's asset/liability management committee. Prior to joining Dime Savings in 1990, Mr. Daras was senior vice president and chief financial officer at Cenlar Federal Savings Bank. Mr. Daras holds a B.B.A. degree from George Washington University and an M.B.A. degree from St. John's University.

Gregory Kitter

Mr. Kitter is a director in the marketing area of the Americas Group at Dow Jones/Telerate, Inc. He spent 20 years in the securities industry, where he was a financial economist, and a trader on both the buy and sell sides of the market. Mr. Kitter teaches a course in money and capital markets trading at New York University's School of Continuing Education. He received an M.B.A. from the New York University Graduate School of Business Administration.

Alexander Levin

Dr. Levin is a senior quantitative analyst at the Dime Savings Bank, the fifth largest thrift in the United States. Prior to joining Dime Savings, Dr. Levin was a quantitative developer at Ryan Labs, Inc., a fixed-income research and money-management company. Dr. Levin holds Soviet equivalents of an M.S. in applied mathematics and a Ph.D. in control and dynamic systems from the University of Naval Engineering and Leningrad State University, respectively, both in St. Petersburg, Russia.

Douglas A. Love

Dr. Love is president of Devonshire Capital Management, Inc., and managing director with Ryan Labs. Previously, he was managing director of fixed-income investing and options/futures strategies at Matrix Capital Management, and he was vice president of BEA Associates, where he covered equities, fixed-income, and derivative strategies. He was the founder and chairman of Buck Pension Fund Services, Inc., a money-manager search and selection firm with advanced performance analytics and asset/liability modeling technologies. He has extensive experience in the financial engineering of fixed-income products and derivatives, and in fixed-income portfolio management. Dr. Love is a registered investment advisor, and a commodities and futures trading advisor. Dr. Love has published extensively. He currently serves on the Advisory Board of the Investment Management Institute, the Bureau of National Affairs Reporter, and the Society of Quantitative Analysts. He holds a Ph.D. in economics from Columbia University, an M.S. and M.B.A. from New York University, and a B.M.E. from Cornell University.

Sean F. McShea

Mr. McShea is vice president in charge of asset/liability management products and asset investment advisory systems with Ryan Labs. Additionally, he has project-management responsibilities in the firm's asset/liability products for plan sponsors and insurance companies. Prior to joining Ryan Labs, Mr. McShea worked for Andersen Consulting as a project manager in their financial services group, and he earned recognition with the Andersen "Excellence Award" in 1990. Mr. McShea holds an M.B.A. from Columbia University and a B.S. in industrial engineering from Worcester Polytechnic Institute.

Martha C. Monteagudo

Ms. Monteagudo, director of product development, is responsible for product development and system management at Ryan Labs. She was the product leader on building the Ryan Labs Treasury Composite Index, and she directs Ryan Labs' proprietary SMART, TOPS, and DAILY systems. All new product dvelopment is managed by her. Previously, Ms. Monteagudo was a functional designer at Telerate/Dow Jones Development Group. Her specialty was in bond and mortgage data analytics. Also, she was an analyst at the Ryan Financial Strategy Group specializing in index analytics. Ms. Monteagudo has a B.S. degree in finance from Seton Hall.

Frank Reilly

Dr. Reilly is an advisor to RLAM and its parent, Ryan Labs. He is currently the Bernard J. Hank professor of business administration at the Business School at the University of Notre Dame. His experience includes serving as a stock and bond trader for Goldman Sachs and as a consultant for the World Bank. He was also the dean of the College of Business at Notre Dame and a professor at both the University of Wyoming and the University of Kansas. Dr. Reilly has published extensively on the subject of investments and on related topics. He received his B.B.A. from Notre Dame, his M.B.A. from Northwestern University, and his Ph.D. from the University of Chicago.

Ronald J. Ryan

Mr. Ryan is president of Ryan Labs, Inc., which manages over $3 billion in assets. Previously, he headed Ryan Financial Strategy Group (RFSG), which created the first daily bond index in the United States—the Treasury Yield Curve. This index is syndicated throughout the world. From 1977-1982, Mr. Ryan was director of research at Lehman where he created and supervised the Lehman indices, which included the Lehman Government/Corporate Index. Since 1982, Mr. Ryan and his staff at Ryan Labs, Inc., have developed over 900 indices, including the first liability index. Ryan Labs provides index databases totaling over 850 indexes. Mr. Ryan received a BBA and an MBA from Loyola University.

Robert G. Smith III

Mr. Smith is president of Sage Advisory Services, Ltd. Prior to forming Sage Advisory Services of Austin, Texas, in 1996, Mr. Smith was the executive vice president and member of the investment committee at Smith Affiliated Capital Corp. in New York. Previously with Merrill Lynch, Mr. Smith was an advisor to the Saudi Arabian Monetary Agency in Riyadh, where he managed the foreign reserves of the Central Bank. Prior to that, he was with Moody's Investors Service. Mr. Smith's research and comments have been featured in a wide variety of publications. He has over 20 years of investment experience in domestic and international research. Mr. Smith is a member of the New York Society of Security Analysts and the Association of Professional Financial Consultants. He was selected to serve on the Suffolk County Financial Advisory Board. Mr. Smith received his M.B.A. from New York University.

John Wibbelsman

Mr. Wibbelsman is the acting/managing director of internal asset management for NYNEX Asset Management Company. He is responsible for $3 billion of internally managed pension and savings plan assets for NYNEX. He is also the portfolio manager for NYNEX's international equity futures portfolio and NYNEX's structured government bond portfolio. Mr. Wibbelsman received his undergraduate degree in finance from Villanova University. He received an M.B.A. from Columbia University's Graduate School of Business. He is a chartered financial analyst and a member of the New York Society of Security Analysts.

David J. Wright

Dr. Wright is an advisor to RLAM and its parent, Ryan Labs. He is currently an associate professor of finance in the School of Business at the University of Wisconsin, where he teaches investments, working capital management, and corporate finance. Previously, he worked at the University of Notre Dame in the College of Business. Dr. Wright has done extensive research in the field of bonds, with special emphasis on bond indices and their implications for fixed-income portfolio performance measurement. He has published numerous articles in prestigious publications. Dr. Wright received his B.S., M.B.A., and Ph.D. from the University of Illinois.

PART I

Bond Market Overview

CHAPTER 1

Bond Market Solar Systems

Ronald J. Ryan, CFA
President
Ryan Labs, Inc.

The American bond market is an awesome creature measuring over 1,000 government securities, over 10,000 corporate bonds, and well over 700,000 mortgage-backed securities. The total market value of such enormity is hard to calculate but is certainly in excess of four trillion dollars (see Table 1).

Pricing for each security is an arduous task even for an army of bond traders. So what drives the bond market? Where do yields come from? How is one bond priced differently than another?

Thirty years experience in the bond business suggests the truth of the old adage that the more things change the more they are the same. The core or foundation of the bond business is built on a base yield from which all bonds derive their ultimate price or yield. That base yield is

TABLE 1. Bonds Outstanding (as of 12/31/95)

	Bonds Outstanding ($)
Government	2,394,662
Corporates	793,223
Mortgages	1,291,196
Total	4,479,081
Others	57,913
Gross	4,536,994

Source: Lehman Brothers Aggregate Bond Market Index.

always the Treasury yield curve since bonds were federal debt when first issued in America. There is reason to believe that this will not only continue but be reinforced in the future as the Treasury yield curve becomes even more developed and defined by the Treasury STRIPS curve (zero-coupon curve).

The Treasury Yield Curve

Since bonds are loans, it is proper to begin the history of the Treasury yield curve with the first U.S. loan. On June 3, 1775, the Continental Congress approved the first domestic loan of £6,000,000 to buy gunpowder for the American Revolution. This first loan was stated in British sterling. By October 3, 1776, the second American loan was approved for $5,000,000, so stated in dollars in defiance of the British currency system.[1] From that humble beginning, the United States would become the largest debtor nation in the world.

It is amazing that the Federal debt is growing so fast. Since 1970, the total interest-bearing debt has risen by a factor of 12 times in 25 years, or by an average of 10.94 percent per annum! (See Table 2). The last 10 years have witnessed a 171.9 percent increase in debt, or a 10.52 percent per year growth. At that rate for the next 10 years, the total interest-bearing debt would amass to $13,458,946.

It is news to many that a stable Treasury yield curve is a rather young creation. There was no orderly or continuous auction series until

TABLE 2. Interest-Bearing Debt

	Interest-Bearing Debt ($ millions)			
			% Growth	
Year	Total Debt	$ Growth	Last 5 yrs	Since 1970
1970	369,026			
1975	532,122	163,096	44.2	44.2
1980	906,402	374,280	70.3	145.6
1985	1,821,010	914,608	100.9	393.5
1990	3,210,943	1,389,933	76.3	770.1
1995	4,950,644	1,739,701	54.2	1,241.5

Source: Treasury Bulletin (various years).

---

1. Gene Hessler, *An Illustrated History of U.S. Loans,* 1988.

the 1970s. Now we have monthly and quarterly auctions for each maturity series. This auction process has truly defined the bond market and made bond trading the art or science it has evolved into over the last two decades. A review of the Treasury auctions histogram reveals the true bond-market lineage. It was not until 1973 that there was a continuous auction series for any maturity series. Prior to that time, auctions were irregular and quite delinquent (see Table 3).

Bond Planetary Systems

If each bond is priced off of a base price which is the Treasury yield curve for the auction issue closest to its effective maturity, it follows logically that each bond must move similarly to the Treasury bond that derives its price. In bond market terms, the *yield spread* is the yield difference between any issue and the Treasury auction issue yield of its "pricing" bond.

It is useful to think of each Treasury auction issue as the sun of a bond solar system. For example, consider the three-year planetary system where all bonds, priced off the three-year Treasury auction issue, reside. Let us think of all three-year equivalent bonds as the planets. Each bond planet is priced and moves around the Treasury auction sun inside a yield-spread orbit. Depending on that bond's credit and liquidity features, it may move in an elliptical orbit such that its yield spread changes through time. But the key observation is that it moves with the Treasury "sun." If interest rates were to spike up swiftly from six percent to seven percent on the three-year Treasury auction issue, every bond priced off

TABLE 3: Treasury Auction History

Auction Series	First Auction Date	Days since Last Auction
2 year	9/04/73	250
3 year	2/15/74	365
4 year	6/30/79	245
5 year	9/05/79	518
7 year	11/15/67	1402
10 year	11/15/77	456
15 year	7/08/77	1239
20 year	1/12/81	2510
30 year	5/15/73	3053

Source: Ryan Labs.

this key issue would move approximately, if not exactly, up 100 basis points. Yield spreads would most probably stay the same as proof that these bonds are locked in a yield-spread orbit around this auction sun.

Currently, there are five major bond solar systems (ignoring the cash market). These five bonds price thousands of bonds, if not millions of loans, every day (see Table 4).

Systematic Risk

Empirical proof of the reality of the bond solar system is apparent in itemizing the interest rate risk or systematic risk inherent in all bonds. Similar to the gravitational pull of any large body, all bonds' behavior patterns are heavily influenced by the base yield and movement of the Treasury yield curve. Correlating monthly total returns over time for any bond sector versus the Treasury yield curve would support this risk/reward dependence. Table 5 shows that historical returns for any bond are highly correlated with the Treasury yield curve. Some 90 percent to 99 percent of the return behavior of any bond sector is explained by Treasury yield curve changes (see Table 5).

Other Markets

To show the enormous influence of the Treasury yield curve, consider the correlation of other markets to it. The S&P 500 is a good proxy for the domestic stock market. Common stocks are not thought of as being par-

TABLE 4. Investment-Grade Bond Market

	Bonds Rated AAA to BAA as of June 30, 1996 # of Bonds in System	
Bond Solar System	**Government**	**Corporate**
1 year	116	116
2 year	113	257
3 year	141	478
5 year	199	1006
10 year	147	1050
30 year	_51_	_945_
Total	787	3852

Source: Salomon Brothers Broad Investment Grade Index.

TABLE 5. Correlation of Monthly Returns

Bond Sector versus Treasury Yield Curve	Last 10 yrs	Last 7 yrs	Last 5 yrs	Last 3 yrs	Last 1 yr
Lehman Aggregate	.985	.987	.988	.987	.998
Lehman Govt/Corp	.994	.995	.996	.996	.999
Merrill Corporate	.957	.980	.991	.996	.999
Salomon Mortgage	.897	.898	.884	.892	.979

Source: Ryan Labs Risk Reward Monitor.

ticularly interest rate dependent or correlated. Yet there is growing proof that stocks are more interest rate related than in the past.

Table 6 shows the correlation of the S&P 500 to the Treasury yield curve as a moving average over the last 10, 5, and 3 years. In addition, the years 1990 and 1994 are isolated observations. There seems to be a definite trend toward a closer return behavior pattern. During 1990 and 1994, stocks and bonds were quite highly correlated.

Table 6 also shows the correlation of the Merrill Lynch Global bond index returns to Treasury-yield-curve changes. International yields are generally thought to be more dependent on international events than the American markets. Once again, there is evidence that international yields and returns correlate more to the Treasury yield curve then to international environments. There is a consistent correlation of over 50 percent direct correlation to the Treasury yield curve.

TABLE 6. Correlations of Monthly Returns

	Periods Ending 6/30/96	
	S&P 500	**ML Global**
Last 10 years	.2961	.5414
Last 5 years	.4098	.6584
Last 3 years	.6516	.5479
Year 1990	.7712	.6853
Year 1994	.8244	.5144

Source: Ryan Labs Risk Reward Monitor.

Conclusion

In today's health-conscious world, where the physical and ecological environment receive so much attention and focus, financial health should be given special attention. The Treasury yield curve is a key to how the American economy will fare for the foreseeable future. We should understand its effect on all bonds, all loans, and on the total economic environment.

The U.S. Treasury STRIPS: Valuation, Liability, and Asset Allocation Frontier

Douglas A. Love, Ph.D.
Managing Director
Ryan Labs, Inc.

Sean F. McShea
Vice President
Ryan Labs, Inc.

U.S. Treasury STRIPS (separate trading of registered interest and principal of securities) are zero-coupon bonds which pay an even $1,000 at maturity, and are manufactured *(stripped)* from U.S. Treasury debt instruments held in trust to secure the payment of the STRIPS. When pricing opportunities arise, portfolios of STRIPS are assembled *(reconstituted)* in exchange for coupon bonds. Coinciding with interest and principal payments from Treasury debt, STRIPS have maturities ranging over a period of 30 years and pay quarterly, on the fifteenth of the month, for the months of February, May, August, and November. Hence, close to 120 STRIPS are outstanding at any one time. STRIPS derived from coupon versus principal payments are separately designated and demonstrate small price differences for identical payment dates.

History of STRIPS—February 1985 to February 1995

On August 16, 1984, Secretary of the Treasury Donald T. Regan announced a new program to facilitate separate trading of registered interest and principal of securities (STRIPS), with eligible securities commencing on the quarterly refunding of February 15, 1985. Prior to that date, stripped U.S. Treasury zero-coupon bonds existed as a series of proprietary programs at major Wall Street brokerage houses.

This chapter is not to be quoted without permission of the authors.

Under the new STRIPS program, selected Treasuries may be maintained in the Federal Reserve's book-entry system in a manner permitting separate trading and ownership of the interest and principal payments. For the first time, the fixed-income market had the opportunity to trade zero-coupon instruments in book-entry form as direct obligations of the U.S. Treasury.

The Ryan Labs STRIP index (RLS) was created on the same day that the first Treasury stripped 30-year coupon bond was created. The RLS is a daily *total return* index for each annual spot on the STRIP curve and an equally-weighted composite total for all years. STRIPS roll to the most current annual maturity on a quarterly basis. Since all STRIPS have maturities that are three months apart (February 15, May 15, August 15, and November 15), the rolls take place at the midpoints of these dates. The Data Appendix for this chapter shows return and volatility for one through 30-year STRIPS. Figure 1 relates STRIPS performance to other major asset classes.

STRIPS Financial Properties

Because of their unique properties, U.S. Treasury STRIPS are increasingly relevant to more sectors and operations in the financial community We will list and explore their importance in three areas: asset pricing, liability pricing, and asset allocation.

Taken together, the several properties of U.S. Treasury STRIPS are propelling them to the forefront of modern finance and investment. These properties include

- uniformly high liquidity
- absence of credit risk, prepayment risk, or other cash-flow uncertainty
- a wide and complete range of maturities and volatilities
- homogeneous tax treatment (absence of coupon effects)
- simplicity

Valuation/Pricing

Price Discovery and Treasury Auction Issues

Bond market practitioners are conscious of the fact that, by industry practice, all bonds are priced off of the current Treasury auction issues (1-, 2-, 3-, 5-, 10-, and 30-year) whose maturity most closely matches the effective

FIGURE 1. Asset/Liability Monitor (10-Year Period Ending 12/31/95)

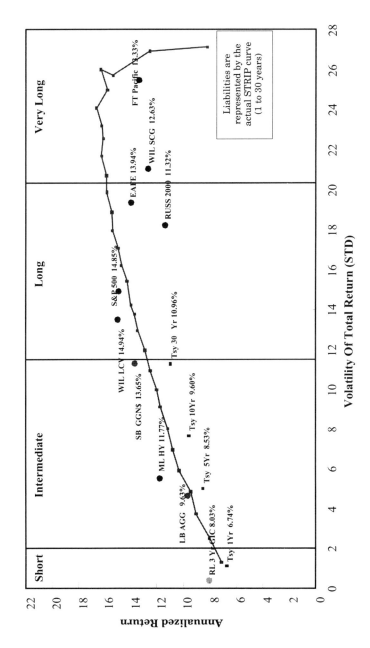

Source: Ryan Labs, Inc.

maturity of the bond in question. This structure is consistent with the economics of price discovery, whereby the prices of less liquid, less-frequently traded issues are derived by interpolation from the prices of liquid, frequently traded bonds.

Academics and financial engineers, however, view bonds as portfolios of cash flows, with those flows having individual prices—so-called cash-flow *sculpturing*. The STRIPS curve is the bridge between these two worlds. Subject to the costs and time required to *strip* and *reconstitute,* the two approaches must produce the same valuations. Whether or not this is true is an empirical issue which questions the limits of arbitrage. In any case, for today's financial engineers, the STRIPS market *is* the bond market.

Forward-Rate Determinations

Securities whose future cash-flows are interest rate dependent (so-called dynamic assets) are increasingly prevalent. These securities include bond options, callable and putable bonds, mortgage bonds and CMOs, swaps, swaptions, caps floors, collars, and nonmaturing deposits. Central to the valuation of all dynamic securities is the evolution of forward rates. Traditionally, these rates have been interpolated from the prices of Treasury coupon bonds. However, while computationally sound, this approach is fraught with empirical problems. First, there are large gaps in coupon-bond market auction maturities (currently nothing between 10 and 30 years, for example). Second, one or more of the available coupon issues may be on speical in the repurchase (repo) market, causing an artificially low yield. A much smaller proportion of STRIPS are so affected at any one time. Third, tax-induced coupon effects are generally observed in the coupon-bond market. All things considered, the STRIPS market should be the preferred domain for forward-rate measurement. Zaretsky (1995) has found that forward rates measured in the STRIPS market are fully consistent with (though more complete than) those estimated from Treasury coupon bonds.

Continuous Time Finance and STRIPS Instantaneous Return and Risk

Because of the central role that forward rates play in modern stochastic pricing models and because of the advanced treatment of new material on the subject, it is instructive to introduce the application of continuous, instantaneous mathematics to STRIPS in order to appreciate key return and volatility properties in the modern context.

Let, $P_T(t)$ equal the price of a $1 STRIPS maturing at time $t+T$. For convenience, let $P_T(0) = P_T$ and its spot rate y_T and instantaneous short forward rates $f_0(t)$ be

$$P_T = e^{-y_T T}, y_T = \frac{1}{T}\int_0^T f_o(\tau)d\tau. \tag{1}$$

Hence, the spot rate is the average forward rate for the period $(0,T)$. The instantaneous forward short-rate at T is

$$f_0(T) = d(y_T{}^T)/dT.$$

Hence,

$$dP_T/dt = -P_T[d(y_T{}^T)/dT]dT/dt = f_0(T)P_T,$$

since

$$dT/dt = -1.$$

With no change in term structure, a STRIP returns $f_0(T)$, the instantaneous short forward rate at time T.

For a change in term structure, $dP_T/dy_T = -Te^{-y_T T}$ and $d^2P_T/dy_T{}^2 = T^2e^{-y_T T}$, or the well-known result that for a pure discount bond its duration is its maturity T and its convexity is T^2.

A Taylor series expansion of the change in bond price, with substitutions from above, gives

$$dP_T = f_0(T)P_T dt - TP_T dy_T + \frac{1}{2}T^2P_T dy_T{}^2 + \varepsilon.$$

Dividing by P_T, the bond's return (ignoring the small ε) is

$$R_T = f_0(T)\, dt - T\, dy_T + \frac{1}{2}\, T^2 dy_T^2. \tag{2}$$

Economic content is added by consideration of market expectations about arbitrage-free interest-rate changes and a term structure of volatility $E(dy_T{}^2)$.

By various cash-flow structures and the inclusion of interest rate options, it is possible to obtain any arbitrary combination of duration and convexity. Hence, two equilibrium risk prices need to be considered; one for extension (duration) and one for optionality (convexity). As a consequence, a pure discount bond's price, and by extension any coupon bond's price with riskless cash-flows, is dictated by its duration and convexity.

It is noteworthy that a long STRIP position demonstrates properties parallel to an options position, as shown in Table 1.

The attributes of Equation (1) and the reference to options is useful, but limited in the following ways:

1. The Taylor series expansion is an approximation (in the small amount ε).
2. The measures of duration and convexity are conventional sensitivities with respect to the bond's own yield, not with respect to the yield on some reference bond or other factor.
3. The equation is definitional and without economic content until arbitrage-free conditions are imposed.
4. While the parameter similarities with options are important, the similarity is limited. An option is a derivative (i.e., arbitrage is possible between the option and its underlying security). Since the price and spot rate of a STRIP are simply alternative characterizations of the same security, there is no possible arbitrage, and the similarity to an option is potentially misleading. Nevertheless, the coincidence of convexity and optionality and the ability to sculpture convexity in the interest-rate options market must be recognized.

Multiple Cash-Flows

Considering any bond, bond portfolio, or index as a portfolio of cash flows, two pricing properties follow. First, since both duration and convexity are value additive, as with pure discount bonds, so are riskless

TABLE 1. Bond and Option Risk/Reward Parallels

	Option	Bond STRIPS
db/dt	Time Value (1)	Instantaneous Forward Rate (f)
db/dx	Hedge Ratio (∂)	Duration (D)
db²/dx²	Gamma (ə)	Convexity (ə)

coupon-bond prices dictated only by their duration and convexity and marketwide parameters. Second, for any duration, a pure discount bond has minimal convexity.

Value Additivity   The duration of a bond is equal to the present-value-weighted time to all of its future payments (i.e., the durations of its constituent STRIPS). Similarly, for a bond portfolio, portfolio duration is the market-value-weighted sum of the duration of its constituent bonds. The same value-additivity principles hold for convexity. It should be expected, therefore, that (omitting tax effects) yield and risk/return premiums adjusted for duration and convexity should be the same for coupon bonds and STRIPS.

Minimal Convexity of STRIPS   Consider an equally weighted dumbbell-construction of two pure discount bonds having durations of $T + x$ and $T - x$.

   The duration D of the portfolio is $D = .5(T{-}x) + .5(T{+}x) = T$, and the convexity C of the portfolio is $C = .5(T{+}x)^2 + .5(T{-}x)^2 = T^2 + x^2$. The convexity disparity goes to zero as x goes to zero (cash-flow matching).

The Cost of Convexity   Immunization analysis shows that it is not possible to immunize two cash flows (a dumbbell) with a single intermediate-term cash flow (STRIPS). The STRIPS will lose ground on any change in rates because, while duration is matched, the STRIP has insufficient convexity. Conversely, if two cash flows are used to immunize a single flow, the resulting portfolio will gain on any change in rates. Hence positive convexity is an unambiguous "good," which commands a higher price (lower yield). Such a portfolio necessarily has a lower yield and will be expensive relative to cash-flow matching. Hence, an immunized portfolio must have at least one more cash-flow than the liabilities have if it is not to underperform liabilities, and therefore must be at least as expensive. These considerations are at the heart of modern mathematical optimization of immunized portfolios.

   Additional losses or gains in a volatile market are associated with the cost of convexity. Thus, investors must require a higher yield (lower price) for lower or negative convexity, such as for a callable bond or a mortgage-backed security. The yield premium must be such as to equate the expected risk-adjusted return on bonds with differing duration and convexities and with similar liquidity in order to be the same. Since a multiple-cash-flow bond always has more positive convexity than a STRIP with the same duration, the bond must have a lower yield.

Liability Pricing

Securities, accounting, banking, and insurance regulators are increasingly demanding that all relevant institutions continually mark their liabilities to market. Risk-based capital requirements and risk-management control and reporting, including value at risk (VAR) measures, are becoming more prevalent.

Problems with Traditional Accounting

Future-Value Land
So long as bonds are held to maturity and their cash-flows are unconditional, if an institution held more future cash-flows (assets) than it was short (liabilities), it was considered to be safely solvent. This simplistic framework comes undone as soon as trading to "improve yield" is undertaken, let alone any required reinvestment. The introduction of dynamic assets, such as callable debt and certainly mortgages, upsets the stability in differences between asset and liability future cash-flows. Under these real world conditions, the statutory cost-based accounting paradigm for financial institutions is rapidly crumbling.

Present-Value Land
Marking-to-market compares market-based present values *and* their respective sensitivity to interest rate and other changes. This is the only possible framework for establishing and meeting asset-management objectives. This framework is very unfamiliar ground to the management of many institutions, and becomes particularly problematic when incentive compensation is based on the traditional framework. Meaningful asset/liability management requires continual marking to market.

Paradigm Shift
The formal paradigm shift began with pension accounting in 1987.

Accounting For Pension Liabilities: FAS-87
After considerable review and controversey, the Financial Accounting Standards Board broke with the traditional accounting model in adopting the marking to market of corporate pension liabilities. Paragraph 44 of FAS-87 (1987) states

> Assumed discount rates shall reflect the rates at which the pension benefits could be effectively settled. It is appropriate in estimating those rates to look to available information about available annuity rates implicit in cur-

rent prices of annuity contracts that could be used to effect settlement of the obligation (including information about available annuity rates currently published by the Pension Benefit Guaranty Corporation). In making these estimates, employers may also look to *rates of return on high quality fixed-income investments currently available and expected to be available during the period to maturity of the pension benefits."* [emphasis added]

Assumed discount rates are used in measurements of the projected, accumulated, and vested benefit obligations, and the service and interest-cost component of net periodic pension cost.

And further at paragraph 199:

Interest rates vary depending on the duration of investments; for example, *U.S. Treasury bills, 7-year bonds, and 30-year bonds have different interest rates.* Thus, the weighted-average discount rate (interest rate) inherent in the prices of annuities (or a dedicated portfolio) will vary depending on the length of time remaining until individual benefit payment dates. A plan covering only retired employees would be expected to have significantly different discount rates from one covering a work force of 30-year olds. The disclosures required by this Statement regarding components of the pension benefit obligation will be *representationally faithful if individual discount rates applicable to various deferral periods are selected."* [emphasis added]

The Financial Accounting Standards Board [1989] subsequently went further in its Statement 106 paragraph 186:

The objective of selecting assumed discount rates is to measure the single amount that, if invested at the measurement date in a portfolio of high-quality debt instruments, would provide the necessary future cash-flows to pay accumulated benefits when due. Notionally, that single amount, would equal *the current market value of a portfolio of high quality zero-coupon bonds whose maturity dates and amounts would be the same as the timing and amount of the expected future benefit payments."* [emphasis added]

The FASB goes on to note within the same paragraph:

Because cash inflows would equal outflows in timing and amount, there would be no reinvestment risk in the yields to maturity of the portfolio." [emphasis added]

Herein is expressed the rationale for the traditional, book-value statutory accounting model. The Statement then goes on to break the mold and to endorse marking to market:

However, in other than a zero-coupon portfolio, such as a portfolio of long-term debt instruments that pay semiannual interest payments or whose maturities do not extend far enough into the future to meet expected benefit payments, the assumed discount rates (the yield to maturity) need to incorporate expected reinvestment rates available in the future. Those *rates should be extrapolated from the existing yield curve at the measurement date. Assumed discount rates should be reevaluated at each measurement date. If the general level of interest rates rises or declines, the assumed discount rates should change* in a similar manner." [emphasis added]

On September 22, 1993, the Securities and Exchange Commission [1993] made the following pronouncement on pension disclosure:

[T]he staff believes that the guidance that is provided in the *paragraph 186 Of FASB 106 . . . for selecting discount rates . . . is appropriate for measuring the pension benefit obligation."* [emphasis added]

Nevertheless, it is clear that most companies do not adhere to Financial Accounting Standard Board (FASB) standards. According to a recent Kwasha Lipton study of the largest corporation pension plans, the average discount rate for pension liabilities was 7.56 percent for measurement dates as of December 31, 1995, when the average yield of the Treasury STRIP curve was 6.08 percent, a difference of –1.48 percent. Table 2 converts this difference into liability valuation differences using an average duration of liabilities.

Accordingly, there is evidence that liabilities are on average undervalued by between 5 and 15 percent per year attributable to the use of inflated discount rates. Notice in Table 2 for the year ending 1990, the difference was only 34 basis points or 5.1 percent. For years ending 1991 to 1992, however, when the STRIP rate fell to 7.24 percent and 7.18 percent respectively, companies retained their discount rates in the 8.25 percent range to smooth pension expense. This caused about a 15 percent difference between actual and reported present value of liabilities.

TABLE 2.   Comparison of Average Discount Rate (Corporate) to the Average Yield on STRIP Yield Curve as of December 31, 1995

Year (A)	Average STRIP % (B)	Average Discount (C)	Yield Difference (D)	Average Duration (E)	Present Value Difference (F)
1995	6.08	7.56	–1.48	15	–22.20
1994	7.95	8.28	–0.33	15	–4.95
1993	6.27	7.29	–1.02	15	–15.30
1992	7.18	8.17	–0.99	15	–14.85
1991	7.24	8.33	–1.09	15	–16.35
1990	8.25	8.59	–0.34	15	–5.10

In 1993, when the average STRIP rate fell further to 6.27 percent, the Securities and Exchange Commission alerted corporations that discount rates above 7 percent would be under review. Companies quickly deflated their discount rates to 7.29 percent, although maintaining a much higher spread (about 100 basis points) as compared to 1990.

In 1994, when rates rose approximately 170 basis points (from 6.27 percent to 7.95 percent), companies increased their discount rates by only about 100 basis points (from 7.29 percent to 8.28 percent), narrowing the spread marginally to 33 basis points. This is an indication that corporations are either moving to more realistic market rates, or they are trying to smooth their pension expense by averaging market rate changes.

Table 2 displays the difference between the market price of liabilities (column B) and the price corporations are using to discount their liabilities (column C). By multiplying the yield difference (column D) times the average modified duration of the Ryan Labs generic Liability index™ (column E), we calculate that the present value difference to be –22.20 percent for 1995. U.S. corporations have mispriced their promise to defined-benefit pension plan participants by 22.2 percent.

Asset-Liability Management

Traditional asset allocation using mean variance analysis pursues allocations which consider asset returns and volatility only. As a result, stocks and intermediate-duration bonds have been favored. The true objective of asset allocation should focus on optimal return and volatility, inclusive of liabilities.

Each plan sponsor has a unique liability term-structure depending on company demographics and plan design—no two pension liability schedules are identical. (See Figure 2.) In FAS 87, paragraph 199, the Financial Accounting Standards Board recognizes these differences: "A plan covering only retired employees would be expected to have significantly different discount rates from one covering a work force of 30-year-olds." Logic dictates that term structure of liabilities should dictate the shape of asset allocation.

Unfortunately, most asset allocation models do not incorporate liability characteristics. Without a client's liability structure (as in Figure 2), all clients tend to get the same asset allocation alternatives. According to Table 3, the annual *Pension & Investments* survey of the top 1,000 defined benefit pension plans, asset allocation ratios have been static.

It is hard to imagine that this asset allocation fits most liability schedules. It is also hard to imagine that asset/liability (surplus/deficit)

FIGURE 2.   Projected Pension Fund Payments

(Present Value $)

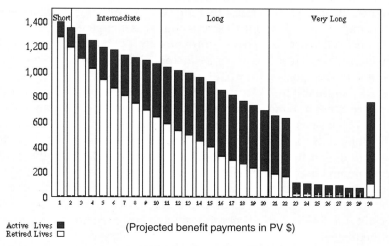

Active Lives ■
Retired Lives □   (Projected benefit payments in PV $)

ratios remains so static that dynamic asset-allocation shifts are not required.

Historically, pension assets are given generic market indices as their performance objective. Performance is measured by comparing the total return of an asset class (e.g., stocks and bonds) versus the generic market index for that asset class. Money managers are hired and fired based on their performance versus an asset index as well as their corresponding universe of fellow managers.

TABLE 3. *Pension & Investments* Survey of Corporate Asset Allocation (%)

	1989	1990	1991	1992	1993	1994	1995
Equity	46.6	43.6	45.7	48.0	48.9	53.9	56.2
Bonds	33.3	36.0	35.8	35.7	35.5	33.6	32.4
Cash	8.9	8.7	6.2	5.9	4.1	3.9	3.2
Real Estate	4.1	4.8	3.9	3.4	3.2	3.3	3.0
Other	7.1	6.9	8.4	7.0	8.3	5.3	5.2

This situation persists in large measure because pension liabilities are traditionally only calculated annually, and they are reported months after the fact. What is more important is that the calculation, or present value pricing, of liabilities is very subjective currently, and it is unclear to the asset side how this process is done. It is difficult or even impossible, for an asset manager to manage against such a benchmark.

Solution: Custom Liability Indices

What is needed is a custom liability index system that correctly prices plan sponsor liabilities in conformity with FASB, and that is delivered *daily* to investment management. The asset side understands the behavior pattern and design strategies that are necessary to beat the liability growth rate. Performance measurement can then be assessed as the present value growth-rate of assets versus the present value growth-rate of liabilities.

The appropriate benchmark for monitoring pension assets is a custom liability index representing the present-value growth of the plan sponsor's liability schedule. Generic indices that measure asset classes (e.g., the S&P 500) are, obviously, not appropriate measurements of liability growth. Only a liability index can represent the client. Liability indices should conform to FASB regulations and should be priced off the Treasury STRIPS yield curve.

Ryan Labs delivered the first liability index in January 1991. These indices are completely customized and weighted to individual plan sponsor liability schedules. In the absence of a clients' liability schedule, a Ryan Labs generic market liability index that equally weights all maturities can be substituted as an approximation. The returns and volatility of this generic index provide a practical analytic input for asset allocation and performance measurement (see Table 4).

As Table 4 indicates, using generic indices for asset objectives, instead of a liability index, results in significant funding variability. Traditional assets are a poor proxy for liabilities and should not be the objective of the assets.

It is critical that each clients' objective is supported. Until a custom liability index is tailored to accurately calculate liability present-value and growth, the plan sponsor will not be well served. Asset allocation (including stocks as well as bonds) is dependent on the liability term-structure. Performance measurement is dependent on a custom liability index in order to accurately assess asset growth versus the liability growth being funded.

TABLE 4. Asset/Liability Total Return Analysis

Index	1990	1991	1992	1993	1994	1995	1990–1995
RL Liability™	3.23	19.26	7.87	22.46	−12.60	41.16	100.65
RL Cash	8.73	7.42	4.12	3.51	3.94	7.11	40.13
RL 3 Yr GIC	8.71	8.61	7.77	6.58	5.66	5.82	51.62
RL Treasury	7.87	15.27	6.31	11.35	−4.98	20.13	68.03
LB G/C	8.28	16.13	7.58	11.03	−3.51	19.24	72.82
LB AGG	8.96	16.00	7.40	9.75	−2.92	18.52	71.36
Salomon BIG	9.09	15.97	7.59	9.89	−2.85	18.55	72.28
S&P 500	−3.15	30.45	7.64	10.07	1.29	37.57	108.58
MS EAFE	−23.32	12.48	−11.85	32.95	8.06	11.56	21.85

For asset managers to function, a custom liability index should be calculated frequently. Asset allocation and performance measurement can be best understood when the weight and growth rate of each liability maturity sector (term structure) is calculated. The term structure of liabilities is critical. Without liability term-structure definitions and measurements, plan sponsors face ambiguous asset-allocation decisions and performance-measurements comparisons. Without accurate liability term-structure measurements, plan sponsors face the greatest risk there is—mismatching assets versus liabilities by term structure. The savings and loan crisis is too vivid a memory of what can happen with mismatched term-structure exposure. The savings and loan crisis of yesterday may very well be the Pension Benefit Guaranty Corporation crisis of tomorrow.

Asset Allocation—The STRIPS Frontier

STRIPS bear no return premium for cash-flow uncertainty (whether credit related or from prepayment uncertainty) or illiquidity. Consequently, relative to their volatility, other asset classes should be analyzed relative to STRIPS in asset-allocation analyses. The STRIPS market spans a large range of return and volatility (see Figure 1). The range of STRIPS volatility compares favorably with the entire range employed in full asset-allocation studies. This span is important, because many financial institutions (notably retirement funds) have long cash-flow liabilities which need pricing and hedging or benchmarking. The STRIPS frontier serves notice as to how high average discount rates are for long *nominal* payments, and to the volatility of the payments' present values. The STRIPS yield curve conveys the market's current appraisal of long-dated cash flows. In short, investing against long nominal liabilities requires aggressive investing whether in STRIPS or other asset classes.

STRIPS are uniquely pristine. They have no credit, event, or prepayment risk, and they are highly liquid. As such, STRIPS' only premium derives from their instantaneous price (interest rate) volatility. By comparison, all other asset categories contain premiums for various forms of cash-flow uncertainty and illiquidity. Because expected return/volatility "efficient frontiers" do not capture illiquidity premiums, it must be expected that assets having less liquidity than STRIPS should fall above the STRIPS frontier. In addition, expected return/volatility frontiers do not deal with optionality—not just standard options, but embedded options, such as prepayment and call provisions and with convexity in general. That Treasury coupon bonds fall below the STRIPS frontier (lower average return for the same volatility) is noteworthy. While the solution to these problems is beyond the scope of this chapter, it is suggested that the STRIPS frontier be a component of any full scale asset-allocation analysis, and serve as the baseline for calibrating term-structure models and defining options adjusted spreads (OAS).

Since the history of STRIPS is still young, there is insufficient history for formal analysis. However, there appears to be a tendency for the average return and volatility of many major asset-classes to converge over time toward the STRIPS frontier (see Figure 1). This might suggest that risk premiums for different factors in units of return volatility may not differ greatly.

Stocks versus Bonds

One allocation issue is worth noting with reference to a long-standing homily about stocks versus bonds: that on average, stocks beat bonds. The 14-year STRIP has had over short and longer periods comparable volatility to that of the S&P 500 (see Table 5 and Figure 1), and a superior return over the first 10 years. It is important to note that whether this superior return continues, the standard bond indices, used to empirically justify the homily, have only about one-third the volatility of the S&P 500. In a rational market, one cannot expect to consistently attain S&P 500 level returns with an asset having only one-third the volatility. The old adage that, in the long run stocks beat bonds, is then merely the consequence of the misapplication of a more fundamental truth: that, in the long run, more volatile, diversified assets outperform less-volatile assets. This has nothing to do with stocks versus bonds, per se.

For the first 10 years of STRIPS data (February 1985 to February 1995), the 11-year through the 28-year STRIPS outperformed the S&P 500. Since the duration of STRIPS is equal to their maturity, their duration can extend as far as 30 years. This is approximately three times the previous longest duration of bonds and about three times the price volatility of bonds for identical interest rate movements. Treasury bonds could now compete effectively with stocks in average return and volatility. The new long-duration structure of Treasury STRIPS makes the price return competitive to the price volatility of stocks. For a total return volatility basis, the S&P 500 appears similar to a 14-year STRIP in standard deviation. (See Table 5.)

TABLE 5. Horizon: February 28, 1985 to February 28, 1995

Risk/Reward Statistics	STRIP 14	S&P 500	Difference
Risk			
1. Annualized Standard Deviation	15.18	15.22	−0.04
2. Minimum Periodic Return	−8.32	−21.52	13.20
3. Maximum Periodic Return	15.12	13.45	1.69
4. Volatility to S&P (Beta)	0.36		
5. R-Squared	13.2		
6. Correlation	36.3		
7. Mean Absolute Tracking Deviation	337 basis points		
8. Shortfall Frequency	51.7		
9. Average Shortfall	319 basis points		
Reward			
10. Annualized Total Return	15.30	14.14	1.16
11. Cummulative Total Return	315.13	275.31	39.82
12. Excess Return Frequency	48.3		
13. Average Excess Return	357 basis points		
Risk Adjusted Ratio			
14. Sharpe Ratio (New)	0.06		

STRIPS and Bond-Market Indices

The popular bond indices are market weighted and require detailed knowledge of the value of bonds outstanding. Stripped Treasuries are reported gross of coupon, or not at all, and most bond indices do not incorporate STRIPS. Consequently, broad market and Treasury indices are significantly underweighted in Treasury STRIPS, and therefore understate both the volatility and return of the bond market. Since February 1985, the U.S. Treasury has been stripping notes and bonds, thereby reducing the par-value amount outstanding. The Appendix Tables B–1 and B–2 display the amount of total Treasury stripping as of 1995.

Since the term structure of interest rates is the dominant contributor to bond market returns and volatility, it is not surprising that all investment-grade bond market indices are highly mutually correlated with the Ryan Labs STRIPS index (Table 6)—the common denominator of them all.

Conclusion

U.S. Treasury STRIPS are rapidly growing in their analytical importance to all major sectors of the financial industry In every case, their pristine properties recommend them as the baseline or frontier against which other cash-flows are priced, hedged, and invested. STRIPS will increasingly become identified as *the* term structure. It is noteworthy that their inherent value is being recognized by both private and public debt issuers around the world (see Table 6).

TABLE 6. Ryan Labs STRIPS Index Equally Weighted for 10 Years Ending December 31, 1995

	Correlations
Lehman Aggregate	.9231
Lehman Government/Corporate	.9355
Salomon Brothers BIG	.9229
Merrill Lynch Domestic Master	.9288

References

Financial Accounting Standards Board. *Employers Accounting for Pensions, Statement No. 87,* Stamford, Connecticut, 1987.

Financial Accounting Standards Board. *Employers Accounting for Postretirement Benefits Other Than Pensions, Statement No. 106,* Stamford, Connecticut, 1989.

Kwasha Lipton. "Corporate Pension Survey." March 1996.

Pension & Investments, "Corporate Survey," May 13, 1996.

Securities and Exchange Commission. Letter to Corporations, September 22, 1993.

Zaretsky, Michael. "Generation of a Smooth Forward Curve for U. S. Treasuries." *Journal of Fixed Income* 5, no. 2 (September 1995).

APPENDIX

Tables follow on pages 27–32.

TABLE A–1. STRIPS Returns and Volatility
Volatility (February 28, 1985 – December 31, 1995)
Annualized Standard Deviation of Returns

STRIPS	1986	1987	1988	1989	1990	1991	1992	1993	1994	1995
RL S01	1.45	1.77	1.12	1.35	0.86	0.63	1.09	0.64	1.06	0.95
RL S02	2.66	3.25	2.03	2.78	1.97	1.40	2.46	1.63	2.06	1.70
RL S03	4.58	4.14	3.39	4.20	3.18	2.31	4.14	2.52	2.68	2.58
RL S04	6.16	5.18	4.56	5.19	4.48	3.05	5.24	3.62	3.63	3.40
RL S05	7.65	6.38	5.63	5.97	5.73	3.73	6.18	4.23	4.56	4.16
RL S06	9.87	7.69	6.81	6.55	6.54	4.38	6.70	4.79	5.24	5.08
RL S07	1.67	9.37	8.05	7.06	7.24	4.93	7.56	5.36	6.13	5.60
RL S08	14.21	10.38	8.63	7.72	8.33	5.80	8.42	6.24	6.84	6.26
RL S09	15.35	11.52	9.67	8.24	9.33	6.43	9.21	6.56	7.74	6.88
RL S10	16.75	13.31	10.70	8.87	10.59	6.98	9.01	7.77	8.43	7.61
RL S11	19.40	14.06	11.60	9.80	11.67	7.24	9.27	8.44	9.36	8.40
RL S12	22.01	15.00	12.52	10.36	12.77	7.74	9.30	9.02	10.02	8.82
RL S13	24.05	14.86	13.87	10.61	13.90	7.99	9.87	8.89	10.66	9.41
RL S14	23.58	15.39	14.75	11.24	14.92	8.36	10.15	9.82	11.39	9.71
RL S15	26.89	16.30	16.74	11.37	16.19	8.80	10.49	9.74	12.06	10.39
RL S16	27.96	17.58	17.61	11.81	17.14	9.40	10.90	10.01	12.38	11.06
RL S17	29.68	18.65	18.78	12.59	18.14	10.41	10.81	9.51	12.55	11.66
RL S18	31.30	19.89	19.49	13.21	19.11	10.90	10.38	10.68	12.90	12.51
RL S19	32.95	20.84	20.24	14.01	20.68	11.37	11.11	11.13	13.50	12.90
RL S20	34.74	22.27	21.36	14.69	21.81	12.36	11.53	11.12	13.83	13.52
RL S21	36.57	22.78	22.35	15.14	22.39	12.78	12.02	12.30	14.08	13.87
RL S22	38.52	24.22	23.57	16.03	23.38	14.09	12.00	12.30	14.62	14.06
RL S23	39.88	24.27	24.81	16.87	24.84	14.61	12.35	12.63	15.07	15.05
RL S24	41.68	22.70	25.79	17.06	25.79	14.86	12.98	13.07	15.50	15.73
RL S25	43.75	22.84	26.97	16.93	26.70	15.44	13.21	14.34	16.12	16.39
RL S26	45.64	24.45	26.23	19.38	26.85	16.07	14.19	15.19	16.41	17.17

TABLE A–1. (continued)

STRIPS	1986	1987	1988	1989	1990	1991	1992	1993	1994	1995
RL S27	47.36	26.01	28.08	19.81	26.46	17.12	15.21	16.90	16.89	17.91
RL S28	44.81	25.63	28.93	20.38	26.37	17.62	15.46	16.29	16.75	18.86
RL S29	43.91	29.64	31.05	20.75	27.89	18.54	17.04	16.73	17.37	19.65
RL S30	35.28	29.49	35.72	21.10	26.84	22.24	16.58	21.89	18.51	22.32
RL S	25.47	16.14	16.46	11.76	16.00	9.59	9.51	9.24	10.68	10.47
RL3GIC	0.09	0.11	0.05	0.02	0.02	0.03	0.08	0.11	0.03	0.02
RL Cash	0.60	0.91	0.46	0.64	0.41	0.28	0.49	0.25	0.49	0.35
RL Tsy	8.09	6.50	5.62	5.39	5.02	3.75	5.05	4.06	4.53	4.14
LB GC	6.12	5.68	5.00	4.77	4.63	3.08	4.35	3.61	4.42	3.62
ML DM	5.70	5.73	5.25	4.70	4.49	2.74	3.83	2.82	4.05	3.42
SB BIG	5.68	5.56	5.19	4.76	4.43	2.69	3.79	2.88	4.13	3.46
SP 500	17.17	29.20	9.64	11.91	17.42	15.10	7.14	5.68	10.16	4.92
EAFE	20.43	22.90	15.08	16.83	28.83	17.70	13.97	17.08	12.48	12.25

TABLE A–2. Nonannualized Total Returns
Reward (February 28, 1985–December 31, 1995)

STRIPS	10 mos. 1985	1986	1987	1988	1989	1990	1991	1992	1993	1994	1995
RL S01	8.46	9.08	6.10	6.28	10.29	9.42	9.69	5.49	4.10	2.64	8.60
RL S02	13.06	11.47	5.30	5.61	11.78	10.20	12.77	6.44	5.62	-0.04	11.95
RL S03	16.47	13.16	5.32	5.47	12.99	10.70	15.78	7.74	7.94	-2.27	14.98
RL S04	20.45	15.87	3.46	5.72	14.74	9.65	16.41	7.84	9.48	-3.91	17.26
RL S05	24.10	18.33	2.31	6.37	16.46	9.75	18.14	7.78	11.65	-4.87	19.96
RL S06	26.67	21.74	-0.03	6.99	17.45	8.63	19.23	7.64	13.47	-5.71	22.44
RL S07	30.52	24.33	-1.97	8.15	18.08	8.11	20.07	7.76	14.28	-7.51	25.37
RL S08	34.47	25.84	-3.57	9.20	19.08	7.71	20.73	8.33	17.01	-8.55	27.74
RL S09	39.62	27.99	-4.45	9.01	19.85	7.00	21.12	8.20	17.75	-8.93	29.70
RL S10	39.04	27.42	-5.38	9.84	21.07	6.77	21.53	10.09	19.14	-9.81	31.94
RL S11	42.74	29.01	-5.09	10.98	22.18	5.70	21.35	9.45	19.75	-10.24	34.55
RL S12	46.08	30.48	-4.39	12.07	22.38	5.25	21.42	9.50	21.18	-11.03	37.14
RL S13	47.18	31.77	-5.29	12.76	22.64	4.92	21.55	8.99	22.66	-11.72	39.02
RL S14	48.79	33.82	-6.05	13.03	23.42	3.83	21.65	9.65	22.72	-12.30	41.53
RL S15	52.26	33.72	-6.91	15.05	23.90	3.91	21.63	9.60	23.17	-12.66	43.39
RL S16	54.62	38.10	-7.91	15.46	25.22	3.11	21.20	9.26	23.85	-12.77	45.35
RL S17	60.15	41.32	-8.89	15.28	26.36	2.36	21.52	8.56	24.66	-13.33	46.97
RL S18	61.15	43.52	-9.39	15.03	27.52	1.73	21.28	8.33	26.92	-13.37	49.24
RL S19	61.84	45.76	-10.18	15.97	28.75	0.04	21.15	7.48	27.25	-14.09	50.65
RL S20	67.78	48.59	-11.11	16.32	31.00	-1.25	21.38	7.25	27.92	-14.80	53.67
RL S21	68.84	50.92	-12.90	16.20	30.69	-0.43	21.79	6.85	28.84	-15.62	54.61
RL S22	71.35	53.94	-13.12	17.00	30.41	-0.28	22.20	6.70	29.42	-16.43	56.66
RL S23	74.23	56.39	-14.26	14.78	31.13	-1.46	22.05	7.10	30.82	-17.76	58.68
RL S24	73.92	60.63	-14.86	14.21	31.21	-1.64	21.23	6.78	31.33	-18.75	61.03
RL S25	57.31	65.13	-15.58	13.56	32.59	-2.28	21.19	6.81	32.42	-18.73	62.55
RL S26	55.90	63.77	-18.35	11.43	36.01	-1.96	19.59	6.38	32.18	-20.46	62.37

TABLE A-2. (continued)

STRIPS	10 mos. 1985	1986	1987	1988	1989	1990	1991	1992	1993	1994	1995
RL S27	56.15	66.31	-16.78	10.28	38.60	-3.47	19.04	6.56	34.62	-20.46	62.72
RL S28	54.18	62.20	-20.11	11.74	38.22	-3.64	16.55	5.34	34.61	-19.29	64.71
RL S29	67.33	66.71	-29.90	6.00	35.66	-3.97	12.58	6.05	32.18	-22.81	65.71
RL S30	79.21	56.43	-31.07	4.04	42.68	-8.70	4.81	6.63	27.51	-33.06	57.72
RL S	48.00	39.40	-8.57	11.58	25.40	3.23	19.26	7.87	22.46	-12.60	41.16
RL3GIC	9.83	10.90	9.48	8.46	8.42	8.71	8.61	7.77	6.58	5.66	5.82
RL Cash	8.01	7.01	6.35	6.46	9.34	8.73	7.42	4.12	3.51	3.94	7.11
RL Tsy	24.54	17.21	0.55	6.12	14.44	7.87	15.27	6.31	11.35	-4.98	20.13
LB GC	21.02	15.62	2.29	7.58	14.24	8.28	16.13	7.58	11.03	-3.51	19.24
ML DM	22.21	15.22	2.40	8.04	14.18	9.10	15.85	7.58	10.02	-2.82	18.52
SB BIG	21.94	15.45	2.60	7.98	14.44	9.09	15.97	7.59	9.92	-2.85	18.55
SP 500	21.07	18.47	5.23	16.81	31.68	-3.15	30.45	7.64	10.07	1.29	37.57
EAFE	54.09	69.94	24.93	28.59	10.80	-23.32	12.48	-11.85	32.95	8.06	11.56

TABLE B–1. Derivation of STRIPS (February 28, 1995)

Treasury Issue			Principal Amount Outstanding (000s)		
Coupon	Note	Maturity	Total	Held In STRIPPED Form	% STRIPPED
8 7/8%	Note A 1996	2/15/95	8,447,058	1,323,200	15.6
7 3/8%	Note C 1996	5/15/96	20,085,643	2,072,000	10.3
7 1/4%	Note D 1996	11/15/96	20,258,810	17,619,610	86.9
8 1/2%	Note A 1997	5/15/97	9,921,237	1,295,600	13.1
8 5/8%	Note B 1997	8/15/97	9,362,836	1,632,000	17.4
8 7/8%	Note C 1997	11/15/97	9,808,329	2,476,800	25.3
8 1/8%	Note A 1998	2/15/98	9,159,068	1,205,760	13.2
9 %	Note B 1998	5/15/98	9,165,387	6,684,387	72.9
9 1/4%	Note C 1998	8/15/98	11,342,646	2,516,000	22.2
8 7/8%	Note D 1998	11/15/98	9,902,875	2,905,600	29.3
8 7/8%	Note A 1999	2/15/99	9,719,623	1,617,600	16.6
9 1/8%	Note B 1999	5/15/99	10,047,103	3,288,000	32.7
8 %	Note C 1999	8/15/99	10,163,644	1,999,650	19.7
7 7/8%	Note D 1999	11/15/99	10,773,960	3,056,000	28.4
8 1/2%	Note A 2000	2/15/00	10,673,033	1,943,200	18.2
8 7/8%	Note B 2000	5/15/00	10,496,230	4,481,600	42.7
8 3/4%	Note C 2000	8/15/00	11,080,646	3,217,600	29.0
8 1/2%	Note D 2000	11/15/00	11,519,682	2,939,200	25.5
7 3/4%	Note A 2001	2/15/01	11,312,802	2,175,200	19.2
8 %	Note B 2001	5/15/01	12,398,083	2,666,150	21.5
7 7/8%	Note C 2001	8/15/01	12,339,185	2,297,600	18.6
7 1/2%	Note D 2001	11/15/01	24,226,102	1,913,840	7.9
7 1/2%	Note A 2002	5/15/02	11,714,397	881,520	7.5
6 3/8%	Note B 2002	8/15/02	23,859,015	1,076,800	4.5
6 1/4%	Note A 2003	2/15/03	23,562,691	332,000	1.4
5 3/4%	Note B 2003	8/15/03	28,011,028	156,000	0.6
5 7/8%	Note A 2004	2/15/04	12,955,077	0	0
7 1/4%	Note B 2004	5/15/04	14,440,372	0	0
7 1/4%	Note C 2004	8/15/04	13,346,467	31,200	0.2
7 7/8%	Note D 2004	11/15/04	14,373,760	0	0
7 1/2%	Note A 2005	2/15/05	13,834,849	0	0
Total Notes			418,301,638	54,620,320	13.1

31

TABLE B-2. Derivation of STRIPS (February 28, 1995)

Treasury Issue			Principal Amount Outstanding (000s)		
Coupon	Bond	Maturity	Total	Held In STRIPPED Form	% STRIPPED
11 5/8%	Bond 2004,	11/15/04	8,301,806	2,638,400	31.8
12 %	Bond 2005	5/15/05	4,260,758	1,597,900	37.5
10 3/4%	Bond 2005	8/15/05	9,269,713	720,800	0.8
9 3/8%	Bond 2006	2/15/06	4,755,916	1,152	0.02
11 3/4%	Bond 2009 14	11/15/14	6,005,584	4,191,200	69.7
11 1/4%	Bond 2015	2/15/15	12,667,799	6,463,360	51.0
10 5/8%	Bond 2015	8/15/15	7,149,916	5,343,040	74.7
9 7/8%	Bond 2015	11/15/15	6,899,859	4,366,400	63.3
9 1/4%	Bond 2016	2/15/16	7,266,854	740,000	10.2
7 1/4%	Bond 2016	5/15/16	18,823,551	557,600	2.9
7 1/2%	Bond 2016	11/15/16	18,864,448	993,760	5.3
8 3/4%	Bond 2017	5/15/17	18,194,169	10,860,320	59.7
8 7/8%	Bond 2017	8/15/17	14,016,858	5,990,400	42.7
9 1/8%	Bond 2018	5/15/18	8,708,639	6,718,400	77.1
9 %	Bond 2018	11/15/18	9,032,870	7,294,600	80.8
8 7/8%	Bond 2019	2/15/19	19,250,798	14,225,600	73.9
8 1/8%	Bond 2019	8/15/19	20,213,832	3,142,720	15.5
8 1/2%	Bond 2020	2/15/20	10,228,868	5,289,200	51.7
8 3/4%	Bond 2020	5/15/20	10,158,883	7,027,520	69.2
8 3/4%	Bond 2020	8/15/20	21,418,606	16,656,800	77.8
7 7/8%	Bond 2021	2/15/21	11,113,373	1,057,600	9.5
8 1/8%	Bond 2021	5/15/21	11,958,888	7,543,680	63.1
8 1/8%	Bond 2021	8/15/21	12,163,482	7,222,080	59.4
8 %	Bond 2021	11/15/21	32,798,394	25,101,800	76.5
7 1/4%	Bond 2022	8/15/22	10,352,790	3,070,400	29.7
7 5/8%	Bond 2022	11/15/22	10,699,626	7,985,600	74.6
7 1/8%	Bond 2023	2/15/23	18,374,361	3,878,400	21.1
6 1/4%	Bond 2023	8/15/23	22,909,044	419,840	1.8
7 1/2%	Bond 2024	11/15/24	11,469,662	475,040	4.1
7 5/8%	Bond 2025	2/15/25	11,725,197	0	0
Total Bonds			389,054,544	161,573,612	41.5
Grand Total			807,356,182	216,193,932	26.8

32

Yield Curves and Market Indices

CHAPTER 3

The Content of Yields and Yield Spreads

Gregory Kitter
Director
Dow Jones—Telerate, Inc.

According to the old adage, "You get what you pay for." Another states, "There's no such thing as a free lunch." Both of these sayings have direct application to the fixed-income markets, particularly when it comes to evaluating the yield on a security. The value of a particular return is only as good as its relationship to yields on securities of both similar and different issuers. It is these comparisons on which many traders and investors spend countless hours, because this is an area where better-than-current market returns can be achieved.

Before we can analyze yield spreads, we need to review the real definition of yield.

What Exactly Is the Concept of Yield?

Most fixed-income securities represent their returns through the determination of an annualized yield, or percentage return over the life of the security expressed on an annual basis. There are three basic yield calculations: *discount yield,* used to calculate returns on money-market securities issued at a discount; *simple interest, or money-market yield,* also used primarily for short-term securities where issuance is at par, with interest accruing until, and payable at maturity; and *yield to maturity,* where periodic interest and, perhaps, principal payments are made until the security matures or is redeemed. It is this final measurement that is most commonly used to measure returns on capital-market securities (due in one year or more).

While yield to maturity is very popular in representing return on fixed-income securities, it presumes all cash flows thrown off from the security will be reinvested at the same initial rate of return. While this is possible, common sense and experience tell us that this scenario is highly unlikely, particularly as the final maturity of the security increases.

An alternative measurement of returns that more closely reflects the actual yield-to-maturity earned on the security is *realized compound yield*. Realized compounded yield (RCY) allows the investor to enter his or her own projected reinvestment rates for future coupon and principal payments. While some would argue that this form of yield calculation is as uncertain as the standard method, the investor has the benefit of viewing future market required returns through a series of derivative securities. The most liquid of these instruments is the Eurodollar futures contract, where three-month returns maturing as far as 10 years in advance are exchange-traded. By combining these returns into coupon equivalents, the investor can lock in a future rate of return by simply purchasing the appropriate futures contracts covering the cash flows of the investment.[1] Clearly, there may be a difference in the degree of risk associated with the Eurodollar futures (based on time deposits) and that of the security being analyzed. Nevertheless, statistical adjustments for risk differentials can be input to create a more relevant rate of return. Table 1 reflects the difference in realized returns resulting from calculating a realized compound yield versus the calculated yield to maturity. *As the reinvestment rates fall, so does the realized compound yield.*

TABLE 1. Realized Compound Yield

The actual or realized compound yield on an interest bearing security is a function of the reinvestment rate of all cash flows associated with that security.			
U.S. Treasury Bond	**Reinvestment Rate**	**Realized Compound Yield**	**Difference from Y-T-M**
Coupon: 6%	5.000%	5.927%	-1.06%
Maturity: 2/15/2026	6.000%	6.443%	-0.54%
Settlement date: 7/15/96	**6.984%**	**6.984%**	0.00%
Price: 87 24/32	8.000%	7.574%	0.59%
Yield to Maturity: 6.984%	9.000%	8.185%	1.20%

------

1. This practice has not been adopted on a widespread basis, although it does enable the investor to develop a better estimate of a realistic rate of return on a coupon security.

One more form of yield is a concept known as *true yield*. Consider the following: On July 15, 1996, a trader purchases a short-term corporate note due on September 7, 1996. This note carries a coupon of 6 percent, and a has a yield to maturity of 6.718 percent, if returns are calculated to the actual maturity date. This date, however, falls on a Saturday, and the issuer does not pay out the proceeds until the next business day (Monday). The trader will lose use of the money for two days (Saturday and Sunday). What is the impact of this loss in terms of actual, or true, yield? Taking these two days into consideration reduces the yield to 6.478 percent (see Table 2). As a practical matter, the difference between true yield and yield to maturity has little impact on overall returns if the cash flows in question are due in more than one year. As a result, money-market traders and investors are particularly interested in the *true yield* concept.

What Determines the Level of a Yield?

The yield, or price, of a fixed-income security is, like all other financial instruments, determined by the market place. An acceptable market level of yield is a function of three basic factors. First, is *creditworthiness*. A fixed-income security is composed of principal and interest payments, the reliability of which is based on the financial stability of the issuer. The risk of default is a major consideration in the determination of an acceptable rate of return on a fixed-income investment.

The second factor is the *maturity* of the security. The representation of a *yield curve* (or series of homogenous risk, fixed-income securities with

TABLE 2. True Yield

Measuring the difference between the standard yield to maturity calculation and **True Yield** on an interest bearing security.

Coupon:	6.000%
Maturity:	9/7/96 (Saturday)
Price:	99.875
Std. Yield:	6.718%
True Yield:	6.478%

The actual payment date for principal and interest will not occur until Monday, September 9. Since the issuer does not pay interest from the maturity date forward, the investor loses earnings power on 9/7 and 9/8. Therefore, the true yield needs to be adjusted to reflect this loss.
Note: 9/7 is a Saturday. Calculations presume 9/7/96.

increasing maturities) is considered to look "normal" when it is upward sloping. In other words, the longer the maturity, the higher the yield. This relates back to the theory of *liquidity preference,* where investors require higher rates of return for investing funds over longer periods of time. Figure 1 is a representation of a normally-sloped U.S. Treasury yield curve, with maturities extending from three months to 30 years. As one can see, the curve flattens out past the 10-year mark, with relatively little pickup in return between 10-30 years as opposed to the yield spreads reflected between the shorter maturities. The reason for this is related to the perceived differences in future economic conditions, the degree of certainty that can be associated with these perceptions, and investors requirements in terms of rates of return over the various time periods. Indeed, forecasting the changes in economic conditions becomes more a function of art than science the farther out one goes in time. For example, it is somewhat easier to estimate economic conditions over the next two years than for the period between 15 and 20 years in the future (it is difficult enough predicting economic conditions three months away).

Generally speaking, longer-term rates don't reflect as much volatility over time as shorter rates, for the simple reason that incremental changes in current fundamental or technical factors affecting interest rates are mostly played out over relatively short periods of time. Over the past 50 years, during periods when the economy heated up and inflation

FIGURE 1.   U.S. Treasury Yield Curve (Normal Yield Curve)

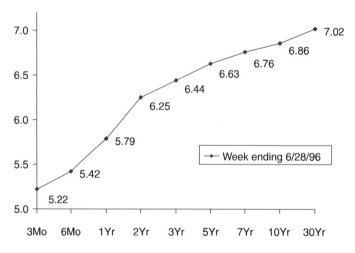

Source: Federal Reserve H.15.

rose, short-term rates rose more dramatically than long-term rates. These situations sometimes led to what is termed an *inverted yield curve* where short-term rates exceeded long-term rates (Figure 2). While there are no strict rules governing the structure and movement of a yield curve over time, these kinds of economic events have traditionally caused the fixed-income markets to react in the manner described above.

The third factor affecting the yield level of a security is *liquidity*. The short to intermediate price/yield movement can easily be affected by the security's age and amount outstanding, impact of demand in the repo markets[2] (where appropriate), and by stripping activities (where appropriate). Generally speaking, the longer a security has been outstanding and the smaller the amount or par value outstanding, the more sensitive its price/yield is to trading activity in the marketplace.

For example, if a trader were interested in purchasing a particular fixed-income security that was issued several years ago, chances are there will not be a large amount of working supply, or trading inventory, available, thereby making the market for this issue considerably less liquid. At this stage of the security's life, it is a good bet that the majority, if not all of the issue has been placed with final purchasers, or the *buy side*. To get this

FIGURE 2.   U.S. Treasury Yield Curve (Inverted Yield Curve)

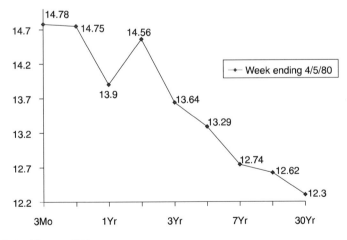

Source: Federal Reserve H.15.

---

2. The repo, or repurchase-agreement, market is in essence a collateralized short-term lending market where both dealers and investors either fund investment positions or provide funds in the form of short-term investment (usually no longer than one month).

security out for trading will require an opportunity for a holder to reap some financial benefit by selling. This may cause the security to rise in price temporarily to get the trade done, before it retreats back to its previous valuation. Recently issued, or actively traded, securities will trade at a much tighter spread than less-active or older issues.

The same liquidity principle applies to the amount of a security outstanding. The larger the issue size, the easier it will be to locate the security, regardless of its age. In the case of Treasury securities, an investor seeking a three-year note will have a much easier time finding a current, or recently issued, three-year security than an old 10-year note with the same three years to maturity. While the creditworthiness is homogenous, the additional liquidity in the recently issued three-year, added to the historically larger issue sizes in current Treasury auctions, translates into a tighter bid/ask quote with less likelihood of a required price/yield shift occurring to get the trade done.

The *repurchase-agreement, or repo, market* can also reflect signs of liquidity impact on an individual security price/yield volatility. Securities dealers sometimes sell securities that they do not own, in anticipation of buying them back at a lower price in the future. The dealers, however, need to deliver the shorted securities at some point. If market conditions are not conducive to covering the short position, the dealer will attempt to borrow the securities to avoid failing to deliver on the trade. The larger the dealer short position, the more pressure there is on the holders of the security to lend it out. When using repurchase-agreement, or collateralized-lending, transactions, dealers are in essence funding the position for the security owner. The bargaining between dealer and owner is over the cost of funding the position. The more desperate the dealer is to borrow the securities, the less he or she will require as compensation for the loan to fund the securities. If, for example, the regular funding rate for a Treasury security is 5 1/2 percent, and an investor can repo a particular security out of his or her inventory at a 1 percent rate, the investor can earn a spread of at least 450 basis points. (If the investor has already paid for the security, he or she can turn the proceeds around and invest them at a more favorable short-term rate. If the investor is putting up the security as collateral in the repo market, the 1 percent funding rate represents a significant reduction in borrowing costs.) In either case, the security has become more valuable due to its low repo cost. To adjust for this borrowing spread, the yield to purchase the security will fall (price rise) to offset the favorable borrowing scenario. This reduced borrowing rate is called a *repo special* to highlight the special borrowing conditions existing in the repo market. Table 3 highlights the price/yield impact of a security on repo special.

TABLE 3. Price Impact from Security on Repo "Special"

Coupon: 6%	**Maturity:** 2/15/26	**Settlement:** 7/15/96
Yield: 6.984%	**RP Term:** 1 week (to 7/22)	
Price: 87 24/32	**Repo Rate (Special):** 1%	**Repo Rate (General):** 5.25%

(per $1million par value)

Coupon accrual for 7 days:	$1,153.88
Financing cost @ 1% for 1 week	$175.46
Financing cost @ 5.25% for 1 week	$921.19
Positive carry @ 1.00% Financing	$978.42
Positive carry @ 5.25% Financing	($232.69)
Difference	$745.73

The additional carry earned amounted to approximately **2 1/2** 32nds of a price point. All other things constant, this security would have a cash price of **87 21+** if the repo cost for financing was **5.25%**. (1/32 per million = $312.50).

Carry represents the difference between daily coupon accrual and cost of financing. Positive carry occurs when the coupon accrual is greater than the cost of financing.

The *stripping,* or separation of principal and interest portions of a fixed-income security reduces the amount of tradable paper in circulation. This can have a similar effect on price/yield volatility as those above-mentioned issues with smaller par-value outstanding. The stripping activity in the U.S. Treasury securities market has also created a process of reattaching, or reconstituting, principal and interest portions of a security.

The difference between these two situations is that the stripped issues can be put back together, or *reconstituted* by the trader. This process will occur when the sum of the parts can be purchased for less than the market value of the whole. At present, reconstitution is an alternative investment strategy only for U.S. Treasuries and for some federal agency issues.

The How, Where, and Why of Constructing Yield Spreads

If one were to be offered a 10-year U.S. Treasury security today at a yield of 8 percent, would it be worthwhile to purchase? How do you know? A yield level of 8 percent on a 10-year note is impossible to measure in terms of whether or not it is a good buy unless the investor knows something about the environment in which the security is being offered. Where has the security been trading over the past few months? The past few days? Has the amount of outstanding par value changed? What are the yields on the five-year and 30-year Treasury issues? What about the yield on a 10-year AAA corporate bond? The investment appeal of any yield is largely a function of its relationship to other securities of similar credit risk and to securities of similar maturity with different credit risks. Once these factors have been determined, the investor has a better framework from which to make an informed decision.

In making the determination as to which securities to compare to a particular issue under consideration, the investor needs to review those issues that most closely relate to the characteristics of that security. As noted above, creditworthiness, maturity, and liquidity, the three major factors in evaluating yield, need to be examined. Many trades get structured based on one or more of these parameters. The investor may feel the yield spread between the five-year and 10-year Treasury note is too wide, indicating either a five-year yield that is too low, or a 10-year yield that is too high. Similarly, the spread between a 10-year AAA corporate bond and a 10-year Treasury may be viewed as too narrow (remember, the larger the implied credit risk, the higher the yield), indicating that the corporate bond is too highly priced, or the Treasury is too cheap.

Interest Rate Risk and Basis Risk

There are two types of market risk associated with a noncallable,[3] fixed-income security yield spread. *Interest rate risk* represents the parallel shift, or simultaneous movement, of multiple rates along the yield curve. In other words, yields of all maturities with a homogenous credit risk, or yields of several levels of credit risk with a similar maturity move the same amount and in the same direction. This can occur from changes in fundamental or technical factors that affect market prices and yields. *Basis risk* represents nonparallel shifts in multiple rates. This is where instances of *steepening* or *flattening* in the yield curve are observed.

There are two ways to take advantage of these perceived differences in yield spreads:

---

3. Securities that are callable are subject to the risk of being called at a date earlier than the stated maturity date. This could cause the investor to lose some portion of return due to early redemption.

1. The investor can either buy or sell a specific security outright, in anticipation of the security falling or rising in yield. This strategy takes on both interest rate and basis risk, in as much as the investor has an immediate gain or loss if the security moves in one direction or the other.

2. A more conservative, yet effective strategy to take advantage of perceived anomalies in yield spreads is to simultaneously purchase and sell the two securities based on the expectations of the direction the yield spread between them will take.

Table 4 reflects how trading strategies (1) and (2) would be set given the assumption that the yield spread between the active three-year and 10-year Treasury securities is too wide.

In the case of the outright purchase or sale of one of the two securities, the investor is subject to both interest-rate and basis risk. A purchase of the 10-year note would result in a loss if interest rates rose in parallel fashion, or if the 10-year yield rose and the three-year note fell or remained unchanged. If, however, the investor sold the three-year note and simultaneously bought the 10-year note, a parallel shift in both interest rates in either direction would leave the current yield spread unchanged, thereby apparently mitigating the interest rate risk. Unfortunately, there is a little more work to be done to actually eliminate this risk.

There are a number of risk measurements that can be used to calculate a hedge ratio. One is called *basis-point value* (BPV), or the dollar price change in a security, given a one-basis-point change in its yield. To calculate this measure, simply determine the security price at .5 basis-points

TABLE 4. Interest-Rate-Risk Management

Settlement Date 7/15/96

U.S.Treasury 3-Year	**U.S. Treasury 10-Year**
6 3/8% Due 5/15/99	7% Due 7/15/2006
Price: 99 26/32	101 2/32
Yield: 6.444%	6.851%
Yield Spread 40.7 basis points	

Strategy 1: Purchase 10-year or sell 3-year Treasuries. Either trade will result in **immediate P/L** when the security changes price.

Strategy 2: Simultaneously sell the 3-year and **buy** the 10-year at a yield spread of 40.7 basis points. This way, if the yield curve moves in a parallel fashion (interest rate risk), the yield spread on the trade will remain constant.

below and above the current yield to maturity. Subtract one from the other, and you have your estimate (see Table 5). BPV is most easily understood when quoted in terms of a change in $1 million present value of a security. It is a "quick and dirty" estimate of price/yield sensitivity.

While BPV is good for calculating short-term changes in the price/yield relationship, a better statistic is a concept known as *duration*. This is a risk measurement developed by Frederick Macaulay in 1938.[4] It represents the midpoint, measured in years, that an investor receives the *middle* dollar of an investment in present value terms (remember, the purchase price of a bond is equal to the present value of the future stream of cash flows associated with the bond). A more practical way to view duration is that a 100-basis-point change in a security's yield will reflect a price change in percent approximately equal to the number of years measured by the duration statistic. For example, a duration of five years indicates a 5 percent change in price given a 100-basis-point change in either direction in yield to maturity.

While duration is helpful as a risk measurement, it assumes continuous compounding of interest over time. A more realistic method of measuring this risk is through a concept known as *modified duration*. Developed by Hicks,[5] this statistic adjusts the compounding factor to the number of coupon payments per annum. In most fixed-income securities, coupons are paid semiannually. The modified duration adjustment (outlined in Table 6) in this case would be

TABLE 5. Basis-Point Value

Basis-Point Value: The dollar price change in a security given a one basis-point change in its yield.		
Coupon: 7%		**VALUE**
Maturity: 7/15/06	Yield: 6.855%	1,010,372
Settlement: 7/15/96	Yield: 6.865%	1,009,652
Yield: 6.86%	Difference (per million present value)	$720
For each move in yield of 1 basis point, the value of 1 million of the above security will change by $720.		

---

4. See Frederick Macaulay's *Some Theoretical Problems Suggested by the Movements of Interest Rates, Bond Yields, and Stock Prices in the United States since 1865* (New York: National Bureau of Economic Research, 1938).

5. See J. R. Hicks, *Value and Capital* (Oxford: Clarendon Press, 1939).

$$\text{Modified Duration} = \frac{Duration}{(1 + YTM/2)}$$

where

YTM	=	Yield to maturity
2	=	number of compounding periods per year.

Table 6 outlines the measurement of modified duration given a 100-basis-point change in yield.

A third, more accurate, measure for small yield-changes, and one used by many traders to calculate hedge ratios for bond swaps, is *dollar duration, or dollar risk*. This statistic is the product of an issue's modified duration and full price (principal plus accrued interest). Table 7 outlines the risk measurement statistic.

The sensitivity of a specific security's price/yield relationship is a function of (1) time to maturity, (2) coupon, and (3) yield to maturity.

Three rules must be remembered:

Rule 1. *The longer the time to maturity, the greater the change in price, given a set change in yield.* The structure of a three-year note contains six

TABLE 6. Duration and Modified Duration

Security:	(1 million present value)
Coupon:	6%
Maturity:	7/15/98
Settlement:	7/15/96
Yield to Maturity:	6.25%

A Cash Flows	B	C Present Value Factor	D (B x C) Present Value	E Period	F (D x E) Adj. Present Value
1/15/97	30,000	0.9697	29,091	0.5	14,546
7/15/97	30,000	0.9403	28,209	1.0	28,209
1/15/98	30,000	0.9118	27,354	1.5	41,031
7/15/98	1,030,000	0.8842	910,726	2.0	1,821,452
					1,905,238

Duration = 1.905 years

Modified Duration = $\dfrac{1.905}{(1 + 0625/2)}$ = 1.847 yrs

For every 100 basis points move in yield to maturity, the price of this security will change by approximately 1.847%.

TABLE 7. Risk (Dollar Duration)

Coupon:		6.00%		
Maturity:		2/15/26		
Settlement:		7/15/96		
Yield:		6.918%		
Price (decimal):		88.497		
Accrued interest per million:		24890.11		
Modified Duration:		12.49531		
Risk =	Principal		884,973	12.49531
	Interest		24,890	x 0.909863
			909,863	**11.36902**

For small changes in yield, the risk statistic can be used as a hedging tool.

coupons and a principal payment. The structure of a 10-year note contains 20 coupons and a principal payment. The price of a fixed-income security represents the present value of a future stream of cash flows associated with a specific security. When the yield to maturity of a security changes, the present value of each of the coupons and of the principal changes as well. Given that there are more than three times the number of coupons in a 10-year note than in a three-year note, the total payments associated with the 10-year note are much greater (see Table 8). As a result, the sensitivity of a price change, given an equal yield change, is much greater for the 10-year note than the three-year note.

TABLE 8. Security Cash-Flow Structure

(per 1 million par value)

Three-year Treasury Note (6 3/8% 5/15/99) has six coupons of $31,875 and a principal payment of $1,000,000.

Total Cash Flow = $1,000,000 + (6 x $31,875) = **$1,191,250**

10-year Treasury Note (7% 7/15/2006) has 20 coupons of $35,000 and a principal payment of $1,000,000.

Total cash flow = $1,000,000 + (20 x $35,000) = **$1,700,000**

The larger total cash-flow of the 10-year note makes it more sensitive to changes in yield.

Rule 2. *The higher the coupon, the lower the price/yield sensitivity of the security.* The total cash flow associated with a bond include both principal and interest payments. As mentioned above, the faster the repayment of these cash flows, the less sensitive the price/yield changes will be. As the coupon of a security increases, proportionately more of the total return of that security will be represented by the coupon payments. As a result, the timing of the cash-flow returns, on average, is reduced. Table 9 reflects two securities with the same maturity date, the same timing of cash flows, and the same price. One security, however, has a 6 percent coupon, while the other has a 12 percent coupon. As one can see, the price/yield sensitivity of the 6 percent coupon issue is greater than that of the 12 percent issue, as the returns, on average, are paid out over a longer period of time for the 6 percent security.

Rule 3. *The higher the yield to maturity (YTM), the lower the price/yield sensitivity of the issue.* As the yield to maturity changes, each cash flow is discounted by the same rate to get to the present value of the security. The lower the yield to maturity, the greater the change in the present value of each cash flow. An easy way to visualize this concept is as follows: 11 percent YTM – 10 percent YTM = 1 percent, with 1 percent equal to a 1/10 relative change. 5 percent – 4 percent also equals 1 percent, but in this case 1 percent is 1/4 of 4 percent. Table 10 reflects a security with the same coupon and maturity under two different yield-change scenarios. It is clear that the 100-basis-point change in yield to maturity between 5 percent and 4 percent creates a much larger price difference than does the same change between yields of 11 percent and 10 percent. You will notice

TABLE 9. Relationship between Coupon and Modified Duration

The higher the coupon, the lower the price/yield sensitivity (assuming identical price and maturity date).

Settlement date:	7/15/96	
Maturity:	7/15/06	
Price:	100	
Yield:	7.00%	
Coupon:	6%	12%
Modified Duration:	7.304	6.429

The higher coupon-rate reduces the average amount of time in which the security pays its returns.

TABLE 10.   Relationship between Yield to Maturity and Modified
             Duration

The higher the yield to maturity, the lower the price/yield sensitivity.

Coupon	7%	Yield to Maturity	Price	Price Difference	Modified Duration
Maturity:	7/15/06	4%	124.527		7.52
Settlement:	7/15/96	5%	115.589	8.938	7.38
		10%	81.307		6.69
		11%	76.099	5.208	6.55

that the modified duration on the lower yield to maturity examples is also higher.

It is important to conceptualize the dynamic relationship between changes in price and yield. As pointed out in the previous examples, the higher the yield, the smaller the price change between equally incremented yield values. While some would expect these differences to be linear in nature, that is not the case. Consider the following:

$$2 - 1 = 1 \qquad\qquad 2/1 = 2.00$$
$$3 - 2 = 1 \qquad\qquad 3/2 = 1.50$$
$$4 - 3 = 1 \qquad\qquad 4/3 = 1.33$$
$$5 - 4 = 1 \qquad\qquad 5/4 = 1.25$$
$$101 - 100 = 1 \qquad\qquad 101/100 = 1.01$$

As you can see, the higher the numbers get in absolute size, the smaller the same one-unit difference becomes in percentage terms. This is reflected in the changing relative weights of the coupons and the principal payment. Holding maturity constant, as yield rises, the coupons take on a larger relative presence in the total present-value dollar return. Remember, the price of a coupon security is nothing more than the present value of all future cash flows associated with the security. Table 11 reflects the differences in price for a security with varying yields to maturity.

Constructing a Yield-Spread Trade Hedging Interest-Rate Risk

Table 12 shows the construction and implementation of a yield spread trade. The trader has determined the yield spread between the active three-year and 10-year Treasury securities is too wide. In order to put on a

TABLE 11. Price Sensitivity at Different Levels of Yield to Maturity

Coupon:	6.00%		
Maturity:	2/15/26		
Settlement:	7/15/96		
Yield		**Price**	**Difference**
3.00%		158.559	
4.00%		134.504	24.055
5.00%		115.355	19.149
6.00%		100.000	15.355
7.00%		87.583	12.417
8.00%		77.447	10.136
9.00%		69.122	8.325
10.00%		62.219	6.903
11.00%		56.447	5.772

curve-flattening trade (three-year yield to rise and/or 10-year yield to fall), the trader needs to calculate the hedge ratio between the two securities. Finding this to be 2.817, the trader sells 2.817 million three-year notes and simultaneously buys 1 million 10-year notes. By putting on the trade with this ratio of three-year to 10-year notes, the trader is insulated from interest rate risk. As the example indicates, a 5-basis-point upward parallel shift in both rates leaves the trader virtually indifferent to the move. If the spread begins to narrow, the trader will earn a little more than $700 (depending on whether the three-year rises in yield or the 10-year falls) for each basis point move. The reverse is true if the spread widens.

There is no simple and inexpensive way to hedge against basis risk. The only readily available format is over-the-counter options, which are both illiquid and expensive.

Convexity
BPV and dollar risk are useful to examine changes in price, given smaller changes in yield. For larger changes in yield, the concept of *modified duration* better quantifies the price/yield sensitivity relationship. The actual change in price is somewhat different from the projected change of the modified duration estimate. This is due to the nonlinear relationship between price and yield (as noted above). In order to adjust for this difference, a second moment of difference, or the change in the change, must be calculated. *Convexity* represents the change in the change of a price, given

TABLE 12.   Hedging against Interest Rate Risk Using the Hedge Ratio

---

Setting the Trade

A trader has determined the yield spread between the active 3-year and 10-year Treasury notes is too wide. As a result, he or she will sell the three's and buy the 10's. But how much of each is needed to mitigate interest rate risk?

Issues Traded

3 year	6 3/8%	5/15/99	Price	99.8125	Yield	6.444
10 year	7%	7/15/2006	Price	101.0625	Yield	6.851
					Current Spread	40.7 bps

Calculate Hedge Ratio

	3 year	10 year	Ratio
Modified Duration	2.53	7.127	2.817

Set the Hedge

Purchase 1 million 10-year notes @ 101.0625

Sell 2.817 million 3-year notes @ 99.8125

Assume a 5 bp upward parallel shift in interest rates.

	Yield	3-Year Price (dec)		Yield	10-Year Price (dec)
	6.444	99.8125		6.851	101.063
+ 5 bps	6.494	99.6850		6.901	100.707
	GAIN	$1,275		LOSS	($3,560)
	X Hedge Ratio	2.817			
	GAIN	$3,592			

$3,592 - 3,560 = $32.00 net gain*

Had the investor not used the hedge ratio in putting on the yield spread the loss on the trade would have been ($3,560 - 1,275) $2,285.

---

*Rounding used in calculations. Note that curvelinear nature of price/yield relationship makes hedge ratio calculation difficult to make P/L = $0 in these transactions.

a change in yield. Combining both modified duration and convexity essentially covers the entire actual change in price, from a specific change in yield. Table 13 measures that portion of actual change in price, given a

TABLE 13.   Measuring the Impact of Convexity in Price/Yield
             Sensitivity

Coupon:	7%	Price:	101
Maturity:	7/15/06	Duration:	7.37 yrs.
Settlement:	7/15/96	Mod Dur:	7.126 yrs.
Yield:	6.86%	Convexity:	64.563

A	B	C	D	E	F	% Change
Yield	Actual Price	% Change from 6.86%	Mod Dur Estimate	% Change from 6.86%	(C - E) Diff.	Measured by Convexity
3.86%	125.846	24.60%	122.592	21.38%	3.22%	2.91%
4.86%	116.791	15.60%	115.395	14.26%	1.34%	1.29%
5.86%	108.535	7.46%	108.197	7.13%	0.33%	0.32%
6.86%	101.000	0.00%	101.000	0.00%	0.00%	0.00%
7.86%	94.120	6.81%	93.803	7.13%	-0.32%	-0.32%
8.86%	87.829	13.04%	86.605	14.26%	-1.22%	-1.29%
9.86%	82.073	18.74%	79.408	21.38%	-2.64%	-2.91%

Out to a 200 bp change in yield, convexity covers virtually all of the price change not
accounted for by modified duration.

change in yield, explained by convexity. As you can see, the actual price
change is almost entirely accounted for by these two statistics.[6]

Positive convexity exists in noncallable bonds. *Negative* convexity
could exist in callable bonds as the likelihood of a call increases. This is
largely a function of changes in required market rates of return for the
particular risk category and maturity represented by the security in question. The following formula gives the percent change in price explained
by convexity:

$$\% \text{ Change} = .5 \times \text{Convexity} \times \Delta \text{Yield}^2 \times 100$$

Yield-Spread Analysis: What Is the Value?

Yield-spread analysis can be viewed in one of two basic forms. Either the
investor is comparing yields of the same maturity with different credit

---

6. Mathematically, modified duration is the first derivative of price with respect to yield,
and convexity is the second derivative of price. The small difference left unaccounted for
can be identified by the third derivative of price. This can be measured thorough a third-
order Taylor series, available in most basic calculus texts.

risks, or similar credit risk with different maturities. The first case is called *intermarket yield-spreads* while the second is called *intramarket yield-spreads.*

In the case of *intermarket analysis,* the major issue is creditworthiness. When investors study this form of yield spread, it is important and efficient from a practical as well as quantitative perspective to have a base, or benchmark, from which all yields can be measured. The U.S. Treasury market is the most eligible candidate for this job, since, from a *creditworthiness* perspective, U.S. Treasury issues have the highest rating of safety. From a *maturity* perspective, there are Treasury issues maturing weekly, monthly, and quarterly out to 30 years. From a *liquidity* perspective, the U.S. Treasury is the largest issuer of debt, containing individual issues within each maturity sector virtually dwarfing the size of even the largest issuers in other fixed-income markets. The Treasury has several standard maturity sectors for which it periodically issues debt. The most recent issue in each sector is considered to be the current, or "on-the-run," issue. Many issuers in other domestic fixed-income segments use these active issues as benchmarks to price their own securities. For example, a new BAA-rated corporate bond could be priced at a 95-basis-point spread over the corresponding Treasury maturity (similar to other issues with the same maturity and credit rating). Then as the issue ages, or *seasons,* it will be spread over the appropriate Treasury on-the-run maturity, again in the same relationship as other similar maturity issues having the same creditworthiness or credit rating. The reason for this is simple: there is a much higher degree of liquidity in Treasury issues than in securities of other issuers. As a result, Treasury securities are more likely to be actively traded in the secondary markets, thereby generating an active, as opposed to interpolated, price.

Intramarket yield-spreads are followed in most markets, but as a practical matter, only actively traded in the Treasury market (once again due to the liquidity issue). The major reason for traders to purchase or sell an intramarket yield-spread is in anticipation of a shift toward a steeper or flatter yield curve. These types of shifts can be a function of changes in fundamental economic factors affecting the markets, of liquidity issues for one or more securities, or of some exogenous factor such as political unrest, war, or a credit crisis for a major bank, agency, or corporation that would cause investors to flee to the safety of short-term Treasury securities (called *flight to quality*).

Traditionally, the trading of these types of spreads in the cash markets was confined mostly to dealers quoting on an *as-requested* basis from the customer, where the dealer would buy or sell a particular spread between two issues at some basis point differential, then purchase from and sell to the customer the securities in question. For example, a dealer sells the 2-year/10-year Treasury active-issue yield spread at a differential of 60 basis points. In this case, the dealer is selling the two-year and buying the 10-year from a counterparty. At this point, the dealer must deliver the two-year note and purchase the 10-year note at a yield spread of 60 basis points, using the appropriate hedge ratio to mitigate interest rate risk. The traded prices of both issues must translate into a yield-spread differential of 60 basis points.

In recent years, the trading of both intermarket and intramarket cash-market spreads has expanded, particularly through the interdealer broker markets. *Curve* trades between several pairs of active Treasury issues are now quoted over Dow Jones Telerate screens by Cantor Fitzgerald, the largest interdealer broker in U.S. Government securities. Market participants are also able to obtain tradable quotes on yield spreads between U.S. government and federal agency securities, spreads between different Federal agency issues, and between and among various Treasury cash securities and principal and interest STRIPS[7] (zero-coupon instrument) maturities. In all cases, the quoting mechanism is reflected in a basis-point yield differential.

Intermarket- and intramarket yield-spread trading are not confined to the cash markets. The futures market traders have also implemented the spread-trade concept in such popular trading relationships as the Treasury bill/Eurodollar (TED) spread.[8] This intermarket trade requires the simultaneous purchase or sale of a three-month Treasury-bill futures contract with an offsetting position in the three-month Eurodollar-time-deposit futures market. Traders buy and sell this spread in anticipation of changes in the yield relationships between Treasury bills and Eurodollars. Historically, the spread widens and narrows as the general level of interest rates rises and falls. The higher the general level of short-term rates, the wider the TED spread. This is due to the greater degree of perceived default risk as the costs of borrowing rise. While short-term Eurodollar time deposits are generally a safe investment, the issuers of the deposits are commercial banks. As a result, the credit risk for these issuers is greater than the credit risk perceived for borrowing from the U.S. Treasury.

Intramarket spreads in the futures markets are also a popular trading tool. Traders use Eurodollar futures to create *calendar spreads*. This is

7. The STRIPS (separate trading of registered interest and principal of securities) program began at the end of 1984. To qualify for stripping, a Treasury issue must have a minimum maturity of 10 years.
8. Treasury-bill and Eurodollar futures contracts are traded on the International Monetary Market of the Chicago Mercantile Exchange.

structured by buying a futures contract of one maturity and selling a contract of another maturity. For example, a trader buying a September 1996 Eurodollar contract at 94.18 (5.82 percent) and selling a December 1996 contract at 93.91 (6.09 percent) for a spread of 27 basis points. Conceptually, the yield on each one of these contracts (yield = 100 − contract price) represents the cost of borrowing or rate of return on investment for the three-month period immediately following the expiration date of the contract. In the example (using a July 15, 1996, trade date), the trader is simultaneously buying a futures contract on a three-month Eurodollar time deposit to begin in September and mature in December, and the trader is selling a futures contract on a three-month Eurodollar time deposit to begin in December and mature in March 1997. The trader believes that the slope of the Eurodollar yield curve will become steeper between these two maturities, between July and September (when the September contract expires), thereby widening the current spread between the two contracts.

Rich/Cheap Analysis: Where Is the Value?

Every morning between 7:30–8:00 A.M. (EST), many dealer trading rooms have a meeting. At this gathering, the sales people listen to their traders from the various market segments discuss the relative merits or demerits of their markets for that particular day. One of the most popular portions of the discussion is the highlights of those issues or yield spreads that are either rich or cheap in value. It is these trading insights which give sales people one reason to call their customers.

Rich/cheap analysis can be calculated by a number of different methods. While this is not the proper venue to get into the more quantitative applications, a quick and dirty method used by many traders, sales people, and portfolio managers is the standard deviation measurement. To determine the relative value in a yield spread, use the following formula:

$$S_{rc} = \frac{Current - Average}{Standard\ Deviation}$$

where:

Current	=	the current value of the spread
Average	=	the average spread value over some period of time.
Standard Deviation	=	the standard deviation of the yield spread over the average time period.
S_{rc}	=	the number of standard deviations that the current spread is over or under the designated historical average.

For example, if the current yield-spread between the two-year Treasury note and the five-year Treasury note is 48 basis points, the average one-month spread is 40 basis points, and the one-month standard deviation of the spread is 4 basis points, the current spread is two standard deviations above the one-month average. What this statistic is telling the user is that over the past month, approximately 98 percent[9] of the spread observations noted were lower than 48 basis points In other words, the current two-year/five-year spread is *statistically wider* than it has been over the past month. The trader could *sell* the two-year note, and *buy* the five-year note (all other things being equal), in the appropriate hedge ratio to take advantage of this apparently temporary widening in the spread. If the trader is correct about the projected movement, the spread will narrow, and the trade will be profitable.

Summary

The most important pricing statistic to a fixed-income investor is yield. Yield is what the investor expects to earn. The determination of yield can be measured in one of several ways, the most important being yield to maturity. While this concept is widely used, it presumes future reinvestment at a constant rate. Realized compound yield allows the user to adjust for changes in future reinvestment rates.

The sensitivity of price/yield relationships in a fixed-income security is a function of maturity, coupon, and yield to maturity. A higher degree of sensitivity will result from a longer maturity, lower-interest coupon, or lower yield to maturity. Popular methods of expressing this sensitivity are basis-point value, yield value of a 32nd, and modified duration. While these measurements are helpful for small yield changes, they are linear in nature and don't entirely account for the actual curvilinear relationship between price and yield. The combination of modified duration and convexity, the first and second derivatives of price with respect to yield (the change in price, and the *change* in the change in price), account for virtually all of the observed price difference, given a large change in yield.

Yield-spread analysis measures the existing relationships among securities of the same maturity, but a different degree of risk (intermarket), and equal risk with different maturities (intramarket). Many fixed-income securities are priced off of the U.S. Treasury curve, due to its

---

9. Under a standard normal distribution, two standard deviations (STDs) above or below the mean indicates a total of .9772 (.5 + .4772) statistical probability that an observation in the sample will be lower than (when 2 STDs above) or higher than (2 STDs below) an observation at this level.

homogenous risk, comprehensive maturity schedule, and high degree of liquidity. The relative value of a yield spread between any two securities can be measured in a number of ways. One of the easiest methods to calculate compares the difference between the current and historical average and divides it by the standard deviation of observations over that time period.

CHAPTER 4

A Methodology for Market Rate Analysis and Forecasting

Alexander Levin, Ph.D.
Senior Quantitative Analyst
The Dime Savings Bank

D. James Daras
Executive Vice President and Treasurer
The Dime Savings Bank

Introduction

A rate forecast can be stated as a problem of finding the rate's average and standard deviation (STD) at a future point of time. More generally, a rate forecast is a problem of finding the probability distribution of a rate at a future point of time but never a concrete or "guaranteed" value that the rate will likely be. We do not predict the rate's specific values as they are random. Instead, we find the probability function and its parameters.

To forecast, one needs to build a model for the unknown variables. That is, a set of equations, inequalities, or other mathematical statements that would identify the process. Since the interest rate market is evolving randomly, the required model has to be stochastic, that is, an unexplainable (input) noise must be a part of it. This is in contrast to deterministic models in which noise arises as the mismatch between the real data and the model and is never treated as a part of the model.

One could wonder how to handle equations containing random (therefore absolutely unknown) input. Fortunately, analytics exist that allow us to solve for all of the needed results. These techniques will be demonstrated further. What is important to understand at this point is that the input noise is not arbitrary. It is called *white noise* and (being absolutely random) is strictly restricted: it has constant mean and STD, and is serially uncorrelated.[1] Since the real interest-rate process has changing distribution parameters and is serially correlated (has a "color"), we can formulate the problem of modeling as finding a filter that would transfer a white noise into the actual interest rate process.

This chapter presents modeling and forecasting methodologies, an application for the three-month Treasury-bill yield, and explains how to use traditional shock scenarios in order to reflect the real (continuous) markets.

The Rate Model

We have built a model, the continuous form of which is as follows:

$$\frac{dr}{dt} = -a(r - r_\infty) + \sigma w \tag{1}$$

where $r(t)$ is the rate process, $w(t)$ is a white noise, a is mean reversion, r_∞ is the long-term average, σ is the process's volatility, which may depend on r and t. Since (1) is a first-order differential equation, one initial condition should be used. Thus, estimates for unknown values of a, r_∞, σ, must be conditional.

Equation (1) can be presented in the following discrete approximation that is traditionally referred to as AR(1) model:

$$r_i = \varphi\, r_{i-1} + \mu(1 - \varphi) + \sigma w_i \tag{1'}$$

where μ is the long-term average, and φ is the AR(1) coefficient.

Two methods were used for estimating the model's parameters, the homoscedastic method and the heteroscedastic method. In the both cases, at any point of time, i of a given historical period, we find the difference between the actual rate and its estimate by formula (2) if there is no noise. This difference is the noise (σw) which is normalized by dividing by its short-term (for instance, 180-day) STD, σ. Finally, the resultant noise $w(t)$ is tested for being now a white noise. If so, the model is built successfully and it is perfectly tractable. If not, we have to make adjustments in the model.

Homoscedastic Model

This is a classical approach where σ=const. It is known [Wei 1990] that the maximum conditional likelihood estimate for a is obtained by minimizing

---

1. In many textbooks, white noise is assumed to be normally distributed, but this is not required for building the model. The only point of the study where normality is assumed is the "mental" interpretation of the distribution percentiles.

the sum of the squares of the noise. That is to say the maximum likelihood estimate for a coincides with the least mean square estimate provided that we use the same initial conditions for the rate process.[2]

Heteroscedastic Model

Volatility of the volatility is a known reality of the fixed-income market. It can be captured by the σ variable. No matter what the volatility model is, we use the following form for the log-likelihood function to be maximized:

$$L(a, \sigma) = -\frac{n}{2}\ln 2\pi - \frac{1}{2}\sum_i \ln \sigma_i^2 - \frac{1}{2}\sum_i \frac{a_i^2}{\sigma_i^2} \qquad (2)$$

where $a_i = \sigma_i w_i = r_i - \varphi r_{i-1} - \mu(1 - \varphi)$, and σ_i is "local" STD of the noise $a(t)$, for instance a 180-day STD. Therefore, the L-function is a function of the model's parameters, φ and μ, and is maximized with respect to them.

Volatility Model

Historical volatility is higher for the periods with high interest rates [Kuberek 1992]. It is important to mention that the "volatility" term refers to parameter σ, the STD of the model's noise, an unexplainable part of the model. If $r(t)$ changes satisfying equation (1) with no noise ($w=0$), we do not associate these changes with volatility.[3]

Some authors were attempting to find a link between yield and volatility. Thus, the Ross-Cox-Ingersoll model [Hull 1993] implies that σ is proportional to $\sqrt{r}$. R. Kuberek [1992] finds that it is rather proportional to the rate r. Our analysis shows that volatility can be fairly well approximated by a linear autoregressive function:

$$\sigma_i^2 = \varphi_\sigma \sigma_{i-1}^2 + (1 - \varphi_\sigma)(\alpha + \beta r) + \varepsilon \qquad (3)$$

where $\varphi_\sigma, \alpha, \beta$ are parameters, ε is the regression's error. A notable advantage of the model (3) is that we can fit the initial, actually observed volatility $\sigma(0)$. This is in contrast to any algebraic formula $\sigma = \sigma(r)$ which approximates "on average," but often results in mismatch between the model and actual data, right at the beginning of the time interval.

---

2. That is why, the estimates are referred to as *conditional*.

3. Thus, function $r(t) = r_\infty(1 - e^{-at}) + r_0 e^{-at}$ perfectly fits model (1) with no noise.

Nonstationary Noise's Drift

One of the problems in stochastic modeling is it requires a sufficiently long historical interval in order to truly represent the market's statistics. Thus, if the length of this period is much greater than $3/a$, the data series used to identify model (1) is long enough. This constraint however is too strict in practice.

Although the stationary nature of the model (1), (3) contradicts the seeming nonstationarity of the data sample, it can be identified to fit the data. The reason is that a short time series may represent a sample from a transient process being observed in a stationary system, much like (1) and (3). Unless we have a very long time-series (but, not necessarily frequent!) with completely diminished transients, we must account for the impact of the initial conditions on the market. That is, we must expect biased estimates for the model's parameters when the observed time series began with other than an "average" initial condition.

An important consequence of this statement is that the average of the model's noise will not be zero as it may be expected. Indeed, if in model (1') μ is accepted as the rate's average for the historical interval, then, the average for the noise term (σw_i) will be $(r_N - r_0)/N$ where N is the length of the interval. If this term is regarded as the nonstationary term, we usually should exclude it from the forecasting model though it was in the model covering the historical period.

It follows from the above discussion that one could view any change in the yield as nonstationary and exclude it from forecasting. The long-term average will be affected by this choice.

Forecasting

Although forecasting can be practically implemented via multiple Monte Carlo simulations with stochastic equations (1) and (3), this method is too time consuming. There are quite simple analytics to reconstruct the average (often called *forecast*) and standard deviation of the yield, at any future point of time. For the both models, we refer to the discrete equation (1').

Homoscedastic Model

Let us assume that μ is the long-term average, and w has a zero mean. The average is easily defined by the following equation:

$$r_i = \varphi\, r_{i-1} + \mu(1 - \varphi) + d_{n/s} \tag{4}$$

where the last term denotes the nonstationary noise drift discussed above. One can mention that this formula has a compact continuous analogue:

$$r(t) = r_\infty(1 - e^{-at}) + r_0 e^{-at}. \tag{4'}$$

We then find the variance of the both sides of equation (1') using the facts that r_{i-1} and w_i are uncorrelated, and the noise w is normalized:

$$\sigma^2_{r_i} = \varphi^2 \sigma^2_{r_{i-1}} + \sigma^2_w \tag{5}$$

Thus, the required uncertainty in the forecast is estimated iteratively.

Heteroscedastic Model

The average is still calculated using formula (4) or (4'). Strictly speaking, an additional term is required because of a nonlinear effect: volatility σ is simulated as an autoregressive function of the rate r, therefore becomes correlated with this rate as well as with the noise w. As a result, the last term in formula (1) has a nonzero mean. This effect however is insignificant (it is within the model's expected accuracy) and does not need to be captured in most cases.

The STD of the forecast is also defined by an iterative formula which becomes more complicated due to volatility equation (3). First, we can formally state that

$$\sigma^2_{r_i} = \varphi^2 \sigma^2_{r_{i-1}} + Var(\sigma_i w_i) + 2\varphi Cov(r_{i-1}, \sigma_i w_i). \tag{6}$$

To simplify the derivations, we again neglect correlations between r's, σ's, and w's in formula (6).

This leads to

$$\sigma^2_{r_i} = \varphi^2 \sigma^2_{r_{i-1}} + \sigma^2_{w_i} + E(\varepsilon_i w_i)^2 \tag{7}$$

Thus, formula (7) for the heteroskedastic case differs from formula (5) for the homoscedastic case in that "instantaneous" volatility is applied rather than the average one, and that the volatility model error is taken into account. Formula (7) shows that statistics of εw should be collected, along with others.

Analysis of the Three-Month Treasury-Bill History: 09/26/88—09/25/95 (Daily)

Estimating the Parameters

The seven-year period represents a seemingly nonstationary data. First, the entire collection of data is very far from being normally distributed (see Figure 1). Second, there is an almost 200-basis-point total drop in the rate (see Figure 2).

The homoscedastic maximum-conditional-likelihood estimate (which is simultaneously the conditional mean least squares estimate) for φ is 0.999329. The heteroscedastic maximum-conditional-likelihood estimate is 0.999342. We would like to give an informal interpretation of this number. For the heteroscedastic mode, the corresponding value of a in equation (1) is $a = 1 - \varphi = 0.000658$. This means a $1/0.000658 = 1520$ (days) $= 4.16$ (years) time constant in the yield dynamics. Roughly speaking, if the market is disturbed by an event (for example, the Federal Reserve changed the rate), the impact of this event will diminish over time by 63 percent in 4.16 years, by 86.5 percent in 8.32 years, and by 95 percent in 12.48 years.

The average STD of the noise is 0.0592 percent, this number becomes σ for the homoscedastic model. A "moving" σ is calculated

FIGURE 1.   Histogram of the Three-Month Yield

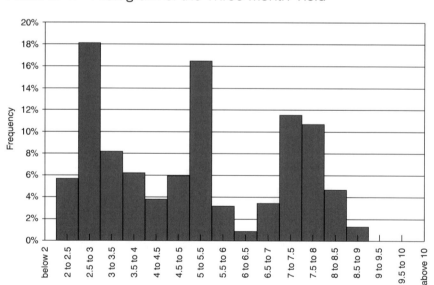

FIGURE 2.   History of the Three-Month Treasury Yield:
Sept. 1988–Sept. 1995

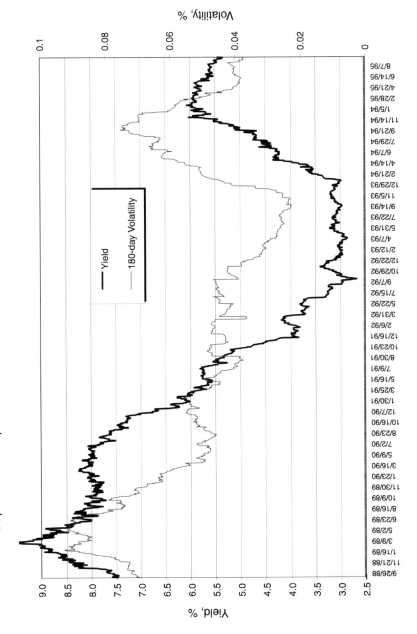

using 180-days intervals. The results are presented on Figure 2. One can see a visible correlation between volatility and the yield. Parameters for the volatility model (3) have been estimated as[4] $\varphi_\sigma = 0.997732$, $\alpha = 7.44_{10} - 6$, $\beta = 2.16_{10} -7$. The daily "volatility of volatility" was $\sigma_\varepsilon = 81.4_{10} - 6$, and the last term in formula (7) was $E(\varepsilon_i w_i)^2 = 6.95_{10} - 9$. The yield's average was 5.54472 percent with the average daily nonstationary drift of -0.00109 percent.

White Noise Test

Figure 3 and 4 give an idea of how the model's noise is closed to a white noise. Theoretical white noise has an autocorrelational function (ACF) equal to zero (except for lag=0) and a uniform spectrum. In our model, the ACF values are small enough. As for the spectrum, it can be corrected (to be uniform) by the model expansion. Namely, the noise spectrum corresponds to the output of a link, transfer function of which is approximately $1/(60s+1)$, where s is the Laplace operator, and input of which is a theoretical white noise. This means that we could include this link in the model making it a second-order system. However, a close look at the above transfer function shows that there is no practical need for the model correction. Indeed, the second-order time constant (60 days) would be insignificant compared to the first-order time constant (1520 days). All we lose in the first-order model is a very fast transient compo-

FIGURE 3.   Autocorrelation Functions for the Process and Noise

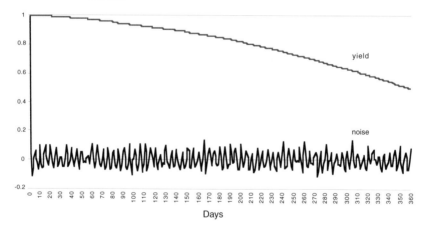

Days

---

4. The least mean squares method was used.

FIGURE 4.   Spectrum of the Noise

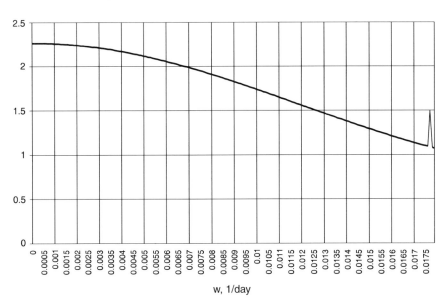

w, 1/day

nent in the market process. For the practical needs we have, these transients are not important.[5] Thus, we conclude that the noise is close to theoretical white noise.

Backcasting Test

Let us attempt to apply the model built to the seven-year historical period (Figure 5). We use forecasting formulas (4) through (7) and actual initial conditions at the left end of the interval. The nonstationarity is captured by including an additional systematic drift of negative 0.00109 percent per day. The 90-percentile is defined as the forecast plus/minus 1.65*STD, the 68-percentile is the forecast plus/minus STD. Table 1 presents the actual number of observations that fit into each of the two forecasted percentiles, for different models used.

One can conclude that inclusion of the nonstationary noise drift and heteroscedasticity improve the forecast, and that all the numbers are below the expectations. We can offer two major explanations of the latter fact: (1) the first two quarters of the period had an abnormal yield change that could not be forecasted by any model and (2) the model incorporates

---

5. If we were concerned about stability of the model, small time-constants would become somewhat important.

FIGURE 5. Model Test (Forecast) for the Historical Period with the Nonstationary Noise Drift

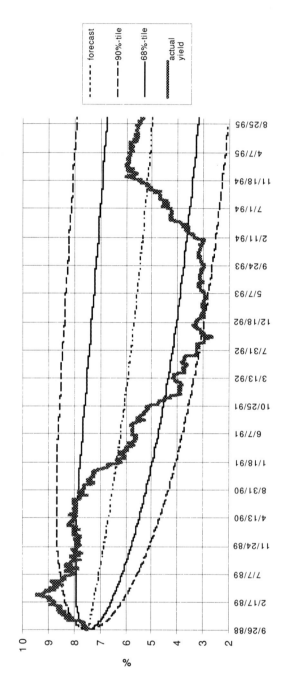

TABLE 1. The Backcasting Test Results

Model	Without Nonstationary Drift		With Nonstationary Drift	
	Observed % Within 90–percentile	Observed % Within 68–percentile	Observed % Within 90–percentile	Observed % Within 68–percentile
Homoscedastic	57.4	37.6	78.6	37.5
Heteroscedastic	62.3	47.0	77.3	43.1

only the average nonstationary noise drift, not its variable part which cannot be modeled.

One-Year Forecast and the Actual Observations

The forecast uses the heteroscedastic model having no nonstationary noise drift. This means that the average yield observed for the historical period (5.54472 percent) is accepted as the long-term yield. We certainly could introduce any biased estimate for the long-term yield. In all other aspects, the model was as presented above.

Figure 6 presents the yield expectation along with the 90-percentile and 68-percentile. Since the long-term average (5.545 percent) is just slightly above today's rate (5.434 percent), and the mean reversion implies a 4.16 year time-constant, there is no essential difference between the forecast and today's value. The percentiles, however, constitute non-trivial information about the rate's distribution.

Adequate Use of the Shock Scenarios

Step-up, step-down style of the yield change is not realistic, but it represents an often used approach to quantifying the risk and serves for certain reporting purposes. We would like to accept this tradition as a given constraint, but to handle shock scenarios in a well-defined mathematical way. Let us look at Figure 7. We see that the yield change within a three-month period has been less than 100 basis points in 80 percent periods and has not reached 200 basis points even once. Does it imply that we have to assign large probabilities for the "flat" scenario, small probabilities for "up100" and "dn100," and ignore all other scenarios? This would be an erroneous conclusion because

1. The pattern of a theoretical shock scenario is different from the actual one. In fact, an average impact of a yield shift (with the

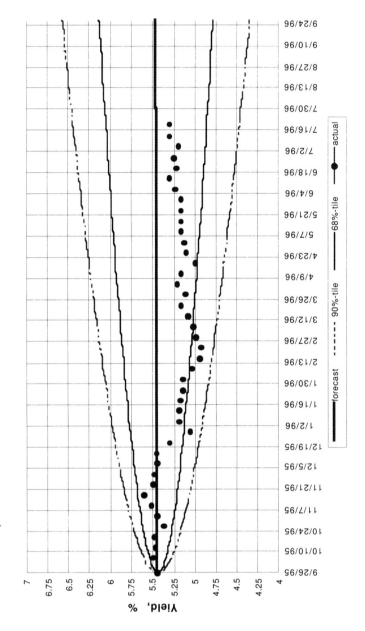

FIGURE 6. Actual Three-Month Treasury Yield versus a No-Noise Drift Forecast for One Year Starting September 26, 1995

FIGURE 7.   Histogram of the Three-Month Treasury Yield
            Change in a 90-Day Period

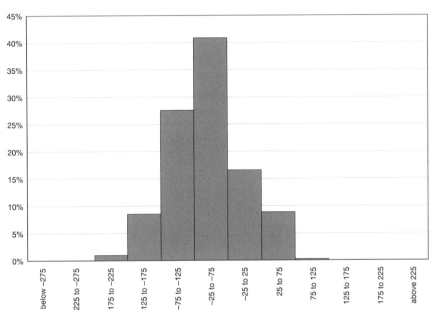

yield remaining constant after the shock) may not be as significant as quite smooth but systematic and long-falling market
rates.

2. The choice of a three-month period was arbitrary. Had we used a
   six-month or one-week interval as indicator of the shift, we
   would have come to absolutely different statistics of the yield
   shift. For the above reasons, the presented statistics of the yield
   change is of little value. The more sophisticated approach should
   account for the integral impact of a yield shift scenario rather
   than on a pattern match with a real continuous process.

The interest rate model that we studied above performs two main
functions: it drifts the yield's average and "shakes" the market around
this average. A question arises: can we use several shock scenarios to
reach "equivalent" effects? We can find the artificial volatility σ and the
drift μ produced by a set of shock scenarios (we call them *step* volatility
and *step* drift, correspondingly) such as to equate average volatility and
average drift of the "real" (continuous) process, over a certain period of
time, T.

For continuous homoscedastic model (1) conditional instantaneous drift (μ_r) and conditional instantaneous volatility (σ_r) are found as

$$\mu_r(t) = (r_0 - r_\infty)e^{-at} + r_\infty \tag{8}$$

$$\sigma_r^2(t) = \frac{\sigma_w^2}{2a}(1 - e^{-2at}). \tag{9}$$

We have to find step volatility, σ, and the step drift, μ. To do this, we assign them to be the average *continuous* volatility and the average *continuous* drift, correspondingly:

$$\mu = \frac{1}{T}\int_0^T \mu_r(t)dt = r_\infty + \frac{r_0 - r_\infty}{aT}(1 - e^{-aT}) \tag{10}$$

$$\sigma^2 = \frac{1}{T}\int_0^T \sigma_r^2(t)dt = \frac{\sigma_w^2}{2a}\left(1 + \frac{e^{-2aT} - 1}{2aT}\right) \tag{11}$$

Formulas (10) and (11) indicate that the time horizon T is an important factor. Indeed, for a security with a short term to maturity, equivalent step drift and step volatility must be smaller than for a security with a long term to maturity, since continuous yield cannot "get diffused" enough. Therefore the "personal mapping" of continuous characteristics into shock characteristics is needed for each particular instrument. McCauley's duration which determines the length of a cash flow weighted by its today's value can serve as a good estimate for T.

Another question is how to use the characteristics computed from (10) and (11). There are several ways to do it. One is simply to assign probabilities calculated from the normal distribution density function with known μ and σ. Thus, scenario with rate r is assigned a probability of

$$\frac{1}{\sigma\sqrt{2\pi}}e^{-\frac{(r-\mu)^2}{2\sigma^2}}.$$

Table 2 gives an indication how McCauley's duration and the mean reversion affect the shock scenario weights. It was assumed that the continuous drift is 1 percent above today's rate and the continuous volatility is 1 percent.

Conclusions we can make here are as follows:

TABLE 2. Weights of the Shock Scenarios for Different Instruments

McCauley's Duration (years)	Mean Reversion	Step drift (%)	Step Volatility (%)	Weights of Scenarios						
				-300	-200	-100	0	100	200	300
1	0.02	0.010	0.702	0.0%	0.9%	20.2%	56.8%	21.0%	1.0%	0.0%
1	0.1	0.048	0.684	0.0%	0.7%	18.0%	58.1%	22.2%	1.0%	0.0%
1	0.2	0.094	0.663	0.0%	0.4%	15.4%	59.6%	23.6%	1.0%	0.0%
2	0.02	0.020	0.987	0.4%	5.0%	23.7%	40.4%	24.7%	5.4%	0.4%
2	0.1	0.094	0.938	0.2%	3.5%	21.6%	42.3%	26.7%	5.4%	0.3%
2	0.2	0.176	0.883	0.0%	2.2%	18.6%	44.3%	29.2%	5.3%	0.3%
3	0.02	0.029	1.201	1.4%	8.0%	23.1%	33.3%	24.0%	8.7%	1.6%
3	0.1	0.136	1.114	0.7%	5.7%	21.3%	35.6%	26.5%	8.8%	1.3%
3	0.2	0.248	1.022	0.2%	3.5%	18.5%	37.9%	29.8%	9.0%	1.0%
5	0.02	0.048	1.530	3.7%	10.9%	21.0%	26.6%	21.9%	11.8%	4.1%
5	0.1	0.213	1.356	1.8%	7.8%	19.9%	29.3%	25.1%	12.5%	3.6%
5	0.2	0.368	1.191	0.6%	4.7%	17.4%	32.1%	29.2%	13.2%	2.9%
7	0.02	0.067	1.787	5.4%	12.0%	19.6%	23.4%	20.4%	13.1%	5.8%
7	0.1	0.281	1.520	2.6%	8.7%	18.8%	26.4%	24.0%	14.1%	5.3%
7	0.2	0.462	1.289	0.8%	5.0%	16.4%	29.3%	28.6%	15.3%	4.5%
10	0.02	0.094	2.096	7.1%	12.7%	18.3%	20.9%	19.1%	13.9%	7.3%
10	0.1	0.368	1.685	3.3%	9.2%	17.7%	24.1%	23.0%	15.4%	7.0%
10	0.2	0.568	1.373	1.0%	5.1%	15.4%	27.1%	28.1%	17.1%	6.1%

1. Step volatility is not very sensitive to duration. Thus, a 10-times increment of duration causes only a double or triple increment of step volatility. It allows to use this method even for instruments with a quite uncertain McCauley duration.
2. Since any increase in mean reversion accelerates the transient process, such increase leads to a higher step-drift and a lower step-volatility. Mean reversion becomes an important factor for long instruments.

The problem with this simple technique is that it is required at least seven to nine scenarios, and it implies normality. An alternative way is explained below. Imagine that we want to estimate certain characteristic such as present value, rate of return, net interest income, interest margin, and so forth. For simplicity, let us denote it as PV and the yield shift as Δ. Let us imagine that we are able to approximate $PV(\Delta)$ by a quadratic function:

$$PV(\Delta) \approx a + b\Delta + c\Delta^2. \tag{12}$$

Several techniques can be used to get a, b, and c in (12). We could find the first three terms in the Taylor expansion. In that case a will be PV at the "central" scenario, b will be the PV's first derivative, and c will be a half of the PV's second derivative. Both derivatives are computed numerically as the first and the second differences correspondingly, at the same central scenario point.

An alternative way is the least mean square approximation where different observation errors are weighted by their probabilities. This seems to be a more accurate technique. But, in any case, three scenarios are enough to estimate all three coefficients in (12).

The model equation (12) is stochastic since Δ is a random variable as is PV. Let us apply the mathematical expectation operator E to the both sides of (12):

$$E(PV) \approx a + b\mu + c(\mu^2 + \sigma^2). \tag{13}$$

The formula obtained estimates one of the major performance measures, the expected PV. We do not have to assign probabilities to different scenarios, formula (13) does the entire job. Similarly, we can obtain a formula for the STD of the PV neglecting all cubic terms:

$$STD(PV) \approx b\sigma. \tag{14}$$

We are now able to analyze both reward and risk associated with the selected underlining measure (PV).

Conclusion

We have presented a methodology for developing homoscedastic and heteroscedastic models for interest rate dynamics. The models can be used for finding the rate's mean and standard deviation at any future instance of time as has been shown for the three-month Treasury rate. We also demonstrated how to "transfer" the results obtained into mathematically well-defined risk and reward measures.

References

Hull, John C. *Options, Futures, and Other Derivative Securities,* Englewood Cliffs, NJ: Prentice Hall, 1993.

Kuberek, Robert C. "Predicting Interest Rate Volatility: A Conditional Heteroscedastic Model of Interest Rate Movements," *The Journal of Fixed Income,* March 1992, pp. 21-27.

Wei, William W. S. *Time Series Analysis*, Redwood City, CA: Addison-Wesley, 1990.

Historical Bond Market Risk/ Reward Patterns

Martha C. Monteagudo
Director—Product Development
Ryan Labs, Inc.

Ronald J. Ryan, CFA
President
Ryan Labs, Inc.

As established in Chapter 1, to understand the bond market is to understand the Treasury yield curve. All bonds are priced off an exact spot, or single auction issue, from the current Treasury yield curve. As a result, all bonds exhibit risk/reward behavior patterns that are very similar to the behavior patterns of the issues from which they are priced or derived. The bond solar system example in Chapter 1 is an interesting and realistic account of how bonds behave. Bonds gravitate around the key Treasury auction issue that forms the base rate, within a yield spread orbit.

Chapter 1 also proved that corporate and mortgage indices have a 90 to 99 percent correlation to the Treasury yield curve. Accordingly, if we analyze and understand the historical return patterns of the Treasury yield curve, we should also have an accurate estimate of the risk/reward behavior patterns of all bonds. Since there are no true yield-curve indices for corporates and mortgages, we are forced to use the Treasury yield curve due to a lack of proper data.

Bond databases are quite young and still rather ambiguous. The *first bond-index* series was developed by Kuhn Loeb in the summer of 1973, shortly before Salomon Brothers delivered its initial bond-index version. Kuhn Loeb was acquired by Lehman Brothers in 1977 and therein started the genesis of the Lehman family of bond indices. The first recorded Treasury yield-curve index and *first daily bond-index* was the Ryan index developed by the Ryan Financial Strategy Group in March 1983. This index broke out distinct subindices for each auction series since 1979 (i.e., 3-month, 6-month, 1-, 2-, 3-, 4-, 5-, 7-, 10-, and 30-year). In 1991, Ryan Labs introduced the *first STRIPS index* as a daily series for each maturity on the

STRIP yield curve plus a composite index. In 1993, Ryan Labs developed a Treasury composite index composed of all Treasuries that were longer then one year and that had historical monthly data since 1949. This may be the most complete and accurate history of the bond market ever developed. The only other bond-index known to go back farther is the Ibbotson long-Treasury index composed on only one bond per calendar year (representing the 20-year Treasury with data since 1926). The Ibbotson index is structurally too narrow to properly represent the well-diversified bond market. Any data evidence from this index should be used with caution.

Reward

The best definition of reward is *total return,* expressed some way (i.e., absolute, relative, annualized, cumulative). Since risk measurements are dependent on returns, our bond market observations have started with the reward side of the equation.

Using the Ryan Labs Treasury Composite Index, we can gain useful insights as to the history of bond market returns. By separating price returns from income returns, we can correctly measure *up markets* from *down markets,* as well as how each market contributes to the total return equation (see Figure 1).

FIGURE 1.   Ryan Labs Treasury Composite Index

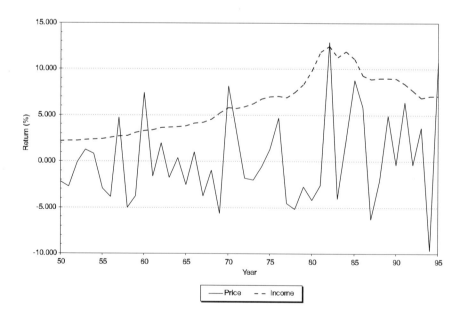

Figure 1 shows, in sharp contrast to common belief, that price return exceeded income return in only four years since 1949. Given the fact that Treasuries have lower income then most other bonds, this observation becomes even more acute for all other bond sectors. This certainly establishes, or certifies, that bonds are income vehicles. Even more amazing is the breakout on cumulative returns. After 46 calendar years, price returns have accumulated to only 2.81 percent return or only 0.21 percent of the total return equation:

Income Return = 1308.01 percent (99.79 percent of total)
Price Return = 2.81 percent (0.21 percent of total)

What is interesting is that, of the 46 calendar years, 19 (41 percent) were up-markets displaying positive price returns, three years (7 percent) were neutral, and 24 years (52 percent) showed negative price returns. If we turn our attention to the return history of the Treasury yield curve (see Figure 2), another clue to the behavior pattern of bonds will be found.

As Figure 2 details, returns are linear in that extending maturity changes returns in a linear and proportional trend. There are six years,

FIGURE 2.   Treasury Yield Curve—Annual Returns

Year	2 year	3 year	5 year	10 year	30 year
1974	7.97	–	–	–	0.12
1975	9.44	9.79	–	–	9.58
1976	10.67	11.61	–	–	19.16
1977	3.51	3.00	–	–	–0.31
1978	4.55	2.91	–	0.36	0.68
1979	8.72	7.64	–	2.49	–0.19
1980	8.34	5.96	3.98	–0.59	–1.39
1981	13.08	11.56	8.11	7.35	2.97
1982	21.42	24.75	29.40	34.80	40.94
1983	8.94	7.83	6.08	4.37	–0.43
1984	14.85	14.23	15.31	14.06	17.07
1985	14.64	16.22	22.46	28.81	34.30
1986	9.80	11.39	13.53	20.01	25.99
1987	5.46	4.11	0.87	–2.40	–6.29
1988	6.02	5.59	5.68	6.02	7.72
1989	10.50	11.61	13.99	17.01	20.09
1990	9.15	9.32	8.42	6.68	4.35
1991	11.75	13.55	14.48	17.21	17.32
1992	6.12	6.46	5.70	6.60	6.71
1993	5.77	7.19	11.23	12.01	20.01
1994	0.55	–1.41	–4.00	–7.87	–11.97
1995	11.45	13.84	17.34	24.98	34.15

Source: Ryan Labs Risk/Reward Monitor.

out of the 22 shown, where this is an exception (1975, 1978, 1984, 1988, 1990, and 1992), but the disparities are not dramatically different.

When the STRIP yield curve was born in 1985, revealing new data was one of the many benefits of this textbook perfect yield curve. Prior to February 1985, it was quite difficult to have bonds exceed durations of 10 or 11 years. But the advent of the STRIP curve produced durations up to 30 years. As a result, price return volatility could be up to three times greater. The magnitude of this achievement is still not fully realized. When STRIPS celebrated their 10-year anniversary, it marked the first time that bonds with 10 to 30 durations had any historical data. What was discovered shocked many bond practioners, but especially stock market experts. Ryan Labs reported that the 11-year STRIP through the 29-year STRIP had outperformed the S&P 500 over the initial 10-year STRIP history.

Those writing textbooks, those creating asset allocation models, and investors need to review their assumptions and traditional beliefs concerning the bond market, because the bond market is now quite different than previous databases suggest. The 15-year STRIPS have best resembled the volatility pattern of the S&P 500. If we compare the annual total returns of these two securities through time, the 15-year STRIPS performs admirably.

FIGURE 3.   STRIPS–Annualized Returns
First 10 Years (2/28/85 –2/28/95)

STRIPS 11 year	14.30
STRIPS 12 year	14.91
STRIPS 13 year	15.07
STRIPS 14 year	15.30
STRIPS 15 year	15.71
STRIPS 16 year	16.19
STRIPS 17 year	16.72
STRIPS 18 year	17.07
STRIPS 19 year	17.06
STRIPS 20 year	17.64
STRIPS 21 year	17.69
STRIPS 22 year	18.12
STRIPS 23 year	18.04
STRIPS 24 year	17.94
STRIPS 25 year	17.10
STRIPS 26 year	16.11
STRIPS 27 year	16.78
STRIPS 28 year	16.60
S&P 500	14.14

Source: Ryan Labs Risk/Reward Monitor.

FIGURE 4.   15-year STRIPS versus S&P 500

Year	15-year STRIPS	S&P 500
1986	33.72	18.47
1987	−6.91	5.23
1988	15.05	16.81
1989	23.90	31.68
1990	3.91	−3.15
1991	21.63	30.45
1992	9.60	7.64
1993	23.17	10.07
1994	−12.30	1.29
1995	41.53	37.57

Source: Ryan Labs Risk/Reward Monitor.

As shown in Figure 4, the 15-year STRIPS outperformed in five of the 10 years. In the best year for stocks (1995), the 15-year STRIPS actually outperformed by a return of 3.96 percent. Returns of 30 percent and 40 percent are now common on bonds, whereas prior to the birth of STRIPS in 1985, the 30-year Treasury only had three years (since 1974) of 30-percent-plus returns.

Risk

Risk has been defined several different ways over the decades. Similar to the pieces of a giant puzzle, each measurement gives us additional insight into the complex world called the bond market. Let us review some of these pieces to see if any clues or consistent behavior patterns are found to help solve the mysteries of the bond market.

Standard deviation is perhaps the most commonly accepted tool used to measure risk. Standard deviation measures the volatility of returns of the index that is under review. The formula requires that the numbers are squared and annualized. As such, these are not the true volatility answers. If an outlier is squared, naturally you will get a larger deviation than the actual volatility. But if all indices are treated equally, a realistic pattern will emerge.

Figure 5 clearly demonstrates that volatility measured by standard deviation is linear. As you extend maturity, you increase volatility proportionally. Not only that, but, on first impressions, these numbers look static. There is little deviation from the 10-year averages to the three-year averages. But averages can lull you into a false interpretation. If we look at the annual history of volatility, we see a different story with more clues in our search for the true risk behavior of bonds.

FIGURE 5.   Historical Standard Deviation

	Periods Ending 6/30/96			
	Last 10 years	**Last 7 years**	**Last 5 years**	**Last 3 years**
Treasury 2 year	2.23	2.11	2.11	2.01
Treasury 3 year	3.16	3.00	3.07	2.87
Treasury 5 year	4.83	4.51	4.61	4.46
Treasury 10 year	7.14	6.76	7.08	7.07
Treasury 30 year	10.41	9.63	9.91	10.60

Source: Ryan Labs Risk/Reward Monitor.

In Figure 6, we gain more information and insight into how bonds behave. The prolonged bear market of 1977 to 1981 certainly had a different volatility pattern than all the bull markets. Amazingly, the three-year Treasury auction series displayed more volatility in 1980 than the 30-year

FIGURE 6.   Standard Deviations—Annual

	Treasury Yield Curve				
Year	**2 year**	**3 year**	**5 year**	**10 year**	**30 year**
1974	2.57	–	–	–	7.40
1975	3.67	4.86	–	–	8.75
1976	2.01	2.48	–	–	4.29
1977	1.62	2.44	–	–	5.70
1978	1.25	2.37	–	3.76	4.46
1979	4.01	5.56	–	8.79	9.94
1980	10.01	12.31	15.42	16.78	19.88
1981	7.02	8.79	10.85	14.94	19.01
1982	4.04	5.29	7.23	8.75	10.98
1983	2.75	3.79	5.56	9.00	11.91
1984	3.39	4.49	6.85	9.80	12.21
1985	2.54	3.53	5.75	9.26	12.44
1986	2.45	3.72	6.33	10.99	16.84
1987	2.71	3.79	5.90	8.44	13.11
1988	2.14	3.04	5.06	7.66	11.70
1989	2.81	3.70	5.44	6.58	9.37
1990	1.84	2.63	4.20	6.90	11.15
1991	1.09	2.05	3.06	5.46	7.63
1992	2.24	3.43	4.98	7.07	7.63
1993	1.52	2.20	3.38	5.31	8.51
1994	1.62	2.38	4.06	6.20	8.92
1995	1.56	2.19	3.62	5.58	8.51

Source: Ryan Labs Risk/Reward Monitor.

has historically (in the last 10 years). Even the two-year Treasury came very close to the 30-year Treasury's historical average volatility.

This suggests that volatility is affected by the type of market environment bonds that we are encountering. In the last long bear-market, bonds were met with an inverse yield curve and negative carry. As a result, Wall Street traders were ordered not to inventory as much as usual. Spreads widened between the bid and ask in order to protect Wall Street from both the negative price returns (bear market) and the negative income returns (negative carry). The natural outcome was increased volatility patterns.

Risk-Adjusted Returns

The Nobel prize winner William Sharpe is credited with the most popular risk-adjusted return measure: the Sharpe ratio. The formula for this ratio is:

$$\frac{\text{Portfolio Return} - \text{Risk-Free Rate}}{\text{Standard Deviation of Portfolio}}$$

The risk-free rate is assumed to be the three-month Treasury bill. This ratio is measuring the amount of return per unit of risk. A high positive number shows significant value added per risk taken versus a low positive number. A negative number would suggest that there was no value added but only value lost. Reviewing the history of the Sharpe ratio for the Treasury yield curve provides another clue in our risk/reward behavior mystery.

The Sharpe ratio is strongly indicating that as you extend maturity you give up value added on a risk-adjusted basis. This is not a popular conclusion, since it suggests that investors should stay short, and that it is difficult for investors to outperform the risk-free rate by enough to compensate them for the extra risk and volatility.

FIGURE 7.   Risk-Adjusted Returns—Historical
(Periods Ending 6/30/96)

	Last 10 years	Last 7 years	Last 5 years	Last 3 years
Treasury 2 year	0.51	0.68	0.83	0.03
Treasury 3 year	0.43	0.61	0.75	−0.09
Treasury 5 year	0.29	0.47	0.67	−0.10
Treasury 10 year	0.21	0.35	0.53	−0.14
Treasury 30 year	0.12	0.28	0.50	−0.07

Source: Ryan Labs Risk/Reward Monitor.

Conclusion

The data suggest that risk is definitely a linear event, such that extending maturity changes your volatility proportionately. Reward or total returns are also linear, but not as consistent as the risk measurement data. Both risk and reward are also affected by the interest rate environment. Bear markets tend to show more risk and volatility, plus they invert the reward process such that shorter maturities outperform longer maturities. On a risk-adjusted basis, reward seems to be a better value on shorter maturities than on longer maturities. Bonds were seen as definite income vehicles, where almost 100 percent of the returns historically were derived from income return and not price returns. This contradicts most active-management beliefs today, and certainly contradicts the goal of Wall Street trading floors. With the advent of STRIPS, the bond market has been greatly expanded, and it is possible to have three times the price return volatility of the pre-1985 era. Maybe STRIPS will become the ultimate Treasury yield curve that derives all bond pricing. Certainly, the STRIP yield curve is the risk-free line where any bond, with similar duration, can be compared for value added or lost.

Bond Market Index Behavior: Applications for Bond Portfolio Management

Frank K. Reilly
Bernard J. Hank Professor of Business
College of Business Administration
University of Notre Dame

David J. Wright
Associate Professor of Finance
School of Business
University of Wisconsin–Parkside

Most investors have a reasonable understanding of the composition and computation of the major equity market indexes such as the S&P 500. In addition, several studies have examined the risks and returns of the equity market indexes and have analyzed the relationships among these series. However, less is known about the relative behavior of the various bond market indexes. There has been limited analysis of the bond indexes' relative risk/return properties, time-series properties, and covariance properties. Part of the reason for a lack of analysis of bond market indexes is the relatively short history of these indexes. Specifically, in contrast to stock market indexes that have been in existence for more than 100 years, total rate-of-return bond indexes were not developed until the 1970s. At that time, with the demand for bond indexes increasing, several major securities firms created aggregate bond indexes, a variety of subindexes, customized indexes, and daily (rather than monthly) indexes.

This chapter analyzes the behavior of the major investment-grade bond market indexes for the 1980–1995 time period and discusses the implications of the results for fixed-income portfolio managers. In addition, the chapter will examine the relationship of bond indexes to each other and with respect to the Ryan Labs Treasury Yield Curve (TYC) indexes. The Ryan Labs TYC indexes are a set of constant-maturity Treasury indexes with maturities ranging from the three-month Treasury bill to the 30-year Treasury bond. The chapter will explore the ability of the constant-maturity Treasury indexes to be used as factors in models for explaining bond-market index behavior.

An analysis of bond market indexes is important and timely for several reasons. First, with the increase in the number and size of bond portfolios, investors and portfolio managers have increasingly come to rely on bond indexes as benchmarks for measuring performance and, in the case of those managing on a performance-fee basis, determining compensation. There are numerous indexes of differing construction that purport to measure the aggregate bond market and the major sectors of the market (government, corporate, and mortgages). An obvious concern is selecting an appropriate index that will provide an accurate benchmark of bond market behavior.

Second, the indexes serve as benchmarks for bond index funds that have become increasingly popular. The behavior of a particular index is critical to fixed-income managers who attempt to replicate its performance in an index fund. Clearly, if all indexes move together, one would be indifferent to the choice of a particular index.

A third reason for examining the bond market index behavior is the growing use of returns-based performance analysis methods such as style analysis which was originally proposed by Sharpe (1992). Style analysis requires the identification of a key number of factors that have a significant influence on investment portfolio returns. After an acceptable set of factors is identified, the goal of style analysis is to estimate a fund's exposures to the specified factors. A fund's set of exposures constitutes its style, while the remaining portion of the fund's return may then be attributed to the choice of specific securities. Style analysis was originally applied to equity portfolios. However, application of style analysis to fixed-income portfolios raises the issue of which factors should be selected. Given the important linkage between a bond portfolio's maturity composition and its return behavior suggests that constant-maturity Treasury indexes could be used as factors in a bond portfolio style-analysis model. Hence, regression tests will be performed to determine whether a set of constant-maturity Treasury return series such as the Ryan Labs TYC indexes may be used as factors in a style analysis model of bond market indexes.

Organization of the Chapter

The initial section of this chapter describes the difficulty of building and maintaining a bond market index compared to the requirements for a stock-market index. The second section contains a description of the investment-grade bond indexes examined in this chapter. The third section describes the issues in applying style analysis to bond portfolio performance measurement. The fourth section presents the empirical analysis, and the fifth section presents the summary and implications.

Building and Maintaining a Bond Index

To construct a stock market index, you have to select a sample of stocks, decide how to weight each component and select a computational method. Once you have done this, adjustment for stock splits is typically automatic and the pricing of the securities is fairly easy because most of the sample stocks are listed on a major stock exchange or are actively traded in the over-the-counter (OTC) market. Mergers or significant changes in the performance of the firms in an index may necessitate a change in the index components. Other than such events, a stock could continue in an index for decades. [On average, the Dow Jones Industrial Average (DJIA) has about one change per year.]

In contrast, the creation, computation, and maintenance of a bond market index are more difficult for several reasons. First, *the universe of bonds is broader and more diverse than that of stocks.* It includes U.S. Treasury issues, agency series, municipal bonds, and a wide variety of corporate bonds spanning several segments (industrials, utilities, financials) and ranging from high-quality, AAA-rated bonds to bonds in default. Furthermore, within each group, issues differ by coupon and maturity as well as by sinking funds and call features. As a result of this diversity, an aggregate bond market series can be subdivided into numerous subindexes; the Merrill Lynch series, for example, contains over 150 subindexes.

Second, *the universe of bonds changes constantly.* A firm will typically have one common stock issue outstanding, which may vary in size over time as the result of additional share sales or repurchases. In contrast, a major corporation will have several bond issues outstanding at any point in time, and these issues will change constantly because of maturities, sinking funds, and call features. This change in the universe of bonds outstanding also makes it more difficult to determine the market value of bonds outstanding, which is necessary when computing market-value-weighted rates of return.

Third, *the volatility of bond prices varies across issues and over time.* Bond price volatility is influenced by the duration and convexity of the bond. These factors change constantly with the maturity, coupon, market yield, and call features of the bond. As maturity changes constantly and market yields become more volatile, which in turn affects embedded call options, it becomes more difficult to estimate the duration, convexity, and implied volatility of an individual bond issue or an aggregate bond series.

Finally, *there can be significant problems in the pricing of individual bond issues*. Individual bond issues are generally not as liquid as stocks. While most stock issues are listed on exchanges or traded in an active OTC market with an electronic quotation system (NASDAQ), most bonds are traded on a fragmented OTC market without a consolidated quotation system. This problem is especially acute for corporate bonds. Several studies have examined this problem and noted the significant effects of using alternative sources for prices.

Description of Alternative Bond Indexes

This section describes the major U.S.-investment-grade bond indexes. We examine the overall constraints and computational procedures employed for each of the aggregate indexes. Our empirical analysis will include the total return series of the Standard and Poor's 500 to compare bond behavior to stocks.

Several characteristics are critical in judging or comparing bond indexes. First is *sample of securities*, including the number of bonds as well as specific requirements for including the bonds in the sample, such as maturity and size of issue. It is also important to know what issues have been excluded from the index. Second is the *weighting of returns* for individual issues. Specifically, are the returns market-value weighted or equally weighted? Third, users of indexes need to consider *the quality of the price date* used in the computation. Are the bond prices used to compute rates of return based upon actual market transactions as they almost always are for stock indexes? Alternatively, are the prices provided by bond traders based upon recent actual transactions or are they the traders' current *best-estimate?* Are prices based on *matrix pricing* that involves a computer model that estimates a price using current and historical relationships? Fourth, what *reinvestment assumption* does the rate of return calculation use for interim cash-flows?

Four firms publish ongoing rate-of-return investment-grade bond market indexes. Three of them publish a comprehensive set of indexes that span the universe of U.S. bonds—Lehman Brothers (LB), Merrill Lynch (ML), and Salomon Brothers (SB). The fourth firm, Ryan Labs (RL), concentrates on the government bond sector.

Figure 1 summarizes the major characteristics of the indexes created and maintained by these firms. Three of the four firms (LB, ML, and SB)

FIGURE 1. Summary of U.S. Investment Grade Aggregate Bond Market Indexes

Name of Index	Number of Issues	Maturity	Size of Issues	Weighting	Pricing	Reinvestment Assumption	Subindexes Available
Lehman Brothers Aggregate	5,000+	Over 1 year	Over $100 million	Market value	Trader priced and model priced	No	Government, gov./corp., corporate
Merrill Lynch Composite	5,000+	Over 1 year	Over $50 million	Market value	Trader priced and model priced	In specific bonds	Government, gov./corp., corporate, mortgage
Ryan Treasury Yield Curve	5	Over 1 year	Current Treasury On-the-Run Auction Issues	Equal	Market priced	In specific bonds	Treasury
Salomon Brothers Composite	5,000+	Over 1 year	Over $50 million	Market value	Trader priced	In one-month T-bill	Broad inv. Grade, Treas.-agency, corporate, mortgage

include numerous bonds (over 5,000), and there is substantial diversity in a sample that includes Treasuries, corporates, and mortgage securities. In contrast, RL computes the Ryan Labs Treasury Yield Curve index which is composed of the returns from the individual Ryan Labs TYC indexes. (RL also produces a Treasury Composite index composed of all available Treasury securities and is the focus of Chapter 10.) The required minimum size of an issue varies from $25 million (ML and LB) to $50 million (SB), while the Treasury issues used by Ryan are substantially larger. All the series include only investment-grade bonds (rated BBB or better) and exclude convertible bonds and floating-rate bonds.

The two major alternatives for weighting are *relative market value* of the issues outstanding and *equal weighting* (also referred to as *unweighted*). The justification for market-value weighting is that it reflects the relative economic importance of the issue, and it is a logical weighting for an investor with no preferences regarding asset allocation. Although this theoretical argument is reasonable, it is important to recognize that, in the real world, it is difficult to keep track of the outstanding bonds, given the possibility of calls, sinking funds, and redemptions. The large-sample indexes of LB, ML, and SB are all market value-weighted.

In contrast, the Ryan Labs TYC index is an equal weighting of the current individual RL TYC indexes with maturities longer than one year. Hence, in the last year of this study (1995), the Ryan Labs TYC index was computed as an equal weighting of the following five issues: 2-, 3-, 5-, 10-, and 30-year Treasuries. Over the 1980–1995 time span, the Ryan TYC index also included the 4-, 7-, and 20-year Treasuries when they were being issued by the government. Equal weighting is reasonable for an investor who has no prior assumptions regarding the relative importance of individual issues. Also, equal weighting is consistent if one is assuming the random selection of issues. Finally, an equally weighted index is easier to compute, and the results are unambiguous because it is not necessary to worry about the outstanding market value of bonds due to calls, and so forth.

As noted, one of the major problems with computing returns for a bond index is that continuous transaction prices are not available for most bonds. RL can get recent transaction prices for its Treasury issues, while SB gets all prices from its traders. As noted, these trader prices may be based on a recent actual transaction, the trader's current bid price, or what the trader would bid if he or she made a market in the bond. Both LB and ML use a combination of trader pricing and matrix prices based on a computer model. It is contended that most of the individual issues are priced by traders, so most of the value of each index is based on trader prices.

The indexes also treat interim cash-flows differently. Both ML and RL assume that cash flows are immediately reinvested in the bonds that generated the cash flows. SB assumes that flows are reinvested at the one-month Treasury-bill rate while LB does not assume any reinvestment of the funds. Obviously, immediate reinvestment in the same bond is the most aggressive assumption, while no reinvestment is the most conservative.

It is not possible to develop a perfect constant-maturity bond index because of the issuing pattern of the U.S. Treasury. However, using a daily-return series of the current, on-the-run, benchmark Treasury issues is an effective empirical approach for constructing a constant-maturity index. The Ryan Labs two-year TYC return series, for example, is based on the most recently issued two-year Treasury note, until it is replaced by a new two-year Treasury note. These daily returns assume immediate reinvestment in the new issue when the auction results are announced. Because recent benchmark Treasury auction issues enjoy very active markets, it is possible to obtain actual transaction prices daily. Consequently, the TYC indexes represent a liquid, purchasable set of securities, and hence, represent a strategy that could be easily followed at low cost in an attempt to replicate bond market returns.

The indexes examined in this chapter are the following:

Lehman Brothers (LB)
- Aggregate Bond Index (LBA)
- Government/Corporate Bond Index (LBGC)
- Government Bond Index (LBG)
- Corporate Bond Index (LBC)
- Mortgage-Backed Securities Index (LBM)

Merrill Lynch (ML)
- Domestic Master (MLD)
- Government Master (MLG)
- Corporate Master (MLC)
- Mortgage Maser (MLM)

Ryan Labs (RL)
- The Ryan Treasury Yield Curve Index (RYAN)
- 3-Month Treasury Bill Index (TBL03)
- 6-Month Treasury Bill Index (TBL06)
- 12-Month Treasury Bill Index (TBL12)
- 2-Year Treasury Bond Index (TSY02)

- 3-Year Treasury Bond Index (TSY03)
- 5-Year Treasury Bond Index (TSY05)
- 10-Year Treasury Bond Index (TSY10)
- 30-Year Treasury Bond Index (TSY30)

Salomon Brothers (SB)
- Broad Investment Grade Index (SBB)
- Treasury/Agency Bond Index (SBG)
- Corporate Bond Index (SBC)
- Mortgage Pass-Through Index (SBM)

Standard and Poor's 500 (S&P500)

Style Analysis and Bond Portfolio Performance Measurement

Style analysis requires construction of an asset-class factor model. The effectiveness of the model is largely dependent on the factors chosen. One desirable characteristic of a set of factors is whether they are exhaustive. The factors should not represent the broad spectrum of influences on the portfolio returns. A second desirable characteristic is whether the factors are mutually exclusive. Do the factors include the same securities? Is the return behavior different among the factors? And third, do the factors represent different risk structures with respect to the magnitude of the factors standard deviations?

     This chapter will explore the ability of the Ryan Labs TYC indexes to be used as the factors in style analysis models for explaining the monthly returns of the broad bond-market indexes over the 1980–1995 time span. The TYC indexes range from the 3-month Treasury bill to the 30-year Treasury bond. However, since the broad-market bond indexes only include securities with maturities of a year or longer, we will restrict our analysis to those Treasury securities with a maturity of a year or longer, and those series that contain a complete history over the 1980–1995 time period of study. As a result, the following TYC indexes will be considered as style analysis factors: TBL12, TSY02, TSY03, TSY05, TSY10, and TSY30. The TYC indexes obviously represent a wide spectrum of bond maturities.

     One test of the usefulness of the TYC indexes is an examination of their correlation matrix. The lower the correlation between factors, the more distinct the asset class that each factor represents. In addition to the factor correlations, the factors should exhibit different volatility patterns, which we will examine using the annualized standard deviations of the

TYC indexes' monthly returns. Another test of the factors is the proportion of the broad-market bond index variance explained by the factor model, measured by R-square. The objective of the factor model building is to select a set of factors which maximize R-square, yet is parsimonious for a given set of factors.

Empirical Results

Risk/Return Characteristics

Table 1 provides the annualized rates of return for the various indexes, along with the annualized standard deviation of monthly returns. Our analysis focuses on the 1980–1995 time period because data for all of the series are available in this time span. Exhibit 2 plots the indexes' risk/return characteristics for the 1980–1995 period. Regressing the annualized returns of the Ryan TYC indexes on their annualized monthly standard deviation yielded a line with an intercept of 8.152 percent (t-statistic of 66.37), a slope of .3244 (t-statistic of 17.92), and a R-square of 98.17 percent.

Examination of Table 1 and Figure 2 suggests several observations. First, as expected, the differences in the maturities of the TYC indexes produce considerably different levels of risk. But notably, the TYC indexes are very linear in the risk/return space displayed in Exhibit 2. The R-square of the regression line representing the TYC indexes suggests that over 98 percent of the variance between TYC index returns may be explained by their risk level. Second, the clustering of observations is consistent with the composition of the indexes. Specifically, the three points with the lowest returns and standard deviations are the pure government indexes. The next-lowest grouping represents the aggregate indexes and the combined government/corporate index. The third grouping includes the pure corporate bond series. The highest-risk grouping contains the three mortgage series. A third observation is that all four clusters of indexes are located between the TYS03 and TSY10 indexes in terms of risk, and all are above the regression line. The position of the indexes along the risk axis is dictated primarily by the indexes' average maturities which range between three and 10 years. The location of the clusters above the regression line is most likely a function of the indexes' diversification, which provides higher return per unit of risk than a single-asset series, and of the liquidity premiums for these securities compared to on-the-run Treasuries. Finally, the RYAN index is located approximately midway between the TSY02 and TSY30, as one would expect given the equal weighted properties of the index.

TABLE 1. Rate of Return and Variability Statistics for Alternative Bond Indexes and Stocks: 1980-1995

Variable	Annualized Total Return	Annualized Monthly Std. Dev.	Minimum	Maximum
	1980 - 1995 Monthly Returns			
Ryan Indexes				
RYAN	10.95	7.87	-6.42	10.83
TBL03	8.29	1.19	0.18	2.32
TBL06	8.48	1.55	-0.19	3.36
TBL12	8.92	2.53	-1.48	5.07
TSY02	9.79	4.03	-4.07	7.72
TSY03	9.96	5.20	-5.59	8.72
TSY05	10.50	7.13	-6.70	11.01
TSY10	11.24	9.71	-7.92	12.29
TSY30	12.28	13.03	-7.66	13.45
Govt. Indexes				
LBG	11.03	6.34	-5.13	9.58
MLG	10.99	6.41	-5.67	9.74
SBG	10.98	6.27	-5.43	9.69
Corp. Indexes				
LBC	11.98	8.52	-6.94	12.89
MLC	11.86	8.31	-7.36	11.97
SBC	11.80	8.32	-6.32	12.16
Mortgage Indexes				
LBM	11.54	9.11	-7.47	15.43
MLM	11.51	8.99	-5.93	15.26
SBM	11.59	8.92	-6.28	15.06
Aggregate Indexes				
LBA	11.28	7.14	-5.92	11.34
LBGC	11.23	6.96	-5.81	10.76
MLD	11.22	7.09	-6.27	11.02
SBB	11.29	7.03	-5.83	11.22
SP500	15.84	14.85	-21.52	13.43

Correlation Results

Does it make any difference which series is used to evaluate portfolio performance or to build an index fund? An analysis of contemporaneous correlations indicates how the competing series track each other on a

FIGURE 2. Annualized Cumulative Return versus the Standard
          Deviation of Alternative Index Returns (1980–1995)

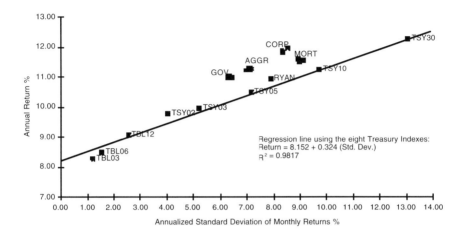

monthly basis. Significant deviations from index to index could be critical
to a manager's choice of an appropriate target index. In addition, correlation analysis provides information for considering the TYC indexes in a
factor analysis model.

The top portion of Table 2 (Panel A) is a correlation matrix of the
TYC indexes and the RYAN index. Correlations between the TYC indexes
with similar maturities were all above .90. However, the correlations
among indexes with considerably different maturities were lower. For
example, the correlation between the TSY02 and the TSY30 indexes was
.792. Although the correlations were all statistically significant, the lower
correlations exhibited between many of the TYC indexes indicate that the
indexes are measuring somewhat different return dimensions. That fact,
coupled with the substantially different TYC index standard deviations
observed in Table 1, suggests that they could be useful as factors.

The bottom portion of Table 2 (Panel A) displays the correlations
between the TYC indexes versus the comprehensive bond market
indexes. Among the TYC indexes, the returns of TSY05 and TSY10 exhibited the highest correlations with the bond market indexes, ranging from
.890 to .982. The results suggest that a single Treasury-issue index, with an
approximately matched maturity, can be highly correlated with broader
comprehensive bond indexes. Furthermore, the Ryan index is interesting
because it is a series with a very limited sample of bonds (five bonds ver-

TABLE 2. Panel A: Correlation of Monthly Returns (1980-1995): Ryan Indexes versus Alternative Indexes

	RYAN	TBL03	TBL06	TBL12	TSY02	TSY03	TSY05	TSY10	TSY30
Ryan Indexes									
RYAN	1.000								
TBL03	0.383	1.000							
TBL06	0.639	0.913	1.000						
TBL12	0.820	0.703	0.906	1.000					
TSY02	0.923	0.558	0.803	0.941	1.000				
TSY03	0.952	0.498	0.751	0.905	0.987	1.000			
TSY05	0.980	0.417	0.675	0.851	0.956	0.977	1.000		
TSY10	0.991	0.347	0.592	0.773	0.886	0.923	0.962	1.000	
TSY30	0.955	0.273	0.504	0.685	0.792	0.837	0.892	0.962	1.000
Govt. Indexes									
LBG	0.990	0.404	0.657	0.834	0.935	0.960	0.982	0.981	0.938
MLG	0.989	0.407	0.655	0.832	0.934	0.959	0.980	0.982	0.938
SBG	0.987	0.409	0.660	0.831	0.933	0.958	0.980	0.980	0.934
Corp. Indexes									
LBC	0.960	0.353	0.621	0.820	0.903	0.924	0.939	0.943	0.907
MLC	0.957	0.342	0.606	0.804	0.895	0.917	0.932	0.942	0.910
SBC	0.954	0.347	0.612	0.810	0.893	0.914	0.928	0.939	0.911
Mortgage Indexes									
LBM	0.914	0.390	0.655	0.831	0.893	0.897	0.906	0.890	0.830
MLM	0.922	0.396	0.647	0.833	0.901	0.908	0.916	0.899	0.835
SBM	0.925	0.400	0.656	0.834	0.904	0.910	0.917	0.901	0.841
Aggregate Indexes									
LBA	0.984	0.400	0.662	0.849	0.938	0.957	0.973	0.969	0.922
LBGC	0.989	0.390	0.652	0.834	0.934	0.958	0.977	0.977	0.935
MLD	0.985	0.393	0.653	0.842	0.935	0.957	0.973	0.972	0.926
SBB	0.986	0.399	0.662	0.848	0.938	0.958	0.974	0.971	0.926
SP 500	0.311	-0.053*	0.065*	0.175	0.204	0.228	0.261	0.319	0.352

* All correlation coefficients are significant at the five percent level except those indicated by the * .

TABLE 2 (Continued). Panel B: Correlation of Monthly Returns (1980-1995): Alternative Indexes

	LBG	MLG	SBG	LBC	MLC	SBC	LBM	MLM	SBM	LBA	LBGC	MLD	SBB	SP500
Govt. Indexes														
LBG	1.000													
MLG	0.997	1.000												
SBG	0.996	0.994	1.000											
Corp. Indexes														
LBC	0.956	0.955	0.946	1.000										
MLC	0.953	0.955	0.942	0.991	1.000									
SBC	0.950	0.951	0.941	0.993	0.992	1.000								
Mortgage Indexes														
LBM	0.903	0.903	0.887	0.946	0.934	0.935	1.000							
MLM	0.910	0.912	0.898	0.951	0.938	0.941	0.984	1.000						
SBM	0.912	0.916	0.901	0.951	0.940	0.944	0.992	0.988	1.000					
Aggregate Indexes														
LBA	0.986	0.984	0.978	0.986	0.980	0.980	0.955	0.958	0.961	1.000				
LBGC	0.993	0.992	0.988	0.982	0.980	0.976	0.929	0.935	0.937	0.996	1.000			
MLD	0.986	0.988	0.979	0.983	0.983	0.980	0.946	0.955	0.956	0.997	0.995	1.000		
SBB	0.986	0.986	0.982	0.983	0.978	0.980	0.947	0.953	0.959	0.998	0.995	0.997	1.000	
SP 500	0.316	0.305	0.309	0.352	0.364	0.344	0.289	0.273	0.270	0.325	0.328	0.320	0.317	1.000

* All correlation coefficients are significant at the five percent level.

sus thousands in the other series) and a weighting scheme (equal weighting) that differs from the other, market-value-weighted series. Even with these notable differences, the correlations of the Ryan index with the other bond indexes range from 0.914 to 0.990—similar to the results for most other comprehensive bond series.

The matrix of correlation coefficients in Table 2 (Panel B) indicates extremely high correlations. The correlation coefficients ranged from 0.887 to 0.997, and all are significant at the 0.05 level. In addition, the correlations between similar series (e.g., the alternative government-bond series) typically exceed 0.98. These strong correlations imply that all sectors of the investment-grade-bond market tend to move together, based on general market interest-rate changes. The extremely high correlations between similar sector series (e.g., corporate bonds) would indicate that the series developed by the various investment firms are generally measuring the same phenomenon.

The S&P 500 exhibits a significant, positive relationship with the comprehensive bond indexes, but only the correlations range from .270 to .364 for the 1980–1995 time period. It is interesting that the longer the maturity of the Treasury series, the higher the correlation with stocks.

Tracking Deviations

Managers of a bond index portfolio must select a target bond index, compare their portfolio performance results with those of the target, and calculate a monthly tracking deviation—the difference between the total returns of the two indexes. An index fund manager attempts to select issues that closely replicate the target index and minimize tracking deviations, since the performance criterion for an index fund is how accurately the fund tracks the target index.

The emphasis on tracking deviations provokes the more fundamental question of how well the three corporate bond indexes (the LBC, MLC, and SBC) track each other on a monthly basis, or the three mortgage indexes, the government bond indexes, or the aggregate market indexes. If the indexes track each other closely, the manager's choice of a particular index is not critical. If there are discrepancies, however, the selection of a particular bond index would be an important decision; in that case, two index funds with identical performance results could have materially different tracking records, depending upon their target indexes.

We define the *monthly tracking deviation* as the difference in total monthly returns between two competing bond indexes. Table 3 displays the tracking deviation analysis of the subindexes within each sector (corporate, mortgage, and government) and the overall broad-market

TABLE 3. Tracking Deviation Analysis of Monthly Returns: 1980-1995

Paired Variables	Mean Absolute Monthly Trk. Deviation (in basis points)	Mean Monthly Trk. Deviation with Sign (in basis points)	Std. Deviation of Monthly Trk. Dev. with Sign (in basis points)	Autocorrelations of Monthly Tracking Deviations with Sign		
				Lag 1	Lag 2	Lag 3
Ryan Indexes vs. LBA						
RYAN-LBA	33.0	-2.0	44.0	-0.081	0.137	-0.005
TBL03-LBA	145.9	-24.9	195.1	0.208*	-0.080	-0.152
TBL06-LBA	135.3	-23.4	179.6	0.209*	-0.074	-0.137
TBL12-LBA	113.1	-19.8	149.2	0.198*	-0.066	-0.137
TSY02-LBA	80.1	-12.7	105.0	0.134	-0.003	-0.148
TSY03-LBA	56.3	-11.0	76.1	0.026	0.032	-0.154
TSY05-LBA	34.8	-5.9	47.7	-0.240*	0.037	0.033
TSY10-LBA	73.1	1.4	95.4	-0.092	0.059	0.001
TSY30-LBA	155.7	12.4	202.3	0.038	0.048	-0.033
Govt. Indexes						
LBG-MLG	8.9	0.2	13.9	-0.329*	-0.139	0.081
LBG-SBG	9.8	0.4	17.2	-0.484*	0.071	-0.139
MLG-SBG	10.7	0.1	20.0	-0.398*	-0.076	-0.002
Corp. Indexes						
LBC-MLC	24.4	1.0	32.3	-0.290*	0.013	-0.065
LBC-SBC	20.1	1.5	29.1	-0.342*	-0.183*	0.228*
MLC-SBC	22.7	0.4	30.9	-0.379*	-0.032	0.039
Mortgage Indexes						
LBM-MLM	23.4	0.3	47.2	-0.555*	0.244*	-0.411
LBM-MLM	17.2	-0.2	32.4	-0.512*	0.015	0.071
MLM-SBM	21.0	-0.5	39.5	-0.525*	0.158*	-0.142
Aggregate Indexes						
LBA_LBGC	12.9	0.5	17.9	-0.043	0.046	-0.148*
LBA-MLD	9.9	0.5	15.0	-0.369*	-0.049	-0.025
LBA-SBB	9.0	0.0	14.7	-0.535*	0.030	0.079
MLD-SBB	9.8	-0.5	15.6	-0.473*	0.037	-0.002

* Autocorrelation coefficient is significant at the five percent level.

indexes. The second column of Table 3 shows the average monthly tracking deviations with sign included. Typically, the average monthly tracking deviation in each sector was less than one basis point, implying that in the long run, the performances of the indexes converge.

Although the mean deviation with sign approaches zero, there may be substantial positive or negative deviations in an individual month. That is, two bond indexes that concur in the long run may diverge in the short run. The standard deviations of the monthly tracking deviations with sign in Table 3 indicate that the variance of the tracking deviations for the corporate- and mortgage-sector indexes were approximately twice as large as those of the government and aggregate indexes. The mortgage indexes exhibited more tracking deviations than the corporate indexes. In contrast, the small tracking deviations between the aggregate bond market indexes were similar to those of the government bond indexes.

These results suggest several key points. First, the tracking deviations vary according to the type of bond index. The large tracking deviations between the corporate indexes are probably caused by pricing uncertainties (i.e., the use of matrix prices for many of the bonds), market illiquidity, the presence of call risk, and the inclusion in these indexes of numerous nonhomogeneous issues. Similarly, the mortgage market is very difficult to track because of numerous and erratic changes in composition. These results suggest that the selection of a target index for the corporate or mortgage sector can have a significant effect on monthly tracking performance, while the selection of a government or an aggregate bond index is not as critical.

Average absolute tracking deviations (that is, deviations without regard to sign) are particularly important for investors attempting to define an acceptable tracking deviation. The means of the absolute tracking deviations are presented in the first column of Table 3. All of the corporate and mortgage tracking deviations exceeded 17 basis points, while the government and aggregate index tracking deviations were approximately 10 basis points or less. Again, the results suggest that the lower limit for acceptable tracking deviations varies significantly across bond sectors.

An analysis of the tracking deviation series with sign indicate that all of the first-order autocorrelations were significantly negative, which means that the tracking deviations tend to alternate around the overall mean. These negative autocorrelations are probably attributable to the difficulties of bond pricing, which cause substantial discrepancies between the short-run estimates of prices and returns of different indexes. Because these short-term price discrepancies tend to reverse themselves, as indicated by the negative autocorrelations, the long-term return estimates tend to converge. In other words, the oscillation in tracking deviation implies that the mean monthly absolute tracking deviations should *decline* as the holding period lengthens. As a result, investors should not place too much emphasis on the monthly tracking performance of their portfolio in relation to a particular target index, but instead should concentrate on longer-term performance (e.g., three or four months).

The top portion of Table 3 provides a tracking deviation analysis between the TYC and LBA. Table 3 indicates that the five-year Treasury is the best single- issue index for tracking the overall market. The tracking of the TSY05 index is the best because its duration is most closely matched to the aggregate market. However, because it is a single-issue index, the TSY05 index exhibits greater monthly tracking deviations than between the aggregate indexes.

Autocorrelation Results

The autocorrelations in Table 4 suggest that bond index returns exhibit substantially more autocorrelation than stock index returns. Stock returns, as shown in a number of previous studies, are not autocorrelated. In contrast, all the bond indexes that were examined exhibit significant autocorrelation coefficients. The autocorrelation with month t-1 is generally a significant positive value, while the autocorrelation for month t-3 is typically a significant negative value. This implies that the size and direction of bond index returns can be predicted by a time-series model that incorporates return information from the previous three months. In contrast, the insignificant autocorrelation of the equity series confirms the results of prior studies.

The autocorrelation of bond index returns reflects the inclusion in monthly bond returns of both accrued interest (or coupon payment) and capital changes. Because the monthly return on short-term bonds is principally accrued interest, which is predictable, one would expect the total return on these bonds to exhibit substantial autocorrelation. But the monthly returns on longer-term bonds are primarily driven by interest rate changes, which affect bond prices, and these interest rate changes do not follow predictable patterns. As a result, one would expect more autocorrelation in the returns of shorter-term bonds than in long-term bond returns. The autocorrelation results in Table 4 for the TYC indexes confirm the extent to which term to maturity explains autocorrelation in bond returns. There were significant autocorrelations in all the TYC bond indexes except for the two bonds with the longest maturities, TSY10 and TSY30.

TABLE 4. Autocorrelations of Monthly Returns for Alternative
          Indexes: 1980-1995 Monthly Returns

Variable	Lag 1	Lag 2	Lag 3
Ryan Indexes			
RYAN	0.177*	-0.065	-0.131
TBL03	0.749*	0.623*	0.596*
TBL06	0.487*	0.257*	0.243*
TBL12	0.289*	-0.003	0.004
TSY02	0.248*	-0.119	-0.097
TSY03	0.232*	-0.105	-0.120
TSY05	0.199*	-0.109	-0.106
TSY10	0.131	-0.050	-0.106
TSY30	0.122	-0.010	-0.132
Govt. Indexes			
LBG	0.196*	-0.088	-0.122
MLG	0.195*	-0.099	-0.131
SBG	0.209*	-0.091	-0.136
Corp. Indexes			
LBC	0.220*	-0.073	-0.165*
MLC	0.215*	-0.084	-0.163*
SBC	0.225*	-0.071	-0.174*
Mortgage Indexes			
LBM	0.125	-0.088	-0.174*
MLM	0.175*	-0.156*	-0.157*
SBM	0.185*	-0.106	-0.203*
Aggregate Indexes			
LBA	0.207*	-0.092	-0.150*
LBGC	0.209*	-0.086	-0.148*
MLD	0.208*	-0.107	-0.152*
SBB	0.223*	-0.092	-0.168*
SP500	0.000	-0.040	-0.064

* Autocorrelation coefficient is significant at the five percent level.

    In sum, there is significant dependence between bond index returns over time. This autocorrelation is not associated with any inefficiencies in the bond market, but rather reflects the accrued interest effect.

Regression Results

A number of alternative regression models were examined to identify a set of factors that may be used in style analysis of fixed-income portfolios. In general, the objective of factor model building is to select a set of independent variables which maximized R-square but is efficient in terms of the added explanatory power provided by the inclusion of additional factors. For the purposes of our analysis, the TYC indexes (TBL12, TSY02, TSY03, TSY05, TSY10, TSY30) were used as independent variables in regression models to explain the returns of the four different LB bond indexes.

Table 5 displays the results of an R-square approach to model selection. The R-square selection method finds subsets of the independent variables that best predict a dependent variable by linear regression. The method finds the best one-variable model, the best two-variable model, and so forth. For example, in the section of Table 5 labeled "Optimal 1-Factor Models," the TYC series that produced the highest R-square for predicting LBA returns was TSY05. TSY05 explained 97.4 percent of the variance of LBA returns, which is the highest of all of the single-factor models for LBA.

For the single-factor models, the R-square was lowest for LBM (.820) and highest for the LBG (.9650). All of the R-squares improved by adding more factors to the models, but the level of improvement in R-square leveled off significantly after adding three factors. The results indicate that beyond three Treasury-index factors, the inclusion of additional factors does not appreciably increase R-square.

The optimal three-factor models for LBG and LBA produced remarkably high R-squares. A fixed weighting of three Treasury issues (TSY02, TSY10, and TSY30) explained over 97 percent of the variance of the comprehensive bond market returns represented by the LBA index. For the LBG index, the TSY02, TSY05, and TSY30 indexes explained 98.68 percent of the return variance. The R-square of 84.66 percent for the optimal three-factor LBM model was not as high. The mortgage market is more difficult to track with a combination of Treasury indexes because of the erratic changes in the mortgage market composition. It is interesting that the optimal LBM model includes the 12-month Treasury series as a factor, unlike the other comprehensive index models which contained the 30-year Treasury issue. The optimal three-factor model for the LBC included the same three factors as the LBA model, but the R-square was somewhat lower at 91.68 percent.

The analysis suggests that a model of three constant-maturity Treasury issues that represent a wide spectrum of maturities can effectively explain the behavior of comprehensive bond-market indexes. Specifically, the 2-year, 5-year, 10-year, and 30-year Treasury issues are important determinants of bond index returns. Hence, the returns for bond market indexes can be effectively replicated with fewer issues than other asset classes such as stocks.

TABLE 5. Optimal Treasury Index N-Factor Models for Predicting Monthly Total Returns of the Lehman Brothers Bond Market Indexes (1980-1995)

N-Factor Models for Dependent Variables: LBG, LBC, LBM, & LBA	*TBL12* Coefficient	(t-Statistic)	*TSY02* Coefficient	(t-Statistic)	*TSY03* Coefficient	(t-Statistic)
Optimal 1-Factor Models						
LBG	–	–	–	–	–	–
LBC	–	–	–	–	–	–
LBM	–	–	–	–	–	–
LBA	–	–	–	–	–	–
Optimal 2-Factor Models						
LBG	–	–	–	–	–	–
LBC	–	–	1.049	14.176	–	–
LBM	–	–	1.098	7.843	–	–
LBA	–	–	0.657	13.140	–	–
Optimal 3-Factor Models						
LBG	–	–	0.325	6.373	–	–
LBC	–	–	0.845	7.752	–	–
LBM	0.672	5.647	0.597	2.110	–	–
LBA	–	–	0.762	14.111	–	–
Optimal 4-Factor Models						
LBG	–	–	0.342	7.125	–	–
LBC	0.230	1.000	0.665	3.167	–	–
LBM	0.540	1.579	1.317	2.282	-0.612	-1.430
LBA	–	–	0.632	7.524	–	–
Optimal 5-Factor Models						
LBG	–	–	0.254	2.988	0.109	1.239
LBC	0.270	1.134	0.437	1.087	0.198	0.667
LBM	0.633	1.788	1.183	1.998	-0.774	-1.697
LBA	0.159	1.325	0.479	3.350	–	–
Complete 6-Factor Models						
LBG	-0.012	-0.174	0.267	2.302	0.106	1.191
LBC	0.282	1.142	0.420	1.017	0.178	0.562
LBM	0.635	1.779	1.180	1.977	-0.775	-1.688
LBA	0.162	1.339	0.455	2.241	0.026	0.167

TABLE 5. *(continued)*

TSY05		TSY10		TSY30		R-Square
Coefficient	(t-Statistic)	Coefficient	(t-Statistic)	Coefficient	(t-Statistic)	
0.873	72.750	–	–	–	–	0.9650
–	–	0.828	39.429	–	–	0.8901
1.157	29.667	–	–	–	–	0.8200
0.974	60.875	–	–	–	–	0.9472
0.632	35.111	–	–	0.148	14.800	0.9839
–	–	–	–	0.336	14.609	0.9140
–	–	0.432	7.448	–	–	0.8432
–	–	0.471	22.429	–	–	0.9681
0.407	40.700	–	–	0.178	17.800	0.9868
–	–	0.256	2.535	0.202	3.544	0.9168
–	–	0.481	7.635	–	–	0.8466
–	–	0.282	5.640	0.117	4.034	0.9707
0.282	6.267	0.166	4.743	0.116	7.250	0.9882
–	–	0.288	2.717	0.193	3.328	0.9173
–	–	0.544	7.065	–	–	0.8482
0.157	1.987	0.210	3.387	0.123	4.393	0.9713
0.258	5.265	0.160	4.571	0.118	7.375	0.9883
–	–	0.261	2.310	0.197	3.397	0.9175
0.267	1.019	0.466	4.275	–	–	0.8491
0.193	2.298	0.216	3.484	0.118	4.069	0.9716
0.255	5.000	0.159	4.417	0.118	7.375	0.9883
0.033	0.181	0.251	1.976	0.197	3.339	0.9175
0.267	1.015	0.473	2.571	-0.004	-0.047	0.8491
0.188	2.112	0.214	3.452	0.118	4.069	0.9716

NOTE: The regression models above were selected selected by the R-Square method. Specifically, for a given number of independent variables, the subset of independent variables with the largest R-Square value is selected.

Summary and Implications

The exceptionally high correlations between similar sector series (e.g., corporate bonds) indicate that the bond market indexes developed by the various investment firms are generally measuring the same phenomena. Investment-grade bonds involve high systematic risk, exhibiting a strong tendency to move together as a reflection of general market interest-rate changes. Over longer periods of time, investors should be indifferent to the choice of a particular provider of an index.

Although bond indexes are highly correlated over longer periods of time, monthly tracking deviations are particularly prevalent in the corporate and mortgage sectors. However, our analysis indicates negative auto-correlation in the index tracking deviations so that long-term performance converges. As a result, investors should not place too much emphasis on the monthly tracking performance of their portfolio in relation to a particular target index, but should instead concentrate on longer-term performance.

Differences in Treasury bond risk are predominantly determined by differences in maturity, which in turn explain over 98 percent of the variance between Treasury returns. An application of style analysis, using a set of constant-maturity indexes as the factors, shows that aggregate bond-market returns may be replicated by as few as three Treasury issues. The maturities of the Treasury indexes should be selected so that they are representative of the entire maturity spectrum. Accordingly, the model will be capable of capturing a wide variety of fixed-income portfolio styles. However, models of specific market sectors, such as mortgages, may need to consider additional factors in order to improve the performance of the style model.

References

Reilly, Frank K.; G. Wenchi Kao; and David J. Wright. "Alternative Bond Market Indexes." *Financial Analysts Journal,* May–June 1992, pp. 48–58.

Sharpe, William F. "Asset Allocation: Management Style and Performance Measurement." *Journal of Portfolio Management,* Winter 1992, pp. 7–19.

PART III

Advances in Stochastic Pricing Models for Dynamic Assets

CHAPTER 7

The Concept of Instantaneous Return

Alexander Levin, Ph.D.
Senior Quantitative Analyst
The Dime Savings Bank

Douglas A. Love, Ph.D.
Managing Director of Asset Management
Ryan Labs, Inc.

Introduction

It is tempting to regard short (instantaneous) return and risk measures as myopic with respect to future cash-flows; particularly for dynamic assets (assets whose future cash-flows are interest-rate dependent, including callable and prepayable securities). This is a misperception. At all points in time, active market participants are well-versed in all of the particulars of a security's promised cash-flows and in the contingencies that govern its short-term holding-period risk. In fact, economic theory suggests that asset prices are determined by buyers and sellers at the margin. Buyers and sellers at the margin are predominantly market makers for whom it is generally recognized that a long-term horizon is anything exceeding twenty minutes.

The practical importance of the instantaneous return model is its ability to directly price dynamic securities, which today are priced by numerically-intensive processes involving either multinomial trees or Monte Carlo simulation. These numeric processes are both cumbersome and slow, and in many cases miscast important dynamics of the target security. Most important, some securities have cash flows which may depend on more than one spot-rate or on the shape of the yield curve, which may be difficult or impossible to adequately represent with trees or simulations, and certainly with single-factor models. The instantaneous return model, however, is easily extendible to multiple factors.

Instantaneous Risk and Return: An "Any-Factor" Stochastic Term-Structure Model

For the consistent pricing of all bonds including dynamic assets (those with interest-rate-determined cash flows), consider a generalized stochastic factor $x(t)$. The factor may be a bond's own yield, the rate on some reference bond, or some other factor or factors. For this general factor, we assume the simplest stochastic process:

$$dx(t) = \mu dt + \sigma dz, \qquad (1)$$

where $x(t)$ is a continuous Weiner process with drift rate μ and volatility rate σ. Any path (scenario) may be referred to as an $x(t)$ *scenario*.

We can define key measures of risk and return relative to changes in this general factor.

The Concept of Instantaneous Expected Return and Variance

Consider a *concept of instantaneous return (IR) measured over an infinitesimal horizon (0,t) where t→0 for any interest-rate path x(t)*. We assume that market price $P(t,x)$ is dependent on time and on a generalized market factor, $x(t)$, and define *instantaneous return* $IR_{x(t)}$ as

$$IR_{x(t)} \equiv lim_{t \to 0}[\frac{1}{t}\,Return(t)]_{x(\tau),\ 0<\tau<t}.$$

Since each scenario is random, so too is instantaneous return conditional on each path $x(t)$.

IR_0 signifies IR for the base-case scenario of no change in the factor $x(t) = 0$; hence,

$$IR_0 = \frac{CF}{P} + \frac{1}{P}\frac{\partial P}{\partial t}\Bigg|_{x=0},$$

where CF is the rate of cash flow per annum. IR_0 is a static return, and plays the same role as time-decay (theta) in options mathematics.

Factor-specific measures of duration and convexity are also defined for the base case:

$$D_x = -\frac{1}{P}\frac{\partial P}{\partial x}\Bigg|_{t\,=\,x\,=\,0}, \quad C_x = \frac{1}{P}\frac{\partial^2 P}{\partial x^2}\Bigg|_{t\,=\,x\,=\,0}.$$

We define *expected instantaneous return (EIR), and variance of instantaneous return (VIR), analytically averaged over all paths:*

$$EIR \equiv E[IR_{x(t)}]$$

$$VIR \equiv Var[IR_{x(t)}]$$

Y. K. Chan (see Diller [1991]) describes the case where the factor is a security's own yield and no cash-flow is received over the very short period. Levin [1996a] shows for the general case that

$$EIR = IR_0 - D_x\mu + \frac{1}{2}C_x\sigma^2 \qquad (4)$$

$$VIR = D_x^2\sigma^2 \qquad (5)$$

Being derived from Ito's Lemma, Equations (4) and (5) are exact formulae (not a series expansion estimate). Certain effects such as changes in outstanding balance, duration and convexity or coupon rates are either taken into account or can be proven to have infinitesimal contributions to either EIR or VIR as $t \to 0$.

Expected Instantaneous Return Spread (EIRS)

Equation (4) typically involves a random market factor with estimable volatility, but unknown drift μ. In the absence of arbitrage, the drift term $D_x\mu$ can be eliminated from Equation (4) by application to both a specified instrument and to a benchmark security (superscript b) with the same duration D_x. We can compute their Expected Instantaneous Return Spread (EIRS) as follows:

$$EIRS = EIR - EIR^b = IR_0 - IR_0^b + \frac{1}{2}(C_x - C_x^b)\sigma^2 \qquad (6)$$

This simple, easy to understand relation is invariant with respect to interest rate expectations, and clearly identifies the cost of convexity. This cost is an adjustment required to get EIRS from a static yield spread.

Equations (5) and (6) reveal important properties of duration and convexity. If risk is defined as return volatility (or some function of it), then duration is a measure of risk since it contributes to VIR *only*. Convexity, however, does not contribute to VIR and is not a risk measure, since positive convexity enhances return regardless of the direction of factor movement. The reward (or penalty) is proportional to volatility squared (e.g., if σ is 1 percent, each unit of convexity is associated with 50 basis points of average gain or loss). Of course, this return enhancement is not for free; convexity does command a price premium (yield discount). Despite widely accepted misperceptions, convexity actually cannot be hedged in the standard sense because it is a certain, not a random, source of return and depends only on realized volatility.

EIRS and VIR have numerous valuation applications as a mathematically well-defined way to assess continuously up-to-date reward and risk measures. Despite its simplicity, it is more strict and sophisticated than what is in common use. This can be illustrated with reference to several immediate applications.

EIRS and OAS

Option-adjusted spread (OAS) is conventionally priced by computer-intensive numerical methods, including multinomial trees and Monte Carlo simulations. In all cases, the modeled processes nonetheless satisfy key theoretical conditions (see for instance, Cheyette [1992]) involving average present values across all arbitrage-free paths $x(t)$, $0 \leq t \leq T$, where T is any arbitrary horizon. The present value operation is applied to all cash flows paid in $0 \leq t \leq T$, as well as to the terminal value. Since the time horizon T is arbitrary and OAS is time-invariant (i.e., is earned homogeneously over time), one can consider any sub-interval including an infinitesimal one. This yields the powerful result [Levin 1996a] that EIRS provides a major time-saving shortcut to OAS because, given the same stochastic model, EIRS is identical to OAS.

VIR and VAR

VAR (value at risk) represents a measure of price volatility which, following adoption by major international regulatory bodies, has experienced rapidly growing popularity. VAR is price volatility adjusted to a specified confidence level. VIR is just VAR (at an 84 percent confidence level) squared. Indeed, in the derivation of VIR [Equation (5)], IR volatility consists entirely of price volatility, as cash flow volatility contributes infinitesimally. As VAR is especially effective under multifactor conditions, so too is VIR (see below).

EIRS has important investment implications:

1. *Figure of Merit:* When choosing from a narrow duration cell, or optimizing a portfolio, weighted-average EIRS, not weighted-average yield, should be maximized.
2. *Implied Volatility:* For securities with known IR_0, D_x, C_x, and EIRS, implied volatility σ can be derived.

3. *Risk and Reward:* EIRS is equal to OAS, and VIR is a simple transformation of VAR.
4. *Software Testing:* Most modern option-adjusted software screen all of the components of Equation (6), and therefore can be quickly and effectively tested.

Factor-Specific Duration and Convexity

Much of the literature about or employing duration and convexity measures utilize measures based on stochastically-invalid market paths (shocks).

Conventional duration and convexity measures employ a three-point interpolation formula:

$$D = \frac{P(0, -\Delta) - P(0, \Delta)}{2P(0, 0)\Delta}, \ C = \frac{P(0, -\Delta) - 2P(0, 0) + P(0, \Delta)}{2P(0, 0)\Delta^2}, \quad (7)$$

which seemingly deals with up scenarios and down scenarios, but in fact are functional sensitivities, not a model of market movements. Once the duration and convexity have been computed, Equations (4) through (6) are derived for continuous markets. The derived reward (EIRS) and risk (VIR) measures do not assume shocks in real markets.

STRIPS Yield-Curve Diffusion Structure

There are many valuation problems which require a model of the entire spot-rate structure. Analysts pricing dynamic securities such as mortgage-related securities, nonmaturing deposits, or options face the following central problems. First, path-dependent or multifactor models necessitate Monte Carlo simulations, in which the entire yield curve cannot be computed. Second, a dynamic cash-flow generator must be constructed which properly responds to each factor. Finally, such generators frequently have only approximately known responses.

Three related questions need to be addressed in the application of IR analysis to the STRIPS (separate trading of registered interest and principal of securities) market.

1. What is the factor that drives the STRIPS market?
2. What constitutes the base path for the factor?
3. How does the factor drive the entire STRIPS curve?

We have explained above that, for stochastically consistent models, EIRS and OAS are equal. Note that Equation (6) produces the same EIRS regardless of the choice of the same-duration benchmark. Under arbitrage-free conditions, all STRIPS have the same EIR, namely the riskless overnight rate *r*. While an infinite number of models meet this constraint (all these models have different base paths), the following choice of answers to the above three questions produces a unique simplest choice.

1. *Factor x(t)* is the deviation of the short rate from its base path.
2. *Base Path* (for each spot rate) is the expected (mean) path for this rate (e.g., $\mu = 0$, and $x = r - Er$). The equation for the base path is determined by a specific stochastic model.
3. *Deviation* of each spot rate from its base path is a function of the factor *x(t)*.

As a consequence of these choices, the term-structure diffusion is a set of perfectly correlated deviations (albeit with different volatilities) that each spot rate experiences from its base path.

In general, it is not possible to establish the base-path equations and the relationship between different rate deviations from their base paths in a closed analytical form. Such closed solutions are, however, obtainable within a linear model. Consequently, our starting point is the Hull-White [1990, 1993] instantaneous short-rate factor model:

$$dr(t) = a(t)[\theta(t) - r(t)]dt + \sigma(t)dz(t) , \tag{8}$$

where $\theta(t)$ is the arbitrage-free "long-term" equilibrium rate, the $dz(t)$ are Brownian motion increments, and $a(t)$, and $\sigma(t)$ are mean reversion and volatility, respectively.

Equation (8) is complimented by an equation for $g(t)$, the natural logarithm of the discount factor $DF(t)$ applied to $1 to be received at time *t*:

$$dg(t) = -r(t)dt. \tag{9}$$

Together Equations (8) and (9) constitute a linear stochastic system in the state variables (r,g).

The value of a $1 STRIPS maturing in *T* years can be stated in terms of an expectation E^{af} with respect to an arbitrage-free interest-rate process as follows (hereinafter, the superscript "af" is omitted):

$$P_T(0,x) = E\,[DF(T)] = E(e^{g(T)}) = e^{E[g(T)] + \frac{1}{2}Var[g(T)]}. \tag{10}$$

The last equality holds because the variables in Equations (8) and (9) above are all normally distributed.

Short-Rate Base (Mean) Path

The expected present value of $1 to be received at time t must also equal the discount factor known from currently observed forward rates, $f(t)$. Hence,

$$E[g(T)] + \frac{1}{2}Var[g(T)] = -\int_0^t f(\tau)d\tau. \tag{11}$$

Thus, Equation (11) is an econometric arbitrage-free condition for the evolution of the short rate. It requires the conditional mean and variance of $g(t)$, given initial conditions $g(0) = 0$ and $r(0)$. The analytic forms for Equations (8) and (9), and the expectations and covariances for the state variables (r,g), are given in Levin [1996b]. For the simplest case of time-invariant mean reversion and volatility $[a(t) = a$ and $\sigma(t) = \sigma]$, the equilibrium long-term arbitrage-free short rate is:

$$\theta(t) = f(t) + \frac{1}{a}\frac{df}{dt} + \frac{\sigma^2}{2a^2}(1 - e^{-2at}), \tag{12}$$

leading to the Hull–White base path for the short rate:

$$E[r(t)] = f(t) + \frac{\sigma^2}{2a^2}(1 - e^{-at})^2. \tag{13}$$

Hence, contrary to intuition, in the presence of volatility, arbitrage-free short rates are not centered around currently observed forward rates. The spread between arbitrage-free forward rates and observed forward rates is volatility dependent and always positive, caused by the nonlinear, positively convex, nature of discounting.

With increasing time, the drift grows asymptotically approaching $\sigma^2/2a^2$. For $a = 0$ (the Ho–Lee model), the systematic drift equals $\frac{1}{2}T^2\sigma^2$ (the cost of convexity for a T-period STRIPS), and increases without limit.

The short-rate variance is:

$$Var[r(t)] = \frac{\sigma^2}{2a^2}(1 - e^{-2at}). \tag{14}$$

Any Spot-Rate Base (Mean) Path

Assuming some short rate $r(t)$ at a future time t, we look to derive the spot rates $r_T(t)$ for any T-maturity STRIPS [the answer to question (3) above]. To achieve this, we need a no-arbitrage condition analogous to Equation (11), which will equate $e^{-r_T(t)T}$ to the expected discount factor $E[e^{g(t+T)-g(t)}]$ applied to the investment period $(t,t+T)$. It is convenient to start the random process in motion at time t rather than at time 0 such that $g(t) = 0$. [The short-term equilibrium rate $\theta(t)$ remains determined by Equation (12) applied to current forward rates and is, therefore, known at $t = 0$]. This gives

$$E[g(t+T)]\Big|_{g(t)=0,\,r(t)} + \frac{1}{2}Var[g(t+T)]\Big|_{g(t)=0,\,r(t)} = r_T(t)T. \quad (15)$$

Levin [1996b] demonstrates that for equation systems (8) and (9), condition (15) leads to the well-known Hull–White spot-rate pricing equations written here in slightly different notation:

$$r_T(t) = A_T(t) + B_T r(t), \quad (16)$$

where $B_T = \frac{1}{aT}(1 - e^{-aT})$;

and

$$A_T(t) = f_T(t) - B_T f(t) + \frac{\sigma^2}{4a^3 T}(1 - e^{-aT})^2(1 - e^{-2at}), \quad (17)$$

where $f_T(t)$ is the rate for a T-maturity STRIPS, t years forward.

Taking expectations of Equation (16) and substituting from the mean short-rate from Equation (13) yields a spot rate's mean path:

$$E[r_T(t)] = f_T(t) + \frac{\sigma^2}{4a^2}B_T[2(1 - e^{-at})^2 + (1 - e^{-2at})(1 - e^{-aT})]. \quad (18)$$

The drift of the mean path above the forward rate curve has a slope of

$$\frac{d}{dt}E[r_T(t) - f_T(t)]\Big|_{t=0} = \frac{1}{2}TB_T^2\sigma^2,$$

and for $t<<1/a$ is approximately $\frac{1}{2}T\sigma^2 t$.

Equations (13) and (18) describe *mean-rate curves* which play a central role in the instantaneous return model. Static IR returns are assessed along this path. Figure 1 shows an example of these curves for July 2, 1996 in BE form for one-month, one-year and 10-year rates (assuming $\sigma = 0.8\%$, $a = 5\%$), versus forward rate curves.

Volatility Term-Structure and Volatility-Adjusted Duration and Convexity

Equation (16) produces spot rates r_T which are linear in the short-rate r with slope B_T, which we treat as *the term structure of volatility*. The second moments of the bivariate distribution (r, r_T) are

$$Var(r_T) = B_T^2 Var(r); \quad Cov(r_T, r) = B_T Var(r); \quad Corr(r_T, r) = 1. \quad (19)$$

Thus, any deviation of the short rate from its mean path $x(t) = r(t) - Er(t)$ causes simultaneous proportional deviations in all other spot-rate paths equal to $x_T(t) = B_T x(t)$. Therefore, *for STRIPS, traditional duration and*

FIGURE 1.   Mean-Rate Curves versus Forward Curves

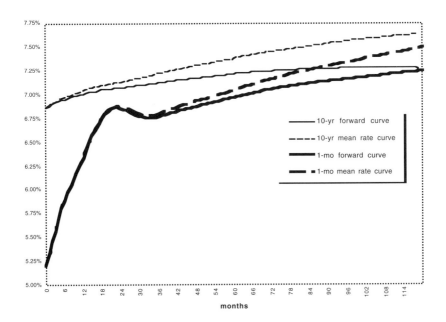

convexity need to be adjusted to reflect the term structure of volatility B_T as follows:

$$D_x = B_T D_{x_T} = B_T T = T^*; \quad C_x = B_T^2 C_{x_T} = T^{*2}. \tag{20}$$

This volatility-term-structure adjusted duration and convexity is reminiscent of Diller [1991], which derived a similar adjustment based on short rate expectation revisions after the important work of Sir John Hicks [1939].

For a general dynamic asset, factor duration D_x and convexity C_x can be computed using the standard three-point method [Equation (7)], for which $P(0,\pm\Delta)$ represents the prices for shock scenarios at $t = 0$. We have shown, for our term-structure model, that each deviation x of the short rate from its base path $(r - Er)$ immediately causes a $B_T x$ deviation of the T-maturity spot rate from its former base path. This implies a certain, immediate change in the entire spot-rate curve for any $\Delta = x(0) \neq 0$. After this shock occurs, the spot, forward, and mean path rates are all shifted in a generally nonparallel fashion implied by the term-structure model.

These changes are easily developed from the above results.

Assume some $x(0) = \Delta \neq 0$, and, therefore, $x_T(0) = B_T \Delta$ defines the entire displaced (shocked) spot curve:

$$\tilde{r}_T(0) = E[r_T(0)] + x_T(0) = r_T(0) + x_T(0).$$

The corresponding shocked forward rates are then

$$\tilde{f}(T) = d[\tilde{r}_T(0)T]/dT = d[r_T(0)T]/dT$$
$$+ d[x_T(0)T]/dT = f(T) + \Delta d(B_T T)/dT \quad .$$

Substituting for B_T and taking the derivative gives

$$\tilde{f}(T) - f(T) = \Delta e^{-aT}. \tag{21}$$

We know from Equation (13) that the spread between the mean rates curve and the observed forward rates is a function of T, and not of rates. Therefore, the left-hand side of Equation (21) is not only the change in the forward rate curve, but the change in mean rates as well.

That is to say that the shocked path for the short rate will differ from the base path by Δe^{-at}. From the term-structure model, the shocked path for a T-maturity spot rate will be displaced from its base path by $\Delta e^{-at} B_T$. For the short rate, Figure 2 illustrates a base path together with four up scenarios and four down scenarios. The shocks are distinctly nonparallel,

FIGURE 2.   The Base (Bold Line) and Shock Paths of the
             Short Rate

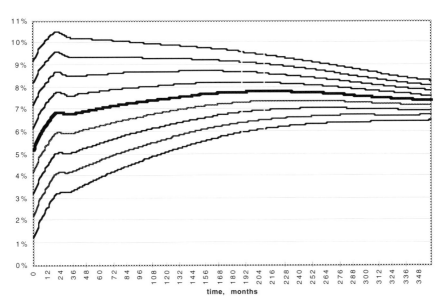

with displacements which diminish over time with a $1/a$ = 20-year time
constant.

Repricing Dynamic Assets

The instantaneous return model is designed to apply to dynamic assets
(those with interest rate dependent cash flows). Many coupon bonds with
various coupon and principal repayment schedules have these parameters dependent on interest rates, including but not limited to short rates.

To derive expected instantaneous return spread (EIRS), Equation (6)
requires knowledge of IR_0, D_x, and C_x. We do know these parameters for
STRIPS (our benchmark assets), for which Equation (4) with $\mu = 0$ can be
resolved for IR_{0T} as follows:

$$IR_{0T} = r - \frac{1}{2}C_x\sigma^2 = r - \frac{1}{2}T^{*2}\sigma^2, \tag{22}$$

where IR_{0T} is the base path instantaneous return for a T-maturity STRIPS.

We do not, however, necessarily know the corresponding parameters for the specified dynamic asset. In fact, for a dynamic asset, duration and convexity as well as cash flows are different from one scenario to another. Practitioners often use rules of thumb such as "constant spread over a same-duration (or average life) Treasury." However, these methods are not mathematically rigorous—at least in that they do not account for changes in the cost of convexity. Our convention will be based on the principle that an asset should retain its relative attractiveness as measured by EIRS for any interest-rate scenario (e.g., that EIRS is x-scenario invariant).

The dynamic asset's cash flows along any x-path can be stripped into corresponding zero-coupon bonds and priced at current spot rates plus the static spread S (differing for different paths). Naturally, $S = 0$ for standard U.S. Treasury bonds. Strictly speaking, further derivations will not be possible without an assumption on how this spread changes over time. For the sake of simplicity, we will illustrate these derivations assuming that S does not change over time, along a path. (This assumption will slightly understate OAS for mortgage-backed securities. While it can play a role of a good initial guess in a professional software system, a more accurate assumption can be made). Thus,

$$IR_0 = \sum v_T IR_{0T} + S$$

where the weights v_T are *relative* STRIPS prices. Substituting from Equation (21) gives

$$IR_0 = r - \frac{1}{2}C_x^{static}\sigma^2 + S, \text{ where } C_x^{static} = \sum v_T T^{*2}, \text{ and } T^* = B_T T. \quad (23)$$

Therefore,

$$EIRS = EIR - EIR^b = EIR - r = S + \frac{1}{2}(C_x - C_x^{static})\sigma^2 = \quad (24)$$

$$S(P) + \frac{1}{2}\left(\frac{1}{P}\frac{\partial^2 P}{\partial x^2} - C_x^{static}(P)\right)\sigma^2.$$

The *repricing equation* (24) is used to compute EIRS (therefore, OAS) given current price or, conversely, price given EIRS. This repricing relationship not only permits EIRS computation, but also provides important measures of duration and convexity in different scenarios.

Equation (24) is a second-order, nonlinear ordinary differential equation in price, for which $S(P)$ is a known function defined by base-path cash flows. The solution requires knowing the base case price $P(0)$

(or EIRS), together with two additional conditions which enable the construction of $\frac{\partial P}{\partial x}(0)$ and the desired unknown, either $P(0)$ or EIRS. The choices depend on the security, and on knowledge of its behavior. For example, for a mortgage-backed security, one may consider two remote boundary scenarios (such as $x = 4.0$ percent, or $x = -4.0$ percent) for which cash flow is practically insensitive to x (e.g., prepayment speed is saturated by burnout, refinancing limitations, or by zero). For this choice of scenario, $D_x(x)$ is close to appropriate static duration. (From a numerical point of view, it is better to specify one boundary condition for each end, rather than two conditions for one end.)

Equation (23) is solved using finite differences, where the grid of scenarios is $x = -i\Delta, -(i-1)\Delta, ..., -\Delta, 0, \Delta, ..., j\Delta$ for sufficiently small Δ and sufficiently large $i\Delta$, and $j\Delta$. The grid reflects the zero-time shock scenarios described by Equation (21). (See Exhibit 2 above.)

The Multifactor Case

When n factors disturb market conditions and a security's cash flows, $x(t)$ needs be interpreted as an n-dimensional Weiner process. (In the discussion that follows, vectors and matrices are denoted by bold letters.) The factors are driven by a drift vector M and covariance matrix V whose element can be represented as $v_{ij} = \rho_{ij}\sigma_i\sigma_j$, where ρ_{ij} is the correlation between changes in the i-th and j-th factors and dx_i and dx_j. Duration D and convexity C become a vector of $D_i = -\frac{1}{P}\frac{\partial P}{\partial x_i}$ and a symmetric matrix

of $C_{ij} = \frac{1}{P}\frac{\partial^2 P}{\partial x_i \partial x_j}$, respectively. The base case becomes $x(t) = 0$.

Under these conditions, the equations for IR, EIR, VIR, and EIRS are completely analogous to those for the single-factor case:

$$EIR = IR_0 - D^T M + \frac{1}{2}tr(VC) = IR^0 - \sum_{i=1}^{n} D_i\mu_i + \frac{1}{2}\sum C_{ij}\rho_{ij}\sigma_i\sigma_j \quad (25)$$

$$VIR = D^T VD = \sum D_i D_j \rho_{ij}\sigma_i\sigma_j, \quad (26)$$

where (as in the single-factor case) all characteristics (IR_0, D and C) are for the base-case scenario.

To achieve EIRS (OAS) in this case requires constructing an equal duration portfolio such that all elements of D are matched. Then, the analog of Equation (6) is

$$EIRS = EIR - EIR^b = IR_0 - IR_0^b + \frac{1}{2} tr[\mathbf{V}(\mathbf{C} - \mathbf{C}^b)]. \qquad (27)$$

Clearly, selecting uncorrected factors is numerically beneficial. It eliminates the cross-convexities that must be estimated. Consider, for example, a mortgage-prepayment model fitted to some function of interest rates, present and past. An important illustration of this is a mortgage-pool prepayment model constructed such that prepayment error, which becomes an additional factor, is independent of interest rates (by least squares estimation, for example). A. Sparks and F. Feiken Sung [1995] conclude that positive (or negative) convexity with respect to prepayment error will increase (or decrease) OAS. However, they do not provide further quantification of, or model this effect comparable to, what is done by Equation (25). Our analysis shows that the explicit inclusion of a prepayment model error factor generates a hidden contribution to OAS, which turns out to be positive for premium mortgages and negative for discount mortgages.

Conclusion

We have demonstrated the concept of instantaneous return, and related it to generic models used for pricing dynamic assets. This approach represents a convenient shortcut to access reward (OAS) and risk (VAR) of holding a dynamic asset in a volatile multifactor environment. While being mathematically rigorous, the method expresses results in traditional effective duration and convexity as their contributions to VAR and OAS have been clearly identified.

References

Chan, Y. K. (1991) cited by Stanley Diller in *Fixed Income Analytics*, ed. R. E. Dattatreya. Chicago: Probus Publishing, p. 123.

Cheyette, O. (1992), "Term Structure Dynamics and Mortgage Valuation," *Journal of Fixed Income*, March, pp. 28–41.

Hicks, J. R. (1939), *Value and Capital*, London: Oxford University Press.

Ilmanen, A. and R. Iwanowski (1996), "The Dynamics of the Shape of the Yield Curve: Empirical Evidence, Economic Interpretations, and Theoretical

Foundations—Understanding The Yield Curve: Part 7," *Fixed-Income Research/Portfolio Strategies,* Salomon Brothers, New York, February 1996.

Levin, A. (1996a), "The Concept of Instantaneous Return Spread," working paper, The Dime Savings Bank.

Levin, A. (1996b), "Linear Systems Theory in Stochastic Pricing Models," chapter 8, this volume.

Sparks, A. and S. F. Feiken (1995), "Payment Duration and Convexity," *Journal of Fixed Income,* March, pp. 7-11.

Linear Systems Theory in Stochastic Pricing Models*

Alexander Levin, Ph.D.
Senior Quantitative Analyst
The Dime Savings Bank

The pricing of dynamic securities such as mortage-backed securities (MBS), nonmaturing deposits, or options presents several serious problems. First, path-dependent or multifactor models necessitate time-consuming numerical experiments (Monte Carlo simulations). In fact, before an asset can be priced, the underlying stochastic process must be calibrated to ensure it correctly prices Treasury bonds. Second, unlike lattice-based algorithms, only predefined model factors can be simulated along Monte Carlo paths, not the entire yield curve. For example, the derivation of a long rate as a function of the short rate (the factor) would require a knowledge of the complete set of future short-rate paths and their probabilities that is simply unavailable to Monte Carlo methods. Therefore, the principle cash flows of mortgage-backed securities normally driven by some "long" rate cannot be built accurately, and pricing assets sensitive to the slope of the yield curve is not possible.

In this chapter, we shall demonstrate that the major goal of Monte Carlo models—computing expected present values of random cash flows—can be achieved via analytical methods of the theory of linear stochastic systems (see Beaglehole and Tenney [1991] for a partial-differen-

*The author is thankful to the colleagues at the treasury department of The Dime Saving Bank for their interest, support, and efforts in the practical implementation of our approach, to Rina Romero of The Dime, and Dr. Douglas Love of Ryan Labs for help in shaping this chapter.

tial-equation-based solution of this problem). From a practical point of view, it means that, if we are able to describe the financial system security/interest-rate market by a set of linear differential and some piece-linear algebraic equations, a closed-form solution for net present value will replace numerical trials. This solution will require an analytic or numeric integration of a system of deterministic linear differential equations. In addition, if option-adjusted spread (OAS) needs to be computed, it will be done much faster than with Monte Carlo methods.

The analytical framework proposed below is not restricted by the number of factors or equations. In contrast, we will find the size of the model and the number of the factors to be somewhat irrelevant to the structure and principle of the method. Programmers and software developers will benefit from the faster processing of certain portfolio segments, while mathematicians may look to the method at a starting point for further analytical research. They will find some important problems that can be solved using this framework. One of them, derivation of the arbitrage-free one- and two-factor gaussian interest-rate models, is presented in the first four sections that follow. In these models, no numerical calibration is needed, and the entire yield curve is linearly expressed through the factors, thus resolving the traditional flaws of the Monte Carlo approach.

Example of a Linear System: Hull–White Interest Rate Model

Linear models are respected for their perfect analytical tractability. A classical example is the Hull–White (HW) [1990, 1993] model:

$$dr(t) = a(t)[\theta(t) - r(t)]dt + \sigma(t)dz(t) \qquad (1)$$

$$dy(t) = -r(t)dt \qquad (2)$$

where $r(t)$ denotes the spot short-rate; $\theta(t)$ is the arbitrage-free "long-term" equilibrium; $y(t)$ is the natural logarithm of the discount rate *(DF)*, which is applied to $1 to be received in time t; $z(t)$ is a standard Brownian motion; and $a(t), \sigma(t)$ are the mean reversion and volatility, respectively. Notice that the model presented here is in the form of linear continuous differential equations and it has to be complemented by initial conditions for $r(0)$ and $y(0) = 0$.

Today's price $P(0,t)$ of a t-maturity zero-coupon bond is computed by the known econometric formula where E^{af} denotes mathematical expectation with respect to an arbitrage-free interest rate dynamics:

$$P(0, t) = E^{af}[DF(t)] = E^{af}(e^{-\int_0^t r\tau d\tau}) = E^{af}(e^{y(t)}) = e^{E^{af}[y(t)] + \frac{1}{2}Var[y(t)]}. \quad (3)$$

The last equality in (3) is valid because all the variables in system (1) and (2) are normally distributed. We, therefore, have to know the conditional mean and variance of $y(t)$, given the initial conditions for model (1) and (2). In general, we have to know the means and covariances for the variables that belong to the system's state space, at any point of time, t. The next section explains how to achieve this goal with the use of the linear system theory.

Linear System Theory: Finding Conditional Expectations and Covariances

The method's principle feature is its ability to provide a closed deterministic form for the required statistical measures. Thus, we can find averages of $r(t)$, $y(t)$, their variances and mutual covariances. More important, we can derive all the statistics needed for more complex securities in a closed analytical form. Further derivation is based on the following mathematical statement.

Let us consider a general (time-dependent) linear system of stochastic differential equations:

$$dX(t) = [A(t)X(t) + C(t)]dt + B(t)dZ(t), \ X(0) = X_0 \quad (4)$$

where X is a vector of n unknowns, Z is a vector of m Brownian motions having a matrix of covariances Q_z, $C(t)$ is a free-term vector, $A(t)$ is an n by n square matrix, $B(t)$ is an n by m rectangular matrix.

Theorem: (see I. Karatzas and S. Shreve [1991], page 355) At any instance of time t, vector $X(t)$ has the following conditional expectation $E[X(t)]$ and conditional autocovariance matrix $Q_X(t,\tau)$ (where $\tau \geq t$)

$$E[X(t)] = \Phi(t,0)X_0 + \int_0^t \Phi(t,\tau)C(\tau)d\tau \quad (5)$$

$$Q_X(t,\tau) = E\{[X(t) - EX(t)][X(\tau) - EX(\tau)]\} = Q_X(t,t)\Phi^T(\tau,t) \quad (6)$$

where

$$Q_X(t,t) = \int_0^t \Phi(t,\lambda)B(\lambda)Q_Z B^T(\lambda)\Phi^T(t,\lambda)d\lambda \tag{7}$$

and $\Phi(t,\tau)$ is the fundamental solution of the homogeneous matrix differential equation $d\Phi(t,\tau)/dt = A(t)\Phi(t,\tau)$ with unit initial conditions $\Phi(\tau,\tau) = I$.

Alternatively, the vector of means $E[X(t)]$ can be computed as the solution of the homogeneous version of equation (4),

$$\frac{d}{dt}E[X(t)] = A(t)E[X(t)] + C(t),\ E[X(0)] = X_0, \tag{8}$$

and matrix of covariances $Q_X(t,t)$ can be found as the solution of the following Lyapunov matrix differential equation:

$$\frac{dQ_X(t,t)}{dt} = A(t)Q_X(t,t) + Q_X(t,t)A^T(t) + B(t)Q_Z B^T(t) \tag{9}$$

with zero initial conditions: $Q_X(0,0) = 0$.

Matrix Φ is symbolically written in the exponential form $\Phi(t,\tau) = \exp[\int_\tau^t A(\lambda)d\lambda]$ and can be built from the Jordan transformation of matrix $\int_\tau^t A(\lambda)d\lambda$ as shown in Appendix A to this chapter.

Thus, one can derive the major conditional statistics for process (4). We should not be surprised that model (4) "produces" a matrix of conditional autocovariances, $Q_X(t,\tau)$, which always depends on two time arguments, not on their difference, even if A, B, and C are constant, time-invariant matrices and vectors. Only the unconditional (long-term) statistics for system (4) will be stationary. Note also that the differential equations (8) and (9) are preferred for large-scale or time-dependent models since they do not involve matrix Φ, and they require less computational and algorithmic efforts than the explicit formulae (5) and (7). In this case, we do not need matrix Φ at all unless the model involves either a time delay or path-dependency.

Let us apply the theorem to the system (1) and (2), and, for simplicity, assume that equation (1) is time-invariant ($a = Const$, $\sigma = Const$). Computing the integrals in (5) and (7), we will get all the statistical moments for system (1) and (2):

$$E[r(t)] = e^{-at}[r(0) + a\int_0^t e^{a\tau}\theta(\tau)d\tau] \qquad (10\text{-}1)$$

$$E[y(t)] = -\frac{r(0)}{a}(1 - e^{-at}) - \int_0^t [1 - e^{a(\tau - t)}]\,\theta(\tau)d\tau \qquad (10\text{-}2)$$

$$Cov[r(t),r(\tau)] = \frac{\sigma^2}{2a}(1 - e^{-2at})e^{-a(\tau\text{-}t)} \qquad (10\text{-}3)$$

$$Cov[y(t),r(\tau)] = -\frac{\sigma^2}{2a^2}(1 - e^{-at})^2 e^{-a(\tau\text{-}t)} \qquad (10\text{-}4)$$

$$Cov[r(t),y(\tau)] = \frac{\sigma^2}{2a^2}(1 - e^{-2at})e^{-a(\tau - t)} + \frac{\sigma^2}{a^2}(e^{-at} - 1) \qquad (10\text{-}5)$$

$$Cov[y(t),y(\tau)] = \frac{\sigma^2}{a^2}[t - \frac{2}{a}(1 - e^{-at}) + \frac{1}{2a}(1 - e^{-2at})]$$

$$-\frac{1 - e^{-a(\tau - t)}}{a}\,Cov[r(t),y(t)]. \qquad (10\text{-}6)$$

Differential equations (8) and (9) for the general, time-dependent case will take the following short forms:

$$\frac{dE[r(t)]}{dt} = -a(t)\{E[r(t)] - \theta(t)\}$$

$$(11)$$

$$\frac{dE[y(t)]}{dt} = -E[r(t)]$$

$$\frac{dVar[r(t)]}{dt} = -2a(t)Var[r(t)] + \sigma^2(t)$$

$$\frac{dVar[y(t)]}{dt} = -2Cov[r(t), y(t)] \qquad (12)$$

$$\frac{dCov[r(t), y(t)]}{dt} = -Var[r(t)] - a(t)Cov[r(t), y(t)]$$

Arbitrage-Free Conditions

So far, we have not been concerned with the choice of function $\theta(t)$. We choose it so as to provide correct pricing for all the zero-coupon bonds by equating price $P(0,t)$ to the cumulative discount factor known from today's forward curve:

$$P(0, t) = e^{E[y(t)] + \frac{1}{2}Var[y(t)]} = e^{-\int_0^t f(\tau)d\tau} \tag{13}$$

where $f(t)$ is the short-rate forward in t years, and hereinafter the "af" index is omitted for brevity. We use the above statistics for $y(t)$, formulae (10-2), (10-6). Constraint (13) yields the following Hull–White arbitrage-free conditions proven in Appendix B to this chapter:

$$\theta(t) = f(t) + \frac{1}{a}\frac{df}{dt} + \frac{\sigma^2}{2a^2}(1 - e^{-2at}) \tag{14}$$

$$E[r(t)] = f(t) + \frac{\sigma^2}{2a^2}(1 - e^{-at})^2 \tag{15}$$

Formula (15) shows that, in the presence of volatility, the short rate is not centered around the forward curve as many practitioners think. A systematic positive drift proportional to volatility squared is caused by the nonlinear, positively convex nature of discounting. As time t increases, this drift grows asymptotically approaching $\sigma^2/2a^2$ if $a>0$. However, if $a = 0$ (the Ho–Lee model), then the systematic drift from the forward curve will equal $\sigma^2 t^2/2$, the cost of convexity for a t-maturity zero-coupon bond.

At any future instance of time t, the entire yield curve is implied by equations (1) and (2) and short-rate $r(t)$. Indeed, the price $P(t,T)$ for a T-maturity zero-coupon bond will equal

$$P(t, T) = exp[-r_T(t)T] = E|_{r(t)} exp\left[-\int_t^{t+T} r(\tau)d\tau \right] \tag{16}$$

$$= E|_{r(t)} exp[y(t + T) - y(t)]$$

where $E|_{r(t)}$ denotes expectation conditional upon knowledge of $r(t)$. To simplify the derivation, we assume that $y(t)$ is set to zero, the short-rate process starts in time t yet follows equations (1) and (14). This transformation excludes $y(t)$ from (16) which leads to

$$-r_T(t)T = E|_{\{y(t)\,=\,0,\,r(t)\}}y(t+T) + \frac{1}{2}Var|_{\{y(t)\,=\,0,\,r(t)\}}y(t+T) \quad (17)$$

The second term in the right-hand side of (17) is simply given by formula (10-6) above in which $t = \tau = T$, whereas the first term is computed by a modification of formula (10-2) in which the starting point is t and the ending point is $t + T$:

$$E|_{\{y(t)=0,r(t)\}} y(t+T) = -\frac{r(t)}{a}(1-e^{-aT}) - \int_{t}^{t+T}[1-e^{a(\tau-t-T)}]\theta(\tau)d\tau.$$

Substituting the required conditional probabilistic measures and expression (14) for $\theta(t)$ in formula (17), we eventually derive the Hull–White formulae presented here in slightly different notations:

$$r_T(t) = B(T)r(t) - A(t,T) \quad (18)$$

where $A(t, T) = f(t)B(T) - f_T(t) - \dfrac{\sigma^2}{4a^3T}(1-e^{-aT})^2(1-e^{-2at})$,

$B(T) = (1 - e^{-aT})/aT$, and $f_T(t)$ is the forward rate for a T-maturity zero-coupon bond, at instance t.

It is seen that there exists a simple linear dependency between all rates, and the volatility term-structure is time-invariant and entirely defined by the $B(T)$ function. Taking the expectation from the both sides of (18) and substituting (15), we derive the mean path for the T-maturity rate:

$$E\{r_T(t)\} = f_T(t) + \frac{\sigma^2}{4a^3T}(1-e^{-aT})[2(1-e^{-at})^2 + (1-e^{-2at})(1-e^{-aT})]. \quad (19)$$

Formulae (15), for the short rate, and (19), for any rate, describe curves, which we call *mean path curves*. It follows from (19) that

$$\frac{d}{dt}\{E[r_T(t)] - f_T(0, t)\}\Big|_{t\,=\,0} = \frac{1}{2}T\sigma_T^2 \quad (20)$$

where $\sigma_T = B(T)\sigma$ is the volatility of the spot rate for a T-maturity zero. Thus, the spread between the mean path rates and forward rates is always positive and, for $t \ll 1/a$, can be approximated by $\frac{1}{2}T\sigma_T^2 t$. In Figure 1, we present an example of these curves for July 2, 1996, built for one-month, and 10-year rates, in the bond-equivalent form, assuming $\sigma = 0.8\%$, $a = 5\%$. Since all rates are perfectly correlated, the long-rate second-order moments are trivial:

$$Var(r_T) = B^2(T)Var(r),\ Cov(r_T y) = B(T)Cov(ry),\ Cov(rr_T) = \quad (21)$$
$$B(T)Var(r)$$

A Two-Factor Gaussian Interest-Rate Model

The one-factor stationary model considered above has at least two practical limitations. First, the yield curve cannot twist and assets sensitive to its slope cannot be priced accurately. Second, the volatility term-structure implied by this model is such that the long-rate volatility cannot exceed the short-rate volatility.

We consider, here, a straight-forward, easy-to-implement multifactor generalization of the Hull–White model. In fact, even the introduction

FIGURE 1.   Mean-Rate Curves versus Forward Curves

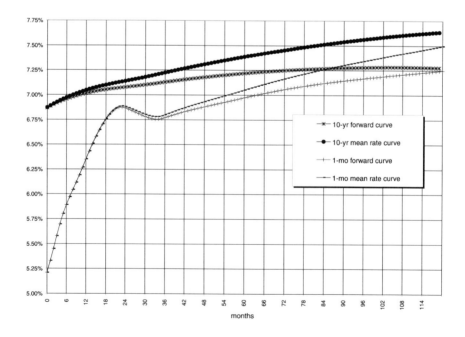

of one additional factor creates enough variability to produce potential twisting of the curve and to fit the observed volatility term-structure without explicit time-dependency of the model parameters. We introduce two pairs of state variables (x_1, y_1) and (x_2, y_2) that satisfy equations analogous to (1) and (2):

$$dx_i(t) = a_i(t)[\theta_i(t) - x_i(t)]dt + \sigma_i(t)dz_i(t), \; i = 1,2 \tag{22}$$

$$dy_i(t) = -x_i(t)dt, \; i = 1,2 \tag{23}$$

where $\theta_2(t)$ can be assumed zero, the two standard Brownian motion increments, $dz_1(t)$ and $dz_2(t)$ have a correlation equal ρ, and the models parameters, a's and σ's will be further treated as constants for simplicity. We define the short rate $r = x_1 + x_2$, therefore, $y = y_1 + y_2$. Matrix A of system (22) and (23) and matrix $\Phi(t,\tau)$ of its fundamental solutions are four-by-four block-diagonal matrices such that each two-by-two diagonal block corresponds to either (x_1, y_1) or (x_2, y_2). The financial meaning of variables x_1 and x_2 is not relevant for either finding the arbitrage-free conditions or the implied term-structure analytics. Indeed, in any linear model with all eigen-values of matrix A being real, a solution must be a weighted sum of exponents, [i.e., the transient solutions of equations (22)]. Therefore, the above definition of the short rate has mathematical meaning only.

Since equations (22) and (23) are identical to (1) and (2) with accuracy of notations, formulae (10) and (11) will be certainly valid if (r, y) is formally replaced by (x_i, y_i), and (a_i, σ_i) is used instead of (a, σ). The mutual covariances not listed in formulae (10) are ($t = \tau$ is assumed)

$$Cov[x_1(t), x_2(t)] = \rho \frac{\sigma_1\sigma_2}{a_1 a_2}[1 - e^{-(a_1 + a_2)t}] \tag{24-1}$$

$$Cov[x_i(t), y_j(t)] = \rho \frac{\sigma_1\sigma_2}{a_j}\left[\frac{1 - e^{-(a_1 + a_2)t}}{a_1 + a_2} - \frac{1 - e^{-a_i t}}{a_i}\right], \; i, j = 1, 2 \tag{24-2}$$

$$Cov[y_1(t), y_2(t)] = \rho \frac{\sigma_1\sigma_2}{a_1 a_2}\left[t - \frac{e^{-a_1 t}}{a_1} - \frac{e^{-a_2 t}}{a_2} + \frac{e^{-(a_1 + a_2)t}}{a_1 + a_2}\right] \tag{24-3}$$

The arbitrage-free econometric condition (13) for the short-rate process holds true regardless the number of factors in a Gaussian model. It results in the following arbitrage-free choice of the long-term drift (proven in Appendix B to this chapter):

$$\theta(t) = f(t) + L(t) + \frac{1}{2}\frac{dVar[y(t)]}{dt} + \frac{1}{a_1}\frac{d}{dt}\left\{f(t) + L(t) + \frac{1}{2}\frac{dVar[y(t)]}{dt}\right\} \quad (25)$$

where $L(t) = -x_1(0)(1 - e^{-a_1 t})/a_1 - x_2(0)(1 - e^{-a_2 t})/a_2$, and, certainly, $Var[y(t)]$ $= Var[y_1(t)] + Var[y_2(t)] + 2Cov[y_1(t)y_2(t)]$.

The short rate's mean path will be defined by

$$E[r(t)] = f(t) + \frac{1}{2}\sum_{i=1}^{2}\frac{\sigma_i^2}{a_i^2}(1 - e^{-a_i t})^2 + \rho\frac{\sigma_1\sigma_2}{a_1 a_2}(1 - e^{-a_1 t})(1 - e^{-a_2 t}) \quad (26)$$

clearly indicating again the progressive positive drift of this curve above the short forward rates.

As the arbitrage-free condition (13) for the short rate has a universal nature, the same is generally true for condition (17) written for any long rate $r_T(t)$. One important notation change is however required:

$$-r_T(t)T = E\big|_{\{y_1(t) = y_2(t) = 0, x_1(t), x_2(t)\}}y(t + T) \quad (27)$$

$$+ \frac{1}{2}Var\big|_{\{y_1(t) = y_2(t) = 0, x_1(t), x_2(t)\}}y(t + T)$$

[i.e., the statistics are conditional upon knowledge of all four (rather than two) state variables of the model]. As in the one-factor case, the required expressions for the conditional expectation and variance can be easily written from formulae (10) and (24) with the following formal substitutions: $t = T$ for the variance, and time instances t and $t + T$ should be taken as the starting and the ending points, correspondingly, when using formula (10-2) for the expectation. The derivation of the following formulae is omitted for brevity:

$$r_T(t) = B_1(T)x_1(t) + B_2(T)x_2(t) - A(t, T) \quad (28)$$

$$E[r_T(t)] = f_T(t) + \frac{1}{2}\sum_{i=1}^{2}\frac{\sigma_i^2}{a_i^2}[2B_i(T)(1 - e^{-a_i t}) - B_i(2T)(1 - e^{-2a_i t})] + \quad (29)$$

$$\rho\frac{\sigma_1\sigma_2}{a_1 a_2}\{B_1(T)(1 - e^{-a_1 t}) + B_2(T)(1 - e^{-a_2 t}) - B_\Sigma(T)[1 - e^{-(a_1 + a_2)t}]\}$$

where

$$B_i(T) = (1 - e^{-a_i T})/a_i T, \quad i = 1,2; \quad B_\Sigma(T) = [1 - e^{-(a_1 + a_2)T}]/(a_1 + a_2)T$$

$$A(t, T) = B_1(T)f(t) - x_2(0)e^{-a_2 t}[B_1(T) - B_2(T)] + \tag{30}$$

$$\sum_{i=1}^{2} \frac{\sigma_i^2}{a_i^2}\left[B_1(T)(1 - e^{-a_i t})^2 - B_i(T)(1 - e^{-a_i t}) + \frac{1}{2}B_i(2T)(1 - e^{-2a_i t})\right] +$$

$$\rho\frac{\sigma_1\sigma_2}{a_1 a_2}\{B_1(T)(1 - e^{-a_1 t})(1 - 2e^{-a_2 t}) - B_2(T)(1 - e^{-a_2 t}) + B_\Sigma(T)[1 - e^{-(a_1 + a_2)t}]\}$$

Formula (29) describes the mean long-rate path as it always evolves above the forward curve. The first two terms in the right-hand side of formula (28) define the volatility term-structure because function $A(t,T)$ is deterministic:

$$Var[r_T(t)] = B_1^2(T)Var[x_1(t)] + B_2^2(T)Var[x_2(t)] \tag{31}$$
$$+ 2B_1(T)B_2(T)Cov[x_1(t), x_2(t)]$$

$$Cov[r_T(t), r(t)] = B_1(T)Var[x_1(t)] + B_2(T)Var[x_2(t)] \tag{32}$$
$$+ \rho[B_1(T) + B_2(T)]Cov[x_1(t), x_2(t)]$$

An important question arising here is how to choose the model's five parameters, a's, σ's, and ρ in order to fit the observed term-structure of volatilities. We assume that one knows the short-rate volatility, σ, some long-rate volatility σ_T, and the correlation ρ_T between those rates. Dividing formulas (31) and (32) by t, and considering the limits as $t \to 0$, we can find today's volatilities and the correlation between the rates. Equating them to the observed market numbers yields to the following algebraic constraints on the model's coefficients:

$$\sigma^2 = \sigma_2^2(1 + \eta^2 + 2\rho\eta) \text{ - for the short-rate volatility;} \tag{33-1}$$

$$\sigma_T^2 = \sigma_2^2 B_2^2(T)(1 + \eta^2\xi^2 + 2\rho\eta\xi) \text{ - for the long rate volatility;} \tag{33-2}$$

$$\rho_T = \frac{1 + \eta^2\xi + \rho\eta(1 + \xi)}{\sqrt{(1 + \eta^2 + 2\rho\eta)}\sqrt{1 + \eta^2\xi^2 + 2\rho\eta\xi}} - \tag{33-3}$$

for the correlation between the rates,

where $\eta = \sigma_1/\sigma_2$, $\xi = B_1(T)/B_2(T)$.

The system (33) may have an infinite number of solutions because it retains two degrees of freedom. However, they may not be redundant. Thus, without a negative correlation ρ between the factors, the system

(33) is not solvable if $\sigma_T > \sigma$. Practitioners can set their own requirements to the yield-curve points (including a possible additional intermediate rate) to be used in fitting the model's parameters.

The Price Premium Formula for Dynamic Assets

In the previous sections, we have considered the pricing of default-free zero-coupon bonds. After all statistics and conditions for the arbitrage-free interest rate process have been derived, we turn our attention to more complicated securities. Eventually, we have to "link" the rate dynamics to the generation and valuation of the interest-rate-contingent cash flows. For an instrument paying interest at a $c(t)$ rate, having a $B(t)$ balance which retires at a $\lambda(t)$ speed (that includes scheduled and prepaid components), the price $P(t)$ satisfies the following equation:

$$P(0) = E \int_0^T B(t)\,[c(t) + \lambda(t)]e^{-y(t)}dt + E[P(T)e^{-y(T)}] \qquad (34)$$

$$\text{where } \frac{dB(t)}{dt} = -\lambda(t)B(t), \text{ therefore } B(t) = B(0)e^{-\int_0^t \lambda(\tau)d\tau}. \qquad (35)$$

The time horizon T is arbitrary in formula (34). The principle cash-flow component is integrated by parts with the use of a terminal balance, $B(T)$:

$$\int_0^T B(t)\lambda(t)e^{-y(t)}dt = -\int_0^T \frac{dB}{dt}e^{-y(t)}dt \qquad (36)$$

$$= B(0)\left[1 - \int_0^T r(t)e^{-y(t)-\int_0^t \lambda(\tau)d\tau}\,dt \right] - B(T)e^{-y(T)}$$

Substituting (35) and (36) in (34), we obtain the following compact formula for the net price (i.e., premium or discount) $p = (P - B)/B$:

$$p(0) = \int_0^T E\{[c(t) - r(t)]e^{-\int_0^t [r(\tau) + \lambda(\tau)]d\tau} \, dt\} + E[p(T)e^{-\int_0^T [r(t) + \lambda(t)]dt}] \quad (37)$$

The obtained formula states that the premium (discount) consists of two components. The first sums the differentials between the paid rate $c(t)$ and the short discount rate $r(t)$. These differentials are discounted at an artificial rate, which is equal to the sum of the actual short rate $r(t)$ and the rate of retirement $\lambda(t)$. The second component is the expected terminal premium value also discounted at the above-mentioned artificial rate.

An equivalent interpretation of formula (37) is as follows. If we transform the economy having all the interest rates (including paid rates) shifted by the time-varying, generally random rate of retirement $\lambda(t)$, formula (37) will be reduced to a constant-par asset's pricing formula. For example, consider a simple one-factor, arbitrage-free tree built for $r(t)$ in the real economy. Since the balance $B(t)$ is not known in the nodes of this tree, one cannot price randomly amortizing assets. However, let us assume that λ is an arbitrary deterministic function of r and t. In the "λ-shifted" economy, the standard tree-based pricing paradigm works perfectly for premiums (discounts) rather than for prices.

Formula (37) can be easily modified if the asset, such as interest rate swaps, swaptions, and so forth, does not pay principle. The model may still account for changes in notional balances, but ignores principle cash-flows:

$$p(0) = \int_0^T E[c(t)e^{-\int_0^t [r(\tau) + \lambda(\tau)]d\tau}]dt + E[p(T)e^{-\int_0^T [r(t) + \lambda(t)]dt}] \quad (38)$$

where p now denotes P/B. In the "λ-shifted" economy, one should not shift $c(t)$, which is now a spread between shifted rates. For clarity of presentation, we will assume that a security pays principal and that it is priced in accordance to formula (37), unless version (38) is explicitly cited.

A choice of the cash-flow horizon, T, is determined by the nature of the asset. For maturing bonds, T can be a finite maturity length, whereas for nonmaturing assets, one can set $T = \infty$. Strictly speaking, the appropriate mathematical assumption to be made here is convergence on proba-

bility of the $\int_0^\infty [r(t) + \lambda(t)]dt$ integral.

Price Computation for Linear Model

We now assume that all the variables in the pricing formula (37), $r(t)$, $c(t)$, and $\lambda(t)$ satisfy a system of linear stochastic equations. In addition, we define the variable y' (instead of y) as the natural logarithm of the artificial discount factor mentioned above:

$$dy' = [-r(t) - \lambda(t)]dt. \tag{39}$$

Let us assume that $p(T)$ is known, denote $x = c - r$ ($x = c$ for (38)) and rewrite (37) as

$$p(0) = \int_0^T E[x(t)e^{y'(t)}]dt + p(T)Ee^{y'(T)}. \tag{37'}$$

The theorem enables us to compute means, variances, and covariances for all state variables. Therefore, we know the parameters for the binormal distribution of the vector $[x(t), y'(t)]$, at any t. In fact, we can always find a unique analytical regression of x with respect to y':

$$x(t) = \alpha(t) + \beta(t)y'(t) + \varepsilon(t), \tag{40}$$

where, for every t, $\beta = Cov(xy') / Var(y')$, $\alpha = E(x) - \beta E(y')$, $Var(\varepsilon) = Var(x) - \beta Cov(xy')$, $\varepsilon(t)$ is independent of $y'(t)$, and all the statistics have been derived. Substituting (40) into (37') and computing the expectation (see Appendix C to this chapter), we obtain the following central formula:

$$p(0) = \int_0^T \{\alpha(t) + \beta(t)[E(y'(t)) + Var(y'(t))]\}e^{E[y'(t)] + \frac{1}{2}Var[y'(t)]} dt \tag{41}$$

$$+ p(T)e^{E[y'(T)] + \frac{1}{2}Var[y'(T)]}$$

Let us summarize the proposed stochastic pricing method. To price a dynamic security, we have to describe both it and the interest rate market by a system of linear stochastic equations, which are complemented by equation (39) for the natural logarithm of the artificial discount factor. Having matrices A and B of the model, we write down the Lyapunov matrix differential equation (9) for covariances along with the vector equation (8) for averages. We integrate (8) and (9) month-by-month concurrently computing (41). Since all the formulae are deterministic, instead of hundreds of Monte Carlo simulations, we need only one loop over all months from settlement to horizon.

Application to OAS Analysis

The difference between the OAS analysis and the above model is that we have to use OAS as the discount rate rather than $r(t)$. Thus, formula (37) is replaced by

$$p(0) = \int_0^T E[(x(t) - s)e^{y'(t) - st}]dt + p(T)Ee^{y'(T) - sT}$$

where s denotes the OAS (note: one should not subtract s from x when formula (38) is used). Having repeated all the derivations that had led to formula (41), we will get

$$p(0) = \int_0^T \{\alpha(t) - s + \beta(t)[E(y'(t)) + Var(y'(t))]\}e^{E[y'(t)] + \frac{1}{2}Var[y'(t)] - s} dt \quad (42)$$

$$+ p(T)e^{E[y'(T)] + \frac{1}{2}Var[y'(T)] - s}$$

Equating the right-hand side of formula (42) to a given premium of the instrument, we obtain a nonlinear equation for s. When iterating for s, we do not build the model's statistics more than once, but rather memorize all needed subintegral terms in (42) computed for $t=1,2,...$etc. Since formula (42) is easily differentiable with respect to s, the Newton-Raphson technique is effective.

Price Computation for Piece-Linear Model

Consider a more general model of the system in which the coupon-rate spread is the sum of a state variable x of the linear system (4), and a piece-linear (generally, time-dependent) function $f(u,t)$ of another state variable u of the same system. That is

$$c(t) - r(t) = x(t) + f(u,t) = x(t) + a_i(t) + b_i(t)u(t), \quad (43)$$
$$\text{for } u_i(t) \le u(t) < u_{i+1}(t), \; i = 0,1,... \, .$$

Most options pay their cash flows according to some piece-linear algorithm. Substituting (43) into (37), we will find that the expected present value of the cash flow received in month t is separated into a "linear" part produced by $x(t)$ and analyzed above, and a "piece-linear" part driven by $u(t)$. Our attention is now turned to this latter part.

First, we state that there exists a unique regression

$$y'(t) = \alpha(t) + \beta(t)u(t) + \varepsilon(t) \tag{44}$$

in which, for every t, ε is independent of u, and

$$\beta = Cov(uy')/\sigma_u^2, \ \alpha = E(y') - \beta\mu_u, \ E(\varepsilon) = 0, \ Var(\varepsilon) = Var(y') - \beta Cov(uy'), \tag{45}$$

where $\mu_u = E(u)$, $\sigma_u^2 = Var(u)$.

Then, for every t, one needs to find the expectation of $f(u,t)e^{y'(t)}$. We can prove (see Appendix C to this chapter) that

$$E[f(u, t)e^{y'(t)}] = \tag{46}$$

$$e^{\alpha + \beta\mu_u + \frac{1}{2}\beta^2\sigma_u^2 + \frac{1}{2}Var(\varepsilon)} \left\{ \sum_i \{a_i + b_i[\mu_u - \beta\sigma_u^2]\}[\Phi(d_{i+1}) - \right.$$

$$\left. \Phi(d_i)] + 2\beta \sum_i b_i\sigma_u^2[p(d_i) - p(d_{i+1})] \right\}$$

where $d_i = [u_i - \mu_u]/\sigma_u - \beta\sigma_u$, $i = 0,1,...$; $\Phi()$ and $p()$ are cumulative and density distribution functions for the standard normal distribution, respectively.

Applications: Swap, Swaptions, Caps

In this section, we describe interest rate derivatives by the required linear or piece-linear models, and we show how to derive closed-form solutions. We consider a continuous swap paying the difference between the short rate, r and a strike rate, r^s. The notional balance is not swapped and may amortize at a predefined (generally time-dependent) rate λ. Since no principal cash flow exists, we use the underlying pricing formula (38) in which $c = r - r^s$.

Standard Swaps

For an at-the-money (ATM) swap, the strike rate r^s is chosen to produce a zero price. For this case, r^s equals the rate r_T^* of a continuously coupon paying bond, maturing in T years and priced at par. Interestingly, this statement holds true even for swaps amortizing at a constant speed, λ. To prove this, we transform the economy shifting all rates by λ: $r' = r + \lambda$, $r'^s = r^s + \lambda$. Formula (38) will take the following form invariant to the speed λ:

$$p(0) = \int_0^T E\{[r'(t) - r'^s]e^{y'(t)}\}dt = 0 \tag{47}$$

where $dy' = -r'dt$. We note that

$$\int_0^T E[r'(t)e^{y'(t)}]dt = 1 - e^{y'(T)} = 1 - P(0, T)$$

$$r'^s \int_0^T E e^{y'(t)}dt = r'^s \int_0^T e^{-r_t(0)t}dt = r'^s P^{Ann}(0, T)$$

where $P^{Ann}(0,T)$ denotes the price of an annuity continuously paying \$1 per annum for T years. Therefore, formula (47) leads to $1 = P(0,T) + r'^s P^{Ann}(0,T)$, an exact formula for the above-mentioned bond, in the transformed economy. Hence, $r^s = r_T^*$ for the ATM swap.

Let us now imagine that $r^s \neq r_T^*$. From (47), we derive a purely deterministic formula:

$$p(0) = \int_0^T E\{[r(t) - r^s]e^{y(t)}\}dt = (r_T^* - r^s)\int_0^T E e^{y(t)}dt = (r_T^* - r^s)e^{-\lambda T}\int_0^T e^{-r_t(0)t}dt \tag{48}$$

Forward Swaps

Forward swaps are similar to the standard swaps except that the starting point in formula (48) has to be moved to the swap's starting date, t:

$$p(0) = E \int_t^{t+T} [r(\tau) - r^s]e^{y'(\tau)}d\tau = E\left\{[r_T^*(t) - r^s] \int_t^{t+T} e^{y'(\tau)}d\tau\right\} \tag{49}$$

The first equality in (49) perfectly fits the required linear model form, and an application of the central formula (41) leads to

$$p(0) = \int_t^{t+T} \{\alpha(\tau) + \beta(\tau)[E(y'(\tau)) + Var(y'(\tau))]\} e^{E[y'(\tau)] + \frac{1}{2}Var[y'(\tau)]} d\tau \quad (50)$$

where $\beta(\tau) = Cov[r(\tau)y'(\tau)]/Var[r(\tau)]$, $\alpha(\tau) = E[y'(\tau)] - \beta(\tau)E[r(\tau)] - r^s$. (51)

For the purpose of swaption pricing (see below), we need to consider the second equality in (49). To simplify the derivations without significant loss of accuracy, one could replace the rate r_T^* for a coupon bearing bond by the spot rate r_{T^*} for some a priori chosen maturity $T^* < T$. This approximation is quite accurate for most maturities actually observed on the swap market and allows us to use one of the spot rate models. Therefore, formula (49) can be rewritten as

$$p(0) = E \int_t^{t+T} [r_{T^*}(t) - r^s] e^{y'(\tau)} d\tau \quad (52)$$

We notice the structural identity with the first equality in (49). In fact, solution (50) is still valid, but, $r(\tau)$ must be formally replaced by $r_{T^*}(t)$ in the expressions for α and β:

$$\beta(\tau) = Cov[r_{T^*}(t)y'(\tau)]/Var[r_{T^*}(t)], \ \alpha(\tau) = E[y'(\tau)] - \beta(\tau)E[r_{T^*}(t)] - r^s, (53)$$

All needed statistical measures have been already derived for the one- and two-factor interest rate processes including computation of the covariance for $t \neq \tau$.

Swaptions

An option expiring at time t on a "pay fixed" swap maturing at $t + T$ will be exercised if and only if $r_{T^*}(t) > r^s$. It leads to an obvious modification of formula (52):

$$p(0) = E \int_t^{t+T} [r_{T^*}(t) - r^s]^+ e^{y'(\tau)} d\tau \quad (54)$$

where, as usual in the mathematics of derivatives, the "+" index means that the negative value is ignored. Thus, we have a piece-linear pricing model and can use formula (46) in which $u = r_{T^*}(t)$, $u_0 = -\infty$, $u_1 = r^s$, $u_2 = \infty$, $a_0 = b_0 = 0$, $a_1 = -r^s$, $b_1 = 1$:

$$p(0) = \int\limits_{t}^{t+T} \{(E[r_{T^*}(t)] - \beta(\tau)Var[r_{T^*}(t)] - r^s)[1 - \Phi(d_1)] + 2\beta(\tau) \quad (55)$$

$$Var[r_{T^*}(t)]p(d_1)\}^* \exp\{\alpha(\tau) + \beta(\tau)E[r_{T^*}(t)] + \frac{1}{2}\beta^2(\tau)Var[r_{T^*}(t)] + \frac{1}{2}Var[\varepsilon(\tau)]\}d\tau$$

where α and β are computed from formula (53),

$$Var[\varepsilon(\tau)] = Var[y'(\tau)] - \beta(\tau)Cov[r_{T^*}(t)y'(\tau)],$$

$$d_1 = \frac{r^s - E[r_{T^*}(t)]}{\sqrt{Var[r_{T^*}(t)]}} - \sqrt{Var[r_{T^*}(t)]}.$$

Thus, we have derived closed-form pricing solutions for homogeneously amortizing swaps and swaptions.

Caps, Floors, Collars

This example is similar to swaps except the interest paid becomes a piece-linear function of the short rate, which is presented below for a collar:

$$
\begin{aligned}
c &= r - r_{cap}, & \text{if } r > r_{cap} \\
c &= 0, & \text{if } r_{floor} \le r \le r_{cap} \quad (56) \\
c &= -r + r_{floor}, & \text{if } r < r_{floor}.
\end{aligned}
$$

The model perfectly fits the general piece-linear form (43), and formula (46) is applicable.

Applications: Nonmaturing Deposits and Mortgage-Backed Securities

Nonmaturing Deposits

We assume that a bank manages its deposit rates to stabilize λ (the rate of redemption or growth) and perfectly achieves this goal. To do so, the bank must adjust the paid rate (c) properly. This process is usually inertial and can be described by a system of differential equations, see OTS [1994]. In a simple case, we can use the following first-order model:

$$\frac{dc'}{dt} = -a_c[c'(t) - r(t) + \theta_c] \quad (57)$$

in which θ_c represent a long-term spread between the short-market rate r and the deposit rate $c(t) = c'(t)$. Thus, we have described the behavior of the deposit by a linear equation and can use the pricing formula (41).

One can complicate the model considering a typically conservative style of a bank's deposit management. Namely, if $c'(t)$ computed from (57) is greater than $r(t) - \theta_c$, only a k-portion ($0 \le k \le 1$) of the "correctly computed" spread is actually paid. This leads to a piece-linear model:

$$c = c' \text{ if } c' - r \le -\theta_c \qquad (58)$$
$$c = k(c' - r + \theta_c) + r - \theta_c \text{ otherwise.}$$

We can use the pricing formula (46) in which $u = c' - r$.

Mortgage-Backed Securites and Adjustable-Rate Mortgages

These securities represent a major, yet the most general, class of dynamic assets (random prepayments, and coupon adjustments to a random index). Pricing will be based on formula (41) or (46), in which the redemption rate λ is required to be a state variable of some linear system. Many developers of prepayment models present the prepayment rate as an arctangent-like function of the spread between the gross coupon (c + service) and some refinancing rate (linked to r_T, with T to be somewhere between four to 10 years). This function has a substantial zone of linearity, but is saturated by the zero (or another minimum) level from the lower side, and by credit limitations on refinancing from the upper side. Successful application of the proposed approach will depend on how far the spread is from the middle point of the prepayment characteristic, and therefore how important the saturations are for MBS valuation.

A possible model to be used in the context of our approach is therefore

$$\lambda = \lambda_0 + k(c - r_T - \theta_c) \qquad (59)$$

where λ_0 is the zero-spread redemption rate, k is the sensitivity to the spread, θ_c accounts for servicing and the typical MBS-TSY spread.

Seasoning and seasonality are easily presented by time-dependent multipliers (recall that our approach has no limitations on time dependency). However, the burnout effect should be modeled by an additive prepayment rate component that is a function of the time and the survival factor. In the latter case, we have to introduce an additional state variable y'' (logarithm of the survival factor) and modify prepayment model (59):

$$\frac{dy''}{dt} = -\lambda(t) \tag{60}$$

$$\lambda = \lambda_0 + k(c - r_T - \theta_c) + ly''. \tag{59'}$$

Lifetime caps for ARMs are modeled exactly as in the above example from the section on swaps, swaptions, and caps.

Conclusion

We have presented an analytical framework that allows for stochastic pricing of interest-rate-contingent dynamic assets via purely deterministic formulae. The asset and the interest rate market are assumed to follow a system of linear stochastic differential equations and some piece-linear algebraic equations. The method derives the price directly from the expectations and covariances of the state variables. Thus, instead of hundreds of numeric trials, one needs to find analytic or numeric solution to a system of deterministic linear equations for the statistics of the state variables.

The approach has been effectively demonstrated on different types of assets, ranging from amortizing interest rate swaps and swaptions to MBS and nonmaturing deposits. It also enables an analytical derivation of arbitrage-free conditions for one-factor and multifactor interest-rate linear models.

References

Beaglehole, D. R. and M. S. Tenney. "General Solutions of Some Interest-Rate-Contingent Claim Pricing Equations." *The Journal of Fixed Income* 4 (1991).

Heath, D. R., R. A. Jarrow, and A. S. Morton. "Bond Pricing and the Term Structure of Interest Rates: A New Methodology for Contingent Claims Valuation." *Econometrica* 50 (1992), pp. 77-105.

Hull, J. C. *Options, Futures and Other Derivative Securities*. Englewood Cliffs, NJ: Prentice Hall, 1993.

Hull, J. C. and A. D. White. "Pricing Interest Rate Derivative Securities." *The Review of Financial Studies* 3 (1990), pp. 573–92.

Karatzas, I. and E. S. Shreve. *Brownian Motion and Stochastic Calculus*. New York: Springer-Verlag, 1991.

The OTS Net Portfolio Value Model. Office of Thrift Supervision, Risk Management Division, Washington, D.C., November 1994.

APPENDIX A

Matrix $\Phi(t,\tau)$ for system (1), (2). The original system is presentable in the general form (4) where

$$A(t) = \begin{array}{|c|c|} \hline -a & 0 \\ \hline -1 & 0 \\ \hline \end{array}, \; B(t) = \begin{array}{|c|} \hline 1 \\ \hline 0 \\ \hline \end{array}, \; Q_Z(t) = \sigma$$

We have to find matrix Φ of fundamental solution for the system. We make use of the following algebraic fact: if J is the Jordan form for matrix $\int_\tau^t A(\lambda)d\lambda$, and P is the matrix of Jordan transformation (that is $\int_\tau^t A(\lambda)d\lambda = PJP^{-1}$), then $\Phi(t,\tau) = Pe^J P^{-1}$. If the Jordan form is diagonal, $J = diag[\lambda_k]_{k=1}^n$ (the most common case), then $e^J = diag[exp(\lambda_k)]_{k=1}^n$. Therefore, finding matrix Φ is a simple three-step procedure.

Step 1. Find the eigen-values and eigen-vectors of matrix $\int_\tau^t A(\lambda)d\lambda =$

$$\begin{array}{|c|c|} \hline -a(t-\tau) & 0 \\ \hline -(t-\tau) & 0 \\ \hline \end{array} : \lambda_1 = -a(t-\tau), \; X_1 = \begin{array}{|c|} \hline -a \\ \hline 1 \\ \hline \end{array}; \; \lambda_2 = 0, \; X_2 = \begin{array}{|c|} \hline 0 \\ \hline 1 \\ \hline \end{array};$$

Step 2. From step 1, $P = \begin{array}{|c|c|} \hline -a & 0 \\ \hline 1 & 1 \\ \hline \end{array}$; Find $P^{-1} = \begin{array}{|c|c|} \hline 1/a & 0 \\ \hline -1/a & 1 \\ \hline \end{array}$.

Step 3. $\Phi(t,\tau) = exp\left[\int_\tau^t A(\lambda)d(\lambda)\right] = Pe^J P^{-1} = P\begin{array}{|c|c|} \hline e^{-a(t-\tau)} & 0 \\ \hline 0 & 1 \\ \hline \end{array}P^{-1} =$

$$\begin{array}{|c|c|} \hline e^{-a(t-\tau)} & 0 \\ \hline \dfrac{1}{a}[e^{-a(t-\tau)}-1] & 1 \\ \hline \end{array}.$$

APPENDIX B

Arbitrage-free conditions in one-factor model. Taking natural logarithm from the both sides of equality (13), we have

$$E[y(t)] + \frac{1}{2} Var[y(t)] = -\int_0^t f(\lambda)d\lambda . \tag{B-1}$$

Substituting the mean and variance of $y(t)$ from formulae (10-2), (10-6) correspondingly (where $t_1 = t_2 = t$) we get

$$-\int_0^t f(\lambda)d\lambda + \frac{r(0)}{a}(1 - e^{-at}) + \int_0^t [1 - e^{-a(t-\lambda)}]\theta(\lambda)d\lambda - \tag{B-2}$$

$$\frac{\sigma^2}{2a^2}[t - \frac{2}{a}(1 - e^{-at}) + \frac{1}{2a}(1 - e^{-2at})] = 0.$$

We differentiate (B-2) with respect to time variable t:

$$-f(t) + r(0)e^{-at} + \int_0^t ae^{-a(t-\lambda)}\theta(\lambda)d\lambda - \frac{\sigma^2}{2a^2}(1 - e^{-at})^2 = 0. \tag{B-3}$$

The obtained condition has an integral term. We exclude it subtracting (B-3) from (B-2) multiplied by a:

$$f(t) - r(0) - a\int_0^t \theta(\lambda)d\lambda + a\int_0^t f(\lambda)d\lambda + \frac{\sigma^2}{4a^2}[2at - 1 + e^{-2at}] = 0. \tag{B-4}$$

Differentiating (B-4) and resolving for the long-term average θ we obtain condition (14).

Arbitrage-free conditions in the two-factor model. Condition (B-1) still holds true, and $\theta(t)$, the unknown function, is entered in the expression of $E[y(t)]$ as follows:

$$E[y(t)] = E[y_1(t)] + E[y_2(t)] = L(t) - \int_0^t \theta(\tau)[1 - e^{a(\tau-t)}]d\tau . \tag{B-5}$$

After substituting (B-5) into (B-1) we obtain the same type of integral equation as (B-2). Applying the same solving technique we arrive to the arbitrage-free condition (25).

APPENDIX C

Derivation of formulae (41), (46). Both formulae are based on the following mathematical statements: if $x \in N(\mu,\sigma)$, then

$$\int_A^B p_{[\mu,\sigma]}(x)e^x dx = e^{\mu+\frac{1}{2}\sigma^2}\left[\Phi\left(\frac{B-\mu}{\sigma}-\sigma\right)-\Phi\left(\frac{A-\mu}{\sigma}-\sigma\right)\right] \quad \text{(C-1)}$$

$$\int_A^B p_{[\mu,\sigma]}(x)xe^x dx = 2\sigma^2 e^{\mu+\frac{1}{2}\sigma^2}\left[p\left(\frac{A-\mu}{\sigma}-\sigma\right)-p\left(\frac{B-\mu}{\sigma}-\sigma\right)\right] \quad \text{(C-2)}$$

$$+ (\mu-\sigma^2)\int_A^B p_{[\mu,\sigma]}(x)e^x dx .$$

In (C-1) and (C-2), p,Φ refer to the standard $[0,1]$-normal distribution whereas $p_{[\mu,\sigma]}$ denotes density of the (μ,σ)-normal distribution. It is seen that the integral in (37′) will be composed of (C-1) and (C-2) with $A = -\infty$, $B = +\infty$ if regression (40) is taken into account. The residual term of this regression produces a zero expectation, as it is centered and independent of y.

The derivation of (46) is quite similar except for two points. First, function $f(u,t)$ is piece-linear, therefore we have to compute integrals on each interval of linearity $[u_i,u_{i+1}]$ and add up the results. Second, the residual term (ε) appears in the exponent although still being centered and independent of the integration variable. It allows for the computing of $E(e^\varepsilon)$ separately and taking this factor out of the "main" integration. The derivation follows below (the time argument t is omitted, and w denotes βu, $w_i = \beta u_i$):

$$E[f(u)e^{\alpha+\beta u+\varepsilon}] = e^{\alpha+\frac{1}{2}Var(\varepsilon)} E[f(u)e^{\beta u}] =$$

$$e^{\alpha+\frac{1}{2}Var(\varepsilon)}\sum_i \int_{u_i}^{u_{i+1}} p_{[\mu,\sigma]}(u)(a_i+b_i u)e^{\beta u} du =$$

$$\frac{1}{\beta}e^{\alpha+\frac{1}{2}Var(\varepsilon)}\sum_i \left\{ a_i \int_{w_i}^{w_{i+1}} p_{[\beta\mu,\beta\sigma]}(w)e^w dw + \frac{b_i}{\beta}\int_{w_i}^{w_{i+1}} p_{[\beta\mu,\beta\sigma]}(w)we^w dw \right\} .$$

Substituting the integrals (C-1), (C-2) leads to formula (46).

A Two-Factor Term-Structure Model

Y.K. Chan, Ph.D.
Director, Mortgage Research
Salomon Brothers

The prevalent wisdom in the financial modeling community is that a one-factor term-structure model is adequate for most purposes, and that the benefit of a two-factor model is outweighed by its cost, both in terms of difficulty in implementation and the computational requirements. Since the first version of this chapter was written in 1993, the importance of a two-factor model in the valuation of complex securities such as collateralized mortgage obligations (CMOs) has been recognized by a growing segment of the investment community. In particular, a version of the model described in this chapter has been implemented on the Salomon Brothers Yield Book and has been used extensively by investors for the pricing of mortgage-backed securities.

A one-factor model may well be sufficient for garden-variety securities where a quick value comparison is all that is needed. However, more

The author wishes to acknowledge helpful critique and suggestions by Scott Richard on an earlier version of this chapter. The author also wishes to thank Michael Waldman and Stanley Diller for numerous conversations on the subject of yield curves, and Gene Cohler for helpful comments. The information contained herein is illustrative and is not intended to predict actual results. We do not guarantee the accuracy or reliability of the assumptions, data, and conclusions referenced herein. Salomon Brothers Inc and/or individuals thereof may have positions in the securities referred to herein and may make purchase or sales thereof while this document is circulating. This document is not a solicitation of any transaction in the securities referred to herein.

derivative securities are now traded which have aspects of both the long and short end of the interest rate spectrum. One example is a CMO inverse floater whose capped coupon is indexed to the short rate, but whose principal amount amortizes as a function of the mortgage rate. A second example is an adjustable-rate mortgage whose prepayment is itself dependent on the spread between the short rate and the mortgage rate.

As the risk characteristics of these instruments need to be more precisely determined, a term-structure model seems desirable which allows for less than certain correlation of the long and short rates.

We view a term-structure and valuation model as a tool with two functions. The first, as the name suggests, is to price a security. The second function, equally important but sometimes ignored by practitioners, is to supply a hedge for the security. The two functions are, of course, inextricably linked. The thrust of the modern option pricing theory, starting with Black and Scholes [1973] and Cox, Ross, and Rubinstein [1979], is that the price of a security is the cost of hedging it with other, actively traded, securities whose prices are known.

The relevant point here is that different term-structure models will produce different hedges and can therefore be judged by the consequences of these hedges. In particular, the question of whether a two-factor model is useful for certain types of securities can be answered by comparing the performance of the hedge produced by a two-factor model with that from a one-factor model.

A perfect term model will produce a dynamic hedge such that the hedged portfolio will behave exactly like a money market account. This means that the value of the hedged portfolio at any time in the holding period is as if the initial investment were invested in the overnight rate and rolled over continuously. Any term-structure model and the accompanying model can be tested according to this criterion over a historical time period using market yield-curve data. No model is expected to perform perfectly. But a better model will produce a hedged portfolio closer to a money market account. The working paper Chan [1993] contains an example of a CMO inverse floater hedged (with the model described here) for its lifetime, which spans the period of May 1986 through December 1990, using treasury yield-curve data for that period. The hedge produced by the two-factor model performs significantly better than that produced by a one-factor model.

The model of Brennan and Schwartz [1979] is probably the earliest two-factor term-structure model in use. It is based on a joint diffusion of the short rate and the console rate. Schwartz [1990] generalizes the model to allow for a time-dependent price-of-risk function which effectively fits the model to the term structure of spot rates. Hogan [1992] shows that with probability one, the Brennan and Schwartz process explodes in finite time. This may or may not be a problem for a limited time horizon like 30 years.

Heath, Jarrow, and Morton [1990] model the forward rates as undergoing simultaneous diffusions driven by the same Brownian motion. The resulting short-rate process is in general not path independent; (i.e., the implementation for the pricing of American options, corporate bonds with embedded options, or other securities with inherently price-driven options would require a high-order Markov process).

Longstaff and Schwartz [1990] presents a two-factor equilibrium model with the short rate and the short-rate volatility as state variables. They obtain closed-form expressions for discount bond options. Langetieg [1980] suggests a model where the short rate is s, a linear combination of multiple macro-economical factors which jointly undergo a linear diffusion.

Recent work on one-factor models, extending those of Ho and Lee [1986] and Black, Derman, and Toy [1990] are mostly in the direction of fitting the initial rate term-structure and volatility term-structure. Among them are the Hull and White [1990] extensions of the Vasicek model and the Cox, Ingersoll, and Ross model. For a discussion of several of these models in the context of numerical integration, see Jamshidian [1991]. We also note the work in Cheyette [1991] which introduces an internal stochastic variable, the cumulative volatility, to influence the short-rate drift and fit the term structure of volatilities exactly, although the rates are perfectly correlated.

We describe below a two-factor model which has the advantage of simplicity, flexibility, and practicality. The two stochastic variables are essential the short rate and its velocity, or, equivalently, the short rate and the normalized slope of the yield curve. By choosing the model parameters properly, we can fit perfectly any initial term structure of rates, the volatility of the short rate, the volatility of the yield-curve slope, the correlation between rate move and changes in slope (yield-curve twisting), the volatility of a long-term rate and that of an intermediate-term rate , and the correlation of the short rate and a long-term rate with designated maturity. The initial term-structure of rates is obtained from the market data. The other parameters are from historical data. Alternatively, some of the parameters can be implied by fitting the model prices of derivative securities to market prices. For example, the volatilities of the short rate, the intermediate-term rate, and the long-term rate can be jointly implied from the market prices of a rate cap and Treasury note and bond options.

We will also present a computationally efficient pricing scheme. We will assume risk neutrality throughout this chapter: the price at time t of a treasury zero-coupon bond maturing at time $t+m$ is calculated as

$$E_t exp\left(-\int_t^{t+m} sudu\right),$$

where s is the short rate and E_t is the conditional expectation given all information up to time t.

The Model—A Second-Order Dynamical System

A general diffusion model for interest rates is given by

$$d\bar{x} = \mu(\bar{x}, t)dt + \sigma(\bar{x}, t)dz ,\tag{2-1}$$

where one component of the vector $\bar{x}$ is the short-rate s or the logarithm of s, μ is the (vector) drift coefficient, σ is the (matrix) coefficient and z is a standard Brownian motion of dimension one or higher.

We propose the following special case:

$$s = a(t)exp(x)\tag{2-2}$$

$$dx = vdt + \sigma_1 dz_1\tag{2-3}$$

$$dv = [-bx - kv]dt + \sigma_2 dz_2 ,\tag{2-4}$$

where s is the short rate and where z_1 and z_2 are standard Brownian motions with correlation coefficient ρ. We will assume that the diffusion starts at the origin, that the diffusion coefficients σ_1, σ_2, and ρ are functions of time t only, and that the coefficients b and k are symmetric in (x,v), [i.e. the values of these coefficients remain the same when (x,v) is replaced by $(-x,-v)$].

The transformation $exp(x)$ is used here for the usual reason: that it is an increasing function which maps any value of x to a nonzero rate s. Other transformations with similar properties can be used. In particular, the transformation $f(x)$ defined by $f(x) = 1 + x + x^2$ (if $x > 0$ and $f(x) = (1 - x)^{-1}$ (if $x < 0$) is usable. The development of our model would follow a similar line. In the following discussion, we will stick to the exponential case, also referred to as the log-normal model.

Interpretation of the variables and parameters are as follows. Because of symmetry, the median of x is 0 and so the deterministic function $a(t)$ is nothing but the median of the short-rate $s(t)$. It is also the rate path if all volatilities are 0. We will therefore refer to $a(t)$ as the equilibrium short-rate path. The variable x is the relative deviation of the short-rate s from this equilibrium. For example, if at time t the equilibrium rate $a(t)$ is 0.08 and x has the value of 0.20, then the short rate is $x = 0.0977$. In the next section, we will show that v is the excess slope of the yield-curve t. (The term excess slope will be precisely defined in that section).

If the coefficients σ_1 and σ_2 are zero, then the model (2-3) and (2-4) is nothing but a second-order dynamic system. The variable v is the velocity. There is an external force $-bx$ which is center reverting where b is positive. The term $-kv$ where k is positive represents a damping force. Our model is then a familiar model of a Newtonian particle subject to a mean reversal force, a damping force, and random disturbances. We will refer to the variable v alternative as the drift, the velocity, or the excess slope.

Our model is guaranteed to be well behaved—no explosion, and a discretization converges to the continuous model—provided the coefficients b, k, σ_1, σ_2, and ρ are continuous and satisfy the Lipschitz conditions. See, for example, Arnold [1974] theorem (6.2.2) on page 105 and corollary (6.3.1) on page 112.

We are especially interested in two special cases:

1. Linear Model—the coefficients b, k, σ_1, σ_2, and ρ are continuous functions of the time variable t only:

$$dx = vdt + \sigma_1 dz_1 \tag{2-5}$$

$$dv = [-b(t)x - k(t)v]dt + \sigma_2(t)dz_2 . \tag{2-6}$$

2. Stationary Model—the coefficients b, k, σ_1, σ_2, and ρ are continuous functions of the rate deviation x only and σ_1, σ_2, and ρ are constants:

$$dx = vdt + \sigma_1 dz_1 \tag{2-7}$$

$$dv = [-b(x)x - k(x)v]dt + \sigma_2 dz_2 . \tag{2-8}$$

The stationary model seems especially appealing. Roughly speaking, this is an assumption that the structure of the financial market is independent of the current and expected economical and fiscal policies, which affect only the equilibrium rate path $a(t)$.

We establish in the next section that the variable v is the excess slope of the yield curve.

Yield-Curve Slope and Yield-Curve Twisting

The advantage of a two-factor model, of course, is that it allows yield-curve twisting which is not perfectly correlated to rate movements. On top of the uncertainty of rate moves, there can be uncertainty in yield-curve slope. The yield curve can flatten or steepen. In this section, we make precise the notion that the excess slope of the yield curve is equal to the velocity variable v.

Given any yield curve, restate the slope at the short end as a fraction of the short-rate s.

$$S = 2(slope)/s \tag{3-1}$$

We will refer to S simply as the (normalized) slope of the given yield curve.

We will assume that the equilibrium rate path $a(t)$ is smooth, (i.e., that it is differentiable). Then we will show that all yield curves in our model have a well-defined slope.

First consider the degenerate case where all volatilities are 0 and therefore $s_t=a(t)$. Let $y_t(h)$ denote the h period continuous compounding rate at time t. Then clearly

$$exp(-hy_t(h)) = exp\left(-\int_t^{t+h} a(u)du\right), \tag{3-2}$$

$$y_t(h) = \frac{1}{h}\int_t^{t+h} a(u)du. \tag{3-3}$$

Differentiation relative to h at $h = 0$ leads to the slope of the yield curve at time t:

$$y't(0) = a'(t)/2. \tag{3-4}$$

Hence,

$$\bar{S}(t) = a'(t)/a(t) \tag{3-5}$$

where $\bar{S}$ signifies the normalized slope S for the equilibrium yield curve.

For the general nondegenerate case, we have the following proposition.

Proposition A—For the system specified above in the defining equations (2-2), (2-3), and (2-4):

$$S(t) = \bar{S}(t) + \frac{\sigma_1^2}{2} + v_t. \tag{3-6}$$

The proof of this proposition is given in the working paper of Chan [1993].

Because of symmetry, the median value of v is 0, and so the median value of $S(t)$, according to the above equation is

$$\tilde{S}(t) \;=\; \bar{S}(t) + \frac{\sigma_1^2}{2}. \qquad\qquad (3\text{-}7)$$

The equation (3-6) can be rewritten as

$$S(t) \;=\; \tilde{S}(t) + v_t. \qquad\qquad (3\text{-}8)$$

In other words, v is the excess of the yield curve's (normalized) slope over the median (normalized) slope. The following terminology is therefore justified:

$\bar{S}(t)$ = slope of equilibrium yield curve

$\tilde{S}(t)$ = median yield-curve slope

v = excess yield-curve slope

As the value of v fluctuates up and down, so the yield curve will twist accordingly. For example, if s=0.05, we see for (3-1) and (3-9) that increasing the value of v by 0.10 has the effect of increasing the (non-normalized) slope of the yield curve by 25 basis points per year.

We could reformulate the system (2-2), (2-3), (2-4) equivalently in terms of the variables x and S. A formulation in terms of the non-normalized slope of the yield curve would, however, involve a second-order term in the drift coefficient. This makes the variable v preferable.

It follows from (2-2), (2-3), (2-4), and (3-6) that

$$\sigma_1^2 dt = E[(d(\log s))^2]$$
$$\sigma_2^2 dt = E[(dS)^2] \qquad\qquad (3\text{-}9)$$
$$\rho\sigma_1\sigma_2 dt = E[d(\log s)dS]$$

Assuming that the coefficients on the left-hand sides of (3-9) are constants, they can be estimated from historical data. The coefficients σ_1, σ_2, and ρ represent respectively the short-rate volatility, the slope volatility, and the correlation between rate-moves and twisting.

Using monthly Treasury zero-coupon bond prices going back five years, and smoothing all the yield curves, we obtain the estimated values:

$\sigma_1 = 0.23$
$\sigma_2 = 0.13$
$\rho = -0.62$

The negative value of ρ indicates that the yield curve tends to flatten when rates rise, although this correlation is not perfect.

Algorithm: The Spline Green-Function in Backward Induction

The usual approach for a numerical algorithm that can handle derivative securities like options is a backward induction. Furthermore, the backward induction is often carried out on a binomial tree which approximates a Brownian motion. (See for example Ho and Lee [1986], and Black, Derman, and Toy [1990] for a description.) For efficiency, certain shared quantities—the Green functions—can be calculated and saved in a forward pass. (See Jamshidian [1991] for a description of the forward induction and the Green function in this context.) In our view, the binomial tree is too restrictive, often becoming the main consideration in the development of the model. A more accommodating method is the backward induction on a multinomial lattice which approximates a diffusion by allowing steps of multiple values, the multinomial probability distribution being selected to reflect local drift and diffusion coefficients. We present a third approach which approximates not the local probability distribution function, but the local expectation. The steps are Gaussian distributed. This will be made more precise in the following. This method results in a smoother and therefore more efficient approximation.

The method also consists of two parts: a forward pass which establishes the state grid and calculates a Green function, and a backward induction which calculates the security values. It should be emphasized that the state grid is not a discretization of the diffusion, as is the case for the multinomial approach, but is merely the support for the spline approximations for continuous functions on the state space.

We present the algorithm only for the case when the volatility coefficients σ_1, σ_2, and ρ are constants. The system (2-3) and (2-4) can be rewritten as

$$dx = vdt + \sigma_1 dz_1 \tag{4-1}$$

$$dv = [-bx - kv]dt + \rho\sigma_2 dz_1 + \sqrt{1 - \rho^2}\,\sigma_2 dz_2 \tag{4-2}$$

where z_1 and z_2 are now uncorrelated standard Brownian motions. A change of variables

$$u = v - \alpha x; \alpha = \rho\sigma_2 / \sigma_1 \tag{4-3}$$

$$v = u + \alpha x \tag{4-4}$$

simplifies the disturbance terms:

$$dx = (u + \alpha x)dt + \sigma_1 dz_1 \tag{4-5}$$

$$du = [-\bar{b}x - \bar{k}u]dt + \bar{\sigma}_2 dz_2, \tag{4-6}$$

where

$$\bar{b} = b + (k + \alpha)\alpha \tag{4-7}$$

$$\bar{k} = k + \alpha \tag{4-8}$$

$$\bar{\sigma}_2 = \sqrt{1 - \rho^2}\sigma_2 . \tag{4-9}$$

We work with the system (4-5) and (4-6) which is simpler in form but equivalent to the original system (4-1) and (4-2).

Divide the time interval (typically 30 years) into a number of time points and the corresponding number of subintervals. Corresponding to each time point t we construct a state space of (x,u) and a grid in the state space, by induction. When $t = 0$ the space and grid are trivial; there is only one point, namely the origin.

Inductively, suppose for time point t at the beginning of the time interval (t,t') we have constructed a

(a) state space which consists of the Cartesian product of an interval I for the variable x and an interval J for the variable μ

(b) grid (x_i) for I and grid (u_j) for J

(c) matrix (A_{ij}) such that for any continuous motion $p(x,u)$ we have

$$Ep \cong \sum_i \sum_j A_{i,j} p(x_i, u_j) \tag{4-10}$$

where E is the expectation at time 0.

We will extend the construction time to t'. We will let (x',u') denote the state at time t'.

Consider the special case of (4-10) where $p(x,u)$ denotes the conditional mean of x' given (x,u), then $p(x,u)$ can be calculated according to (4-5) Hence the unconditional mean of x' can be calculated from (4-10). Similarly, we obtain the second moment, and therefore that standard deviation of the variable x'. We let I' be the interval of x' which contains + or –4 standard deviations from the mean. Likewise construct an interval J' of the variable u. Subdivide I' and J' by grid points (x'_k) and (u'_h) respectively. Choice of the number of grid points determines the accuracy of the algorithm. For any function $p'(x',u')$ defined on the state space $I'xJ'$ at time t', we have a spline approximation

$$p'(x', u') \cong \sum_k \sum_h p'(x'_k, u'_h) F_k(x') G_h(u'), \qquad (4\text{-}11)$$

where (F_k) are the spline basis function for which

$$F_k(x'_{k'}) = \begin{cases} 1 & k = k' \\ 0 & k \neq k' \end{cases},$$

and similarly for the G's. See Press, *et al.* [1986] for spline functions and an algorithm. The functions $F_k(x')$ are smooth, and for each (x_i, u_j) in the grid at time t, have conditional expectation given by the Gaussian integral with the conditional mean and standard deviation calculated according to (4-5), for example by some numerical quadrature. We denote this expectation by

$$E_{i,j} F_k = f_{i,j,k}. \qquad (4\text{-}12)$$

Similarly, for the spline functions G's we have

$$E_{i,j} G_h = g_{i,j,h}. \qquad (4\text{-}13)$$

Combining (4-11) and (4-13), we see that the conditional expectation of p' given (x_i, u_j) is

$$E p' \cong \sum_k \sum_h p'(x_k, u_h) f_{i,j,k} g_{i,j,h}. \qquad (4\text{-}14)$$

The present value of the expected value is obtained by discounting with the short rate, defined by (2-2):

$$disc_i E_{i,j} p' \cong \sum_k \sum_h p'(x_k, u_h) disc_i f_{i,j,k} g_{i,j,h} \qquad (4\text{-}15)$$

$$disc_i = \frac{1}{1 + (t' - t)a(t)exp(x_i)}. \qquad (4\text{-}16)$$

The products $(f_{i,j,k} g_{i,j,h})$ are the spline Green functions. The discounted product

$$disc_i f_{i,j,k} g_{i,j,h} \qquad (4\text{-}17)$$

is the present value, given the state (x_i, u_j), of a security whose payoff is at the next time point with value $F_x G_x$. Note that this payoff has value

1 if $(x,u) = (x_k, u_h)$

0 if $(x,u) = (x_{k'}, u_{h'})$ where $k' \neq k$ or $h' \neq h$,

and is continuous over $I' x J'$. The expression (4-17) is therefore the counterpart of the Arrow-Debreu prices where the state space reduces to the discrete grid itself. The point of using the spline bases F and G and the products (4-17) is that we need fewer of them. A small number of grid points result in a good spline fit.

The induction will be completed if we can calculate the matrix A' for t'. This follows from applying (4-10) to (4-14) to get

$$A'_{k,h} = \sum_i \sum_j A_{i,j} f_{i,j,k} g_{i,j,h}. \tag{4-18}$$

With the grid construction completed up to the time point t', and the three matrices in (4-18) stored for subsequent use, we can price any security up to this time. In particular, the price at time zero of a zero-coupon bond maturing at time t' and paying one dollar at that time is given by

$$\sum_k \sum_h P^{t'}_{k,h}, \tag{4-19}$$

where the matrix $P^{t'}$ is inductively defined by

$$\sum_k \sum_h P^{t'}_{i,j} disc_i f_{i,j,k} g_{i,j,h}. \tag{4-20}$$

At this point, the equilibrium rate $a(t)$ used in (4-16) can be adjusted, via Newton and Raphson, until the price of the t'-period zero-coupon bond in (4-19) matches the price obtained from the given yield curve at time 0.

This completes the forward pass, and we are ready to use backward induction for the valuation of any derivative securities. Start with t' equal to the last time horizon at which time the value $p'(x,u)$ of the security is known with certainty, then go backward and compute the value at the state gird points at time t one time-step before t':

$$P_{i,j} = \sum_k \sum_h p'_{k,h} disc_i f_{i,j,k} g_{i,j,h} + c_{i,j}, \tag{4-21}$$

where c_{ij} is the cash flow at time t given the state (x_i, u_j). Note that if the yield curve is needed to determine the cash flow $c_{i,j}$, equation (4-21) can be used first for all the discount bonds to derive their prices and yields at (x_i, u_j). Furthermore, after p is calculated from (4-21), any price-driven options can be examined for exercise and the value p adjusted accordingly. When the backward induction is completed, we have the price p at time 0.

The working paper of Chan [1993] contains examples of fitting the parameters to historical as well as market volatilities.

The Salomon Brothers two-factor term-structure model implemented on the Yield Book for mortgage-backed securities is in essence the linear model in equations (2-5–2-6) with constant sigmas; the parameters are fitted to seven caps and four swap options.

References

Arnold, L., 1974, *Stochastic Differential Equations: Theory and Applications, Wiley-Interscience.*

Black, F.; E. Derman; and W. Toy, 1990, "A One-Factor Model of Interest Rates and Its Application to Treasury Bond Options," *Financial Analysts Journal,* January–February, pp. 33–9.

Black, F., and M. Scholes, 1973, "Pricing of Options and Corporate Liabilities," *Journal of Political Economics* 81, pp. 637–54.

Brennan, M. J. and E. S. Schwartz, 1979, "A Continuous Time Approach to Pricing of Bonds," *Journal of Banking and Finance 3*, pp. 133–5.

Chan, Y. K., 1993, "Term Structure as a Second Order Dynamical System, and Pricing of Derivative Securities," working paper, Salomon Brothers, Inc.

Cheyette, O., 1992, "Term Structure Dynamics and Mortgage Evaluation," *The Journal of Fixed Income,* March, pp. 28–41.

Cox, J. C.; S. A. Ross; and M. Rubinstein, 1979, "Option Pricing: A Simplified Approach," *Journal of Financial Economics* 7, pp. 229–64.

Heath, D.; R. Jarrow; and A Morton, 1991, "Bond Pricing and the Term Structure of Interest Rates: A Discrete Time Approximation," *Journal of Financial and Quantitative Analysis,* vol. 25, no. 4, pp. 419–39.

Ho, T. S. Y., and S. B. Lee, 1986, "Term Structure Movements and Pricing of Interest Rate Claims," *Journal of Finance* 42, pp. 1011–29.

Hogan, M., 1992, "Problems in Certain Two-Factor Term Structure Models," *Journal of Applied Probabilities.*

Hull, J., and A. White, 1990, "Pricing Interest-Rate Derivative Securities," *The Review of Financial Studies,* vol. 3, no. 4, pp. 573–92.

Jamshidian, F., 1991, "Forward Induction and Construction of Yield Curve Diffusion Models," *The Journal of Fixed Income,* June, pp. 62–74.

Langetieg, T. C., 1980, "A Multivariate Model of the Term Structure," *The Journal of Finance* 35, no. 1, pp. 71–97.

Longstaff, F., and E. S. Schwartz, 1990, *Interest Rate Volatility and the Term Structure: A Two-Factor General Equilibrium Model,* John Anderson Graduate School of Management at UCLA, publication no. 29.

Press, W. H.; B. P. Flannery; S. A. Teukolsky; and W. T. Vettering, 1986, *Numerical Recipes,* Cambridge University Press.

Schwartz, E. S., 1990, "Recent Developments in Term Structure Modelling and Pricing Interest Rate Options," seminar notes from the Fourth Annual Seminar on Pricing, Hedging, and Trading on Interest Rates.

Portfolio Management and Performance Measurement

CHAPTER 10

Introducing a Comprehensive U.S. Treasury Bond Market Benchmark

Frank K. Reilly
Bernard J. Hank Professor of Business
College of Business Administration
University of Notre Dame

David J. Wright
Associate Professor of Finance
School of Business
University of Wisconsin–Parkside

Introduction

Although bonds are a significant factor in most individual and institutional portfolios, and despite the fact that the U.S. fixed-income market is larger than its equity market, total-rate-of-return bond indexes were not developed until the 1970s. At that time, with the demand for bond indexes increasing, several major investment firms created aggregate bond-market indexes, a number of diverse subindexes, customized indexes, and even daily indexes, in addition to the original monthly series [Bildersee (1975), Leibowitz (1985)]. Concurrently, there has been a significant increase in the financial media exposure related to the bond market.

These total return bond-market indexes play a central role in bond portfolio management, because investors and portfolio managers rely on bond indexes for several important functions. One very important use is for measuring portfolio performance, where these indexes are used as benchmarks [Dialynas (1995), Fong, et al. (1991), Peifer (1995)]. In addition, the behavior of the bond indexes is critical to managers of bond index funds who attempt to replicate the structure and return performance of the indexes [Dialynas (1995), Dunetz and Mahoney (1989), Massavar-Rahmani (1995)]. Finally, the historical results for these series can be used to make asset allocation decisions [Dunetz and Mahoney (1989), and Leibowitz (1986)].

A recent study of alternative bond-market indexes indicates that the various investment firms have generally developed similar indexes [Reilly, Kao, and Wright (1992)]. All of these indexes are properly constructed and maintained, use large samples, are value weighted, and compute total rates of return. Unfortunately, the relatively short history of these bond indexes does not allow investigators to analyze the *long-term* total return pattern of the aggregate bond market. Specifically, there are no similarly constructed, market-value-weighted, total-rate-of-return indexes available that measure the behavior of the aggregate bond market before 1973. This chapter describes and analyzes a new market-value-weighted, total-rate-of-return monthly bond index that includes all U.S. Treasury notes and bonds with maturities longer than one year. In contrast to the existing broad-based Treasury indexes, the inception date for this index is December 1949. Consequently, the new index spans 46 years through 1995, which provides a history that is more than twice that of the available Treasury indexes.

Currently, the most widely used total return Treasury-bond indexes available to investors for the years prior to 1973 are the Ibbotson long-term (IBL) and the Ibbotson intermediate-term (IBI) government bond indexes that begin in 1926. However, the methodology used to construct the Ibbotson bond indexes differs substantially from that employed by the creators of the other Treasury bond indexes. The Ibbotson indexes are based upon *one* Treasury-bond issue that is held for at least one year. This sample selection contrasts to the other Treasury market indexes described and analyzed in Reilly, Kao, and Wright (1992), which include *all* Treasury notes and bonds longer than one year. There is a concern that the one-bond portfolio used in the Ibbotson indexes may not represent the performance of the total Treasury-bond market that includes a number of issues over a wide range of maturities. Specifically, it is shown that the number of issues eligible for inclusion in a composite Treasury index at any point in time since 1949 has ranged from 29 to 183 issues. Also the Ibbotson one-bond portfolios have had maturities that ranged from 10 to almost 27 years for the long-term Treasury index, and from 1.46 to 6.54 years for the intermediate-term Treasury index. In contrast, the various Treasury indexes developed by the investment firms typically have had smaller ranges. For example, the range of maturities for the Ryan Labs Treasury Composite Index over the 46 year period was 5.50 to 10.56 years. These differences in index sample and methodology could cause significant tracking deviations between the Ibbotson government indexes and the various large sample bond indexes.

Organization of the Chapter

The initial section contains a detailed discussion of the bond series and the data collection procedures. In the second section, we discuss the several empirical tests of the series that include a comparison of this new series to the other bond series, during the recent time-period when the series are available, and a detailed analysis of the new Treasury series relative to the two Ibbotson bond-series since 1950. The empirical results are presented and discussed in the third section. In the final section, we summarize the results, present our conclusions, and discuss the implications of these results for bond portfolio managers and for those interested in bond market research.

Description of Data

This chapter presents and examines a new U.S.-Treasury-bond database created and compiled by Ryan Labs, a quantitative fixed-income money management firm, with the assistance of the authors. The Ryan Labs Treasury Composite Index [hereinafter referred to as the Ryan Treasury Composite Index (RT)] database includes all outstanding publicly traded U.S. Treasury securities with initial maturities greater than one year. To ensure wide coverage of the U.S. Treasury market, the database includes flower bonds. The resulting database includes 804 individual issues that were traded between 1950 and 1995. The number of U.S. Treasury issues included in any particular month ranged from 25 to 183 issues.

Data were collected for the last trading day of each month starting from December 1949. For December 1949 through December 1988, the pricing sources were *The U.S. Treasury Bulletin* and *The Wall Street Journal.* For the period since 1988, the source of prices was from the New York Federal Reserve quotations. Bid prices were used for all calculations. The data were passed through several filters, which examined price levels and rates of returns in order to detect any errors. The new index is a market-value-weighted, aggregate market series that employs the methodology used by the three investment firms that have created Treasury indexes: Lehman Brothers (LB), Merrill Lynch (ML), and Salomon Brothers (SB).

Index Characteristics

Table 1 contains a summary of the characteristics of the Ryan Treasury Composite Index (RT) compared to the investment firm Treasury bond indexes and the two Ibbotson government bond indexes. This description indicates that the Ryan Treasury Composite Index (RT) and the three

TABLE 1. Characteristics of Alternative Treasury Bond Indexes

	Ryan Treasury Composite Index	Lehman Brothers Treasury Index	Merrill Lynch Treasury Master	Salomon Brothers Treasury Index	Ibbotson Long-Term Government Index	Ibbotson Intermediate-Term Government Index
Maturity	> one year	> or = one year	> or = one year	> or = one year	One bond with maturity of approximately 20 years	One bond—shortest noncallable bond with maturity not less than 5 years
Excluded Issues	Treasury 11/2% notes dated 4/1, 10/1 between 1951-1979	Any Treasury issue with outstanding par value less than $100 million	Any Treasury issue with outstanding par value less than $10 million; all flower bonds	Any Treasury issue with outstanding par value less than $25 million; all flower bonds	Any Treasury issue whose returns "reflect potential tax benefits, impaired negotiability or special redemption or call privileges"	Any Treasury issue whose returns "reflect potential tax benefits, impaired negotiability or special redemption or call privileges"
Weighting	Market-Value and Equal-Value	Market Value	Market Value	Market Value	100% in selected bond	100% in selected bond
Pricing	Bid prices: *U.S. Treasury Bulletin, Wall Street Journal* and N.Y. Fed. Res. Quotations (since 1989)	Market-priced	Bid-side market prices	Bid-side market prices	1926-76 from CRSP government file; since 1977—*Wall Street Journal*	1926-76 from CRSP government file; since 1977—*Wall Street Journal*
Reinvestment of Cash Flows	Pre-1989 at beginning monthly yield; since 1989 in specific bond	None	In specific issue when daily prices available. Previously, not reinvested	In daily average one month Treasury bill for payment month	In specific bond	In specific bond
Beginning Date for Monthly Data	January 1950	January 1973	January 1978	January 1980	January 1926	January 1926
Current Daily Data	Yes	Yes	Yes	Yes	No	No

investment firm indexes are quite similar in terms of the sample. Specifically, all of them have the same maturity factor with small differences in excluded issues. The investment firm indexes differ based on minimum size constraints that probably are not very binding for government issues, and Merrill Lynch and Salomon Brothers exclude flower bonds while Ryan and Lehman Brothers do not. The only other difference is that Ryan excludes an issue that exhibited significant pricing problems (these issues were not a factor for indexes that began after 1979). In addition, all the indexes are market-value-weighted, while Ryan also has an equal-weighted index.

The investment firms all use market-price bids that would have been available to dealers, while Ryan uses public sources for bid quotes. The reinvestment assumptions differ in the following ways: (1) nonreinvestment during the month of the payment by Lehman Brothers, (2) reinvestment in a one-month Treasury bill by Salomon Brothers, and (3) an attempt to simulate reinvestment in the specific bond by Ryan and Merrill Lynch.

As noted, there are several major differences among these four indexes and the two Ibbotson indexes. The most significant difference is the sample wherein the four indexes include all available bonds with small exclusions, while the Ibbotson indexes are one-bond portfolios where the single bond varies over time. Ibbotson attempts to avoid bonds that have potential tax benefits, or special redemption or call features. Notably, over the 69 years, the long-term government bond index has used 21 bonds [Ibbotson, Exhibit 20 in 1996 Annual], which implies that in many instances the bonds were used for several years. The most extreme example is that the same bond was used for the 11-year period, 1942–1953. As a result, the maturity for this index that attempts to be approximately 20 years ranged from 19 to 30 years. The intermediate-term bond index typically changed its sample bond each year with three instances of a two-year holding period and two cases of a three-year holding period. Because of some major changes in coupons, the annual changes in the sample bond resulted in large changes in the duration of the index because of the coupon effect. For example, between 1980 and 1981, the coupon went from 8 percent to 13.50 percent; between 1984 and 1985 it declined from 14.625 percent to 10.50 percent.

In summary, this list of characteristics indicates several differences among the four large sample-indexes and indicates a couple of large differences among these four indexes and the two Ibbotson indexes. The subsequent tests will attempt to determine if these differences have an impact on the empirical relationships among these indexes in terms of return and risk measures, correlation of returns, and tracking deviations.

Return Computations

There is both a Ryan market-weighted Treasury index (RTM) and a Ryan equal-weighted Treasury index (RTE) constructed using the monthly total return of each security in the Ryan Treasury Composite Index (RT) database. Total returns include the following components: price change, coupon payments, accrued interest, and reinvestment of intramonth cashflows. From 1950 through 1988, intramonth cash-flows were invested for the number of days between the coupon payment date and the end of the current month at the beginning-of-month yield on that particular security. After 1988, intramonth cash-flows for a particular bond were invested as received in the specific issue, using daily pricing.

The market-weighted index return was computed using the beginning-of-month market values. At the end of each month, the index was reweighted to reflect new issues, scheduled or early repayment of principal, and the removal of bonds with maturities of one year or less.

There were three return series constructed for both the market-weighted composite index and the equal-weighted composite index as follows: (1) price return, (2) income return, and (3) total return. The series covers the 552 months (46 years) from 1950 through 1995.

Index Summary Statistics

Statistics describing the Treasury market were computed every month for each individual security. The summary index statistics are either a market-weighted average or an equal-weighted average and include the following: coupon, term, price, yield to worst, current yield, and modified duration.

Comparison of Characteristics. Table 2 contains a comparison of the significant characteristics of the Lehman Brothers and RTM indexes. The comparison indicates that the two series are fairly similar with a tendency for the Ryan index to have higher market-values, a longer term to maturity and modified duration, but a slightly lower average yield-to-maturity. Notably, none of these differences are significant.

Specification of Empirical Tests

As noted, the construction of the Ryan Treasury Composite Index (RT) is similar to that of the Treasury bond indexes developed by Lehman Brothers, Merrill Lynch, and Salomon Brothers. It was shown in Reilly, Kao, and Wright (1992) that the alternative government-bond indexes are very similar in terms of correlations (which were typically about 0.98) and

TABLE 2. Index Characteristics of Lehman Bros. and Ryan
Treasury Indexes 1973-1995

Variable	Mean	Standard Deviation	Minimum	Maximum
Market Value ($billion)				
RTM	848,252	NR	NR	NR
LBT	770,255	NR	NR	NR
Yield to Maturity (%)				
RTM	8.49	2.28	4.88	15.63
LBT	8.61	2.39	4.87	16.07
Term to Maturity (years)				
RTM	7.44	1.71	LBT	7.02
1.88	5.49	9.17	3.46	9.38
Modified Duration (years)				
RTM	4.31	0.49	3.32	5.42
LBT	4.14	0.75	2.94	5.54

NR - not relevant

tracking deviations (that averaged about 10 to 12 basis points a month between government indexes). To confirm the similarity of the Ryan Treasury Composite Index (RT) and the investment firm indexes, the first tests examine the relationship between RT and the three investment firm indexes: the Lehman Brothers Treasury Index (LBT), the Merrill Lynch Treasury index (MLT), and the Salomon Brothers Treasury index (SBT), and the two Ibbotson indexes (IBL and IBI) for the longest period that includes all three investment-firm indexes, which is the 15-year period, 1980–1995. This analysis shows the similarity among the indexes based on correlations, tracking deviations, rates of return, and risk measures (e.g., standard deviations).

The second set of tests examines the relationship between the Ryan Treasury Composite Index (RT) and the Lehman Brothers Treasury index which is the investment-firm index with the longest history (i.e., the 23-year period, 1973–1995). This analysis also considers the two Ibbotson indexes in order to determine which indexes have the strongest relationship with the LBT index.

The third set of tests examine the basic characteristics of the Ryan Treasury Composite Index (RT) for the total 46-year period. This analysis considers the overall risk-return characteristics of the series and its components during this period using both the market-value-weighted series and the equal-weighted series. Also, we compare the risk-return charac-

teristics of the Ryan Treasury Composite Index (RT) to the two Ibbotson
government bond series and to other asset classes including the Ibbotson
corporate bond series, the S&P 500 stock series, the Ibbotson small-cap
stock series, Treasury bills, and the consumer price index.

Empirical Results

The empirical results will be presented for the time period (1) when the
results for all the investment-firm indexes are available, (2) that includes
the full history for the Lehman Brothers series, and (3) that includes the
full history for the Ryan Treasury Composite Index (RT) .
   The Treasury index designations that will be used are as follows:
   IBL — Ibbotson Long-Term Government Bond Index
   IBI — Ibbotson Intermediate-Term Government Bond Index
   LBT — Lehman Brothers Treasury Index
   MLT—Merrill Lynch Treasury Index
   RTM — Ryan Treasury Index Market-Weighted
   RTE — Ryan Treasury Index Equal-Weighted
   SBT — Salomon Brothers Treasury Index

Return-Variability Results

Table 3 contains the rate-of-return and variability statistics for the alternative Treasury indexes. Given the seven indexes at the top of the table, the
only obvious difference is IBL which has a higher rate of return but a
much higher standard-deviation of return. This is because it has a much
longer maturity (duration) than the other indexes. This is confirmed by
the comparison with the constant maturity indexes, which show that the
IBL index is similar to the T30 index.
   The other six indexes are reasonably similar, with returns that vary
from 11.93 percent to 12.11 percent and with standard deviations that
vary from 6.94 to 7.5 percent. It is interesting to note that the equal-
weighted RT series is very similar to the RTM series, but has a slightly
higher return and standard deviation.
   The results for the non-Treasury indexes that range from Treasury
bills to small-cap stocks are very consistent with expectations. Specifically, there is a consistent relationship between return and volatility, as
one would expect.
   These results are shown in Figure 1 which indicates a strong positive relationship between return and risk. These results are consistent
with the notion that the multibond portfolios are more diversified and,
therefore, have lower volatility.

TABLE 3.   Rate of Return and Variability Statistics for Treasury
Bond Indexes—Monthly Returns

	1980-1985		1973-1995		1950-1995	
Variable	Annualized Total Return	Annualized Monthly Std. Dev.	Annualized Total Return	Annualized Monthly Std. Dev.	Annualized Total Return	Annualized Monthly Std. Dev.
RTM	10.95	6.55	9.33	5.96	6.15	4.89
RTE	10.97	6.94	9.28	6.33	6.07	5.19
IBI	10.80	7.07	9.21	6.45	6.25	5.25
IBL	12.35	12.25	9.59	11.07	5.67	8.99
LBT	11.06	6.44	9.43	5.81	–	–
MLT	11.06	6.63	–	–	–	–
SBT	10.98	6.43	–	–	–	–
CORPB	12.37	10.94	9.69	10.23	6.13	8.18
SP500	15.84	14.85	11.85	15.45	12.56	13.97
SMCAP	16.10	17.68	16.29	21.11	15.13	19.16
TBILL	7.36	0.89	7.23	0.80	5.16	0.86
CPI	4.44	1.07	5.75	1.21	4.16	1.17

FIGURE 1.   Annualized Cumulative Return versus the Standard
Deviation of Alternative Treasury Index Returns
(1980-1995)

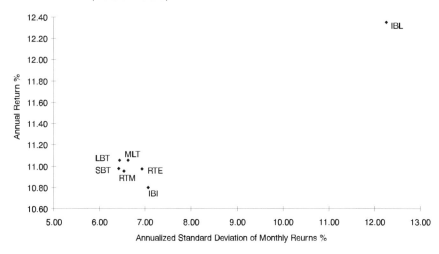

Figures 2 and 3 repeat these results for longer periods (1973–1995 and 1950–1995). It is shown that the return/risk relationship holds, with the IBL always below the average line because of its high risk.

FIGURE 2.   Annualized Cumulative Return versus the Standard Deviation of Alternative Treasury Index Returns (1973-1995)

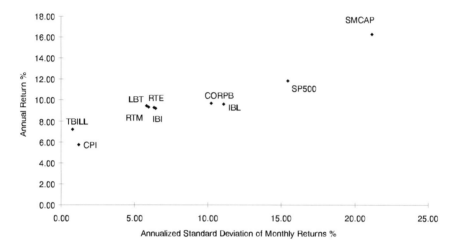

FIGURE 3.   Annualized Cumulative Return versus the Standard Deviation of Alternative Treasury Index Returns (1950-1995)

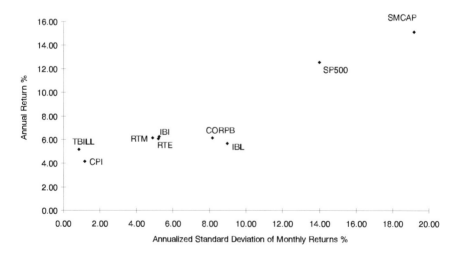

Correlation Results

Table 4 contains the correlation results for monthly rates of return among the seven Treasury indexes for the 1980–1995 time period. All of the correlation coefficients are large and statistically significant. The only differences occur between the Ibbotson indexes and the other indexes. Specifically, the coefficients with the Ibbotson indexes vary from .891 to .969. Except for the correlations with the two Ibbotson indexes, the other correlations average about .97. In contrast, the correlations among the multibond indexes vary from .988 to .997, and average about .994. While these differences in correlation coefficients are not statistically significant, they indicate some impact from the differences in the sample.

The results for 1973–1995 and 1950–1995 that include corporate bonds, large-cap and small-cap stocks, Treasury bills, and inflation, generally provide consistent results. First, the correlations among investment-grade corporate bonds and Treasury bonds are very similar to three that were generated by Reilly, Kao, and Wright (1992)—for example, the correlations are about 0.93 with corporates versus 0.97 among Treasury indexes. The substantial changes occur with large-cap stocks where the correlations with bonds are significantly lower at about 0.30. The correlations with small-cap stocks are even lower at about 0.15 to 0.20.

Although Treasury bills are fixed-income securities, it is clear that the returns are driven by a different set of factors than the over-one-year securities. Specifically, the correlations among the assets are all very low and in many instances insignificant. Finally, the results of the correlations with inflation are consistent with numerous prior studies that show generally negative correlations of inflation with long-term bonds and common stock, which implies that these asset classes are very poor inflation hedges. Notably, the only significant positive correlation was between inflation and Treasury bills, which indicates that these are the best inflation hedges among these assets.

Tracking Deviations

An alternative measure of how various indexes relate to each other is the tracking deviation which is the average difference in basis points between the returns for two indexes. Some observers consider it to be more precise than correlations because it measures the specific deviations in returns, which is the important variable. The variability of tracking deviations is also an important factor. The average tracking deviations can be measured either with or without sign. Again, most observers prefer the absolute deviations because the results are not masked by offsetting deviations.

TABLE 4

1980-1995 Correlation Coefficients Among Treasury Indexes: N=192

	RTM	RTE	IBI	IBL	LBT	MLT	SBT
RTM	1.000						
RTE	0.997	1.000					
IBI	0.944	0.939	1.000				
IBL	0.958	0.961	0.867	1.000			
LBT	0.998	0.994	0.943	0.957	1.000		
MLT	0.997	0.994	0.942	0.957	0.996	1.000	
SBT	0.993	0.989	0.942	0.954	0.996	0.994	1.000

1973-1995 Correlation Coefficients Among Alternative Indexes: N=276

	RTM	RTE	IBI	IBL	LBT	CORPB	SP500	SMCAP	TBILL	CPI
RTM	1.000									
RTE	0.977	1.000								
IBI	0.944	0.938	1.000							
IBL	0.952	0.956	0.865	1.000						
LBT	0.996	0.992	0.944	0.951	1.000					
CORPB	0.923	0.934	0.854	0.939	0.917	1.000				
SP500	0.316	0.321	0.279	0.367	0.303	0.385	1.000			
SMCAP	0.159	0.165	0.132	0.200	0.150	0.226	0.780	1.000		
TBILL	0.143	0.133	0.150	0.059*	0.153	0.044*	-0.067*	-0.087*	1.000	
CPI	-0.151	-0.152	-0.128	-0.195	-0.149	-0.184	-0.207	-0.158	0.421	1.000

1950-1995 Correlation Coefficients Among Alternative Indexes: N=552

	RTM	RTE	IBI	IBL	CORPB	SP500	SMCAP	TBILL	CPI
RTM	1.000								
RTE	0.996	1.000							
IBI	0.944	0.935	1.000						
IBL	0.934	0.946	0.842	1.000					
CORPB	0.877	0.891	0.810	0.898	1.000				
SP500	0.224	0.232	0.200	0.271	0.323	1.000			
SMCAP	0.133	0.138	0.110	0.163	0.222	0.785	1.000		
TBILL	0.233	0.220	0.222	0.130	0.121	-0.085	-0.062*	1.000	
CPI	-0.027*	-0.031*	-0.031*	-0.082*	-0.087	-0.128	-0.114	0.511	1.000

*All correlation coefficients are significant at the five percent level except those indicated by the * .

Table 5 contains the statistics related to the monthly tracking deviations among the alternative Treasury indexes in both absolute and with sign including the standard deviation of tracking deviations and autocorrelation of deviations. The results between IBL and the large-sample indexes for the 1980–1995 time period confirm the substantial differences due to the much longer maturity (duration) of IBL. Not only is the mean tracking deviation quite large (about 135 basis points) but the standard deviation of the tracking deviations with sign is also very large (about 180 basis points).

The results with IBI indicated much smaller and less-volatile tracking deviations. Still, the range is fairly large and a mean tracking deviation of about 37 basis points is fairly large among IBI and the Treasury indexes, as is the standard deviation of 67 basis points These results are in contrast to the mean deviations between the large-sample indexes of about 11 basis points and an average standard deviation of about 18 basis points.

The autocorrelation of tracking deviations indicates how the tracking deviations act over time—for example, is there a tendency for them to be negatively related over time, which means that the series becomes smaller; or is there a positively related series, which implies growing differences between two series.

The tracking deviations with IBL show fairly large monthly tracking deviations and large variability of deviations over time. There is insignificant negative autocorrelation at lag 1, but significant negative autocorrelation at lag 3.

The results for the longer periods (1973–1995 and 1950–1995) have fewer comparisons than the initial panel that covers 1980–1995, but the results are very similar—the analysis with IBL always contains very large tracking deviations that are quite volatile. The tracking deviation results with IBI are smaller and less volatile, and the results between the Lehman Brothers series and the Ryan series are always very small, and the results have large negative autocorrelations of tracking deviations.

Autocorrelation Results

Table 6 contains the autocorrelations for the rate of return series. The results are very similar to those reported in the Reilly, Kao, and Wright (1992) study which showed significant autocorrelations for short lags, due to the impact of accrued interest.

The results for the composite indexes show that the IBL index has insignificant autocorrelation for the first two lags, but a significant negative result for lag 3. The results for the large sample Treasury indexes and

TABLE 5.

Autocorrelations of Monthly Tracking Deviations with Sign

Paired Variables	Mean Absolute Monthly Tracking Deviation (in basis points)	Mean Monthly Tracking Deviation with Sign (in basis points)	Standard Deviation of Monthly Tracking Deviation with Sign (in basis points)	Autocor.-Lag 1	Autocor.-Lag 2	Autocor.-Lag 3
Monthly Tracking Deviation Analysis 1980-1995						
IBI-IBL	152.6	-15.7	203.8	-0.158*	0.068	-0.112
RTM-IBL	136.3	-14.9	181.0	-0.061	0.061	-0.176*
LBT-IBL	137.5	-14.1	183.6	-0.047	0.052	-0.190*
MLT-IBL	135.1	-14.1	179.4	-0.062	0.065	-0.183*
SBT-IBL	137.6	-14.8	185.1	-0.068	0.047	-0.173*
RTM-IBI	37.1	0.9	67.4	-0.320*	-0.048	0.026
LBT-IBI	37.1	1.6	68.3	-0.303*	-0.053	0.016
MLT-IBI	37.1	1.6	68.3	-0.303*	-0.053	0.016
SBT-IBI	38.3	1.0	68.9	-0.309*	-0.076	0.056
RTM-LBT	7.0	-0.7	12.1	-0.147*	-0.132	-0.076
RTM-MLT	10.1	-0.8	16.0	-0.343*	-0.079	0.085
RTM-SBT	12.8	-0.1	22.3	-0.511*	0.081	-0.072
LBT-MLT	10.2	-0.1	17.3	-0.354*	-0.048	0.019
LBT-SBT	11.0	0.6	17.5	-0.555*	0.128	-0.101
MLT-SBT	11.0	0.7	21.1	-0.475*	-0.013	0.108

TABLE 5. (continued)

| | Mean Absolute Monthly Tracking Deviation (in basis points) | Mean Monthly Tracking Deviation with Sign (in basis points) | Standard Deviation of Monthly Tracking Deviation with Sign (in basis points) | Autocorrelations of Monthly Tracking Deviations with Sign | | |
Paired Variables				Autocor.-Lag 1	Autocor.-Lag 2	Autocor.-Lag 3
Monthly Tracking Deviation Analysis 1973-1995						
IBI-IBL	135.8	-6.2	184.1	-0.141*	0.049	-0.069
RTM-IBL	121.7	-5.6	164.8	-0.041	0.045	-0.122*
LBT-IBL	124.5	-4.9	168.2	-0.024	0.030	-0.132*
RTM-IBI	36.2	0.7	61.5	-0.317*	-0.021	0.021
LBT-IBI	36.1	1.4	61.9	-0.301*	-0.033	-0.001
RTM-LBT	9.4	-0.7	15.1	0.022	-0.124	-0.011
Monthly Tracking Deviation Analysis 1950-1995						
IBI-IBL	108.9	2.4	155.3	-0.151*	0.049	-0.083
RTM-IBL	95.6	1.5	137.3	-0.074	0.057	-0.136*
RTM-IBI	30.3	-1.0	50.0	-0.303*	-0.038	0.050

*Autocorrelation coefficient is significant at the five percent level.

TABLE 6. Autocorrelations of Monthly Returns for Alternative Indexes

	1980-1995 Monthly Returns			1973-1995 Monthly Returns			1950-1995 Monthly Returns		
Variable	Lag 1	Lag 2	Lag 3	Lag 1	Lag 2	Lag 3	Lag 1	Lag 2	Lag 3
RTM	0.183*	-0.092	-0.133	0.159*	-0.078	-0.105	0.164*	-0.020	-0.045
RTE	0.180*	-0.086	-0.146	0.158*	-0.074	-0.117	0.159*	-0.020	-0.067
IBI	0.195*	-0.126	-0.131	0.164*	-0.103	-0.111	0.156*	-0.050	-0.043
IBL	0.084	-0.026	-0.171*	0.086	-0.025	-0.123*	0.073	0.005	-0.109*
LBT	0.175*	-0.083	-0.113	0.153*	-0.064	-0.089	–	–	–
MLT	0.175*	-0.087	-0.123	–	–	–	–	–	–
SBT	0.191*	-0.074	-0.133	–	–	–	–	–	–
CORPB	0.154*	-0.052	-0.146*	0.151*	-0.042	-0.064	0.161*	-0.014	-0.057
SP500	0.002	-0.040	-0.064	-0.001	-0.026	0.012	0.020	-0.039	0.009
SMCAP	0.241*	0.010	-0.057	0.141*	-0.055	-0.032	0.169*	-0.028	-0.038
TBILL	0.934*	0.877*	0.824*	0.928*	0.874*	0.838*	0.961*	0.935*	0.918*
CPI	0.607*	0.391*	0.281*	0.650*	0.549*	0.489*	0.642*	0.551*	0.478*

*Autocorrelation coefficient is significant at the five percent level.

the corporate bond are significant and positive for lag 1. The two stock-indexes are quite different. The large-cap index has virtually no autocorrelation, while the small-cap index has larger autocorrelation at lag 1 than the bond indexes. Finally, the Treasury-bill series has very large autocorrelation because of the accrued-interest component, as noted in Reilly, Kao, and Wright (1992).

Summary, Conclusions, and Implications

Summary

The description of the new Ryan Treasury Composite Index (RT) indicated that the sample selection and computational procedures were very similar to the procedures used in the various Treasury bond indexes constructed by the major investment firms: Lehman Brothers, Merrill Lynch, and Salomon Brothers. The major difference is that the Ryan index is available for a longer period than the investment-firm indexes (i.e., it begins in 1950 rather than 1973 or 1980). Alternatively, these large-sample indexes differed from the single-bond series constructed by Ibbotson to represent the long-term and intermediate-term government bond market.

The return/variability, correlation, and tracking deviation results indicated that when the indexes overlap, the Ryan Treasury index is *very similar* to the large-sample indexes. The comparison between the market-value-weighted and the equal-weighted Ryan index (RTE) indicated fairly similar results. This similarity differs from the results when one compares stock indexes with different weightings. The long-term risk/return results for different asset classes were as expected.

The comparisons between the Ibbotson and Ryan indexes consistently indicated differences with the Ibbotson long-term government index (IBL) based on return/variability (IBL had lower returns and higher variability), correlations (lower), and tracking deviations (very large and volatile). The comparisons with the intermediate index (IBI) indicated consistent return/volatility results, and somewhat lower correlations. The big difference with IBI came with the tracking deviations that were larger and more volatile.

Conclusions

An analysis of a new Treasury composite index is important and timely for several reasons. First, a key decision for pension fund managers is the asset-allocation decision, which has traditionally been based upon a comparison of the historical results for different asset classes over the last 30 to 50 years [Dialynas (1995); Fong, Pearson, Vasicek, and Conroy (1991); and Peifer (1995)]. For a measure of stock returns, investors have relied on the S&P 500 index, which is a broad-based, market-value-weighted, total-return index. The most widely used bond index for making asset-allocation decisions based on historical results has traditionally been the IBL index, because the IBI index has only recently been available. Notably, while the two Ibbotson indexes provide a long-run historical record, they are based on a single bond that changes over time. This chapter has examined the relationship of the new Ryan index with the Ibbotson indexes and several well-known large-sample indexes created by various investment firms. That is, how would the results of the asset-allocation models be changed by replacing the Ibbotson long-term government bond index with the Ryan Treasury Composite Index (RT)? Second, the comprehensive Treasury composite allowed analysis of the bond-market-return behavior including autocorrelation tests of bond returns. An analysis of the effect of equal weighting versus market-value weighting on risk/return behavior showed that differential weighting has a limited effect, which is not surprising because all Treasury bonds are heavily impacted by basic macroeconomic factors (see Reilly, Kao, and Wright (1992)].

Implications

The strong similarities among the Ryan index and the other large-sample indexes mean that this index can be used to represent the total Treasury-bond market for a longer period than is available with the other indexes. Besides the basic return/variability results, this index can be used to describe and analyze important Treasury bond market characteristics including its yields, maturity, and duration.

The results with the IBL index indicate that this series is not representative of the U.S. Treasury bond market and probably should not be used to make long-term asset-allocation decisions. The results with the IBI series were more consistent with other large-sample indexes, except that the IBI-series tracking deviations with these other indexes were larger and more volatile. Hence, the IBI series would not be appropriate for short-run tracking tasks such as index funds.

References

Bildersee, John S. "Some New Bond Indexes." *Journal of Business,* vol. 48, no. 4 (October 1975), pp. 506-25.

Dialynas, Chris P. "The Active Decisions in the Selection of Passive Management and Performance Bogeys." In *The Handbook of Fixed Income Securities,* 4th ed.

Edited by Frank J. Fabozzi and T. Dessa Fabozzi. Burr Ridge, IL: Irwin Professional Publishing, 1995.

Dunetz, Mark L. and James M. Mahoney. "Indexation and Optimal Strategies in Portfolio Management." In *Fixed Income Portfolio Strategies*. Edited by Frank J. Fabozzi. Chicago, IL: Probus Publishing Company, 1989.

Fong, Gifford; Charles Pearson; Oldrich Vasicek; and Theresa Conroy. "Fixed Income Portfolio Performance: Analyzing Sources of Return." In *The Handbook of Fixed Income Securities*, 3d ed. Edited by Frank J. Fabozzi. Homewood, IL: Business One-Irwin, 1991.

Ibbotson, Roger C. *Stocks, Bonds, Bills, and Inflation.* Chicago: Ibbotson Associates, Annual.

Leibowitz, Martin L. *Introducing the Salomon Brothers Broad Investment-Grade Index.* New York: Salomon Brothers, 1985.

Leibowitz, Martin L. *Liability Returns: A New Perspective on Asset Allocation.* New York: Salomon Brothers, 1986.

Massavar-Rahmani, Sharmin. *Bond Index Funds.* Chicago, IL: Probus Publishing Company, 1991.

Massavar-Rahmani, Sharmin, "Indexing Fixed Income Assets." In *The Handbook of Fixed Income Securities*, 4th ed. Edited by Frank J. Fabozzi and T. Dessa Fabozzi. Burr Ridge, IL: Irwin Professional Publishing, 1995.

Peifer, Daralyn B. "A Sponsor's View of Benchmark Portfolios." In *The Handbook of Fixed Income Securities*, 4th ed. Edited by Frank J. Fabozzi and T. Dessa Fabozzi. Burr Ridge, IL: Irwin Professional Publishing, 1995.

Reilly, Frank K.; G. Wenchi Kao; and David J. Wright. "Alternative Bond Market Indexes." *Financial Analysts Journal,* vol. 48, no. 3 (May–June 1992), pp. 44-58.

The Risks of a Laddered Portfolio

Robert G. Smith III
President
Sage Advisory Services, Ltd.

In the world of investment management theory, there are few financial axioms or methodologies that remain unquestioned and untested. Traditional investment concepts are subject to constant scrutiny and reevaluation as a result of dynamic changes in the marketplace and the needs of investors.

In the fixed-income investment area, we have witnessed many changes in recent years that have brought new products, concepts, and problems. However, one popular concept that remains unaltered and unquestioned throughout the years is that of the laddered maturity portfolio. It is a concept widely touted by financial advisors as a conservative, low-risk approach to managing a fixed-income security portfolio. However, unlike the popular concept of dollar cost averaging in an equity portfolio, there is very little published on laddered portfolios in academic or professional literature. Our efforts to identify research that analyzed the methodology and historical returns of laddered maturity portfolios produced almost no empirical evidence.

It is rare today to find such a monolithic financial concept without the support of significant and rigorous historical numeric analysis. However, market history offers many examples of popular investment concepts that were simple to understand, but when applied, led to significantly different rewards for investors. Generally, these investment differences had nothing to do with the actual securities selected but, rather, the lack of uniformity in the creation and application of the methodology behind the investment concept. In our view, this is a serious problem, imbedded with unrecognized risk, which lies beneath the ever-popular investment concept of laddered maturity portfolios.

As fixed-income investment professionals, we are often asked to comment on the risks that confront investors in the marketplace. We find that the unqualified acceptance of the laddered-maturity-portfolio concept, as a secure approach to investing, is misleading and risky.

What Is the Objective?

Any investment program or activity must be assessed in terms of an ultimate objective. Its success can then be judged in terms of its ability to satisfy the stated objective. In most fixed-income investment programs, the objectives are clear, generally. They are geared toward income generation, capital appreciation, or they are structured to satisfy a specific liability.

Objectives are often represented either in the form of market indices or by specific cash flow requirements. In either case, the assets within the investment program are competing to match or exceed the stated objectives. As such, it is the relative total return growth of assets in the portfolio versus the objectives over a period of time that is the primary concern.

With a laddered maturity portfolio, the objective is ill-defined. The frequently stated objective is a simple, nebulous term known as *safety*. While it is a desirable feature, it is unacceptable for it to be identified as the lone objective.

The risk of a laddered portfolio is unknown. Traditionally, risk has been defined as the uncertainty of total return or as the volatility of total return. To calculate risk, you must calculate total return. Risk is dependent upon total return data for its measurement. Thus, the greater the uncertainty or variability of total-return patterns, the riskier the investment program. Since laddered-portfolio total returns are not generally known or measured, and since they are subject to variability, this investment approach must contain an undefined degree of risk.

The Ideal and the Reality

Frequently a laddered portfolio is structured along the maturity spectrum of the yield curve, with the final maturity varying depending on the individual investor. Most conventional laddered portfolios avoid the long end of the yield curve, and are usually constructed along a rolling one- to five-year or one- to seven-year maturity horizon.

In a laddered portfolio, the investor is principally driven by one of two factors. These factors are (1) the desire to avoid a loss of principal by holding all securities to final maturity, or (2) the inability or unwillingness to actively manage portfolio cash flows in changing markets.

The investor presumes that, by instituting a laddering process, he or she has created a dynamic yet passive portfolio that avoids the greatest perceived risk (i.e., loss of principal). This process also appeals to those investors seeking a methodical and nonanalytic portfolio management approach. However, there are some contradictions inherent in this approach with regard to investor intent and the reality of historical interest rate movements in the U.S. capital markets.

If one of the primary purposes of a laddered portfolio is to avoid the risk of loss of principal by holding each security to its final maturity at par, then such investors must be considered to be intermediate to longer-term investors. This identification is a function of the final maturity allocation of the laddered portfolio. However, fixed-income investment total returns are comprised of three parts:

1. the change in price of the security from one point in time to another,
2. the coupon income received for a given time frame, and
3. the reinvestment of the coupon income and principal received for a given time frame.

Fixed-income mathematics show us that, in the short run, security price changes can have a measurable effect on total returns. But, the longer the time frame, the more important coupon income and reinvestment of income become in determining total investment returns. Hence, the greatest risk to achieving reasonable returns in a laddered portfolio is not short-run price changes but, rather, reinvestment risk.

The Relative Importance of Price, Coupon, and Reinvestment Returns over Investment Horizons

By neutralizing price risk in the laddered portfolio through a *hold-to-maturity* process, the investor elevates the importance of income and reinvestment in the total return equation. This is troublesome when one considers that most laddered portfolios, in seeking to avoid principal volatility, will be biased toward short to intermediate maturities. Moreover, these biases may be maintained in the portfolio over an extended period of time through the roll-over process espoused in this investment management technique. This creates a problem for the investor because short-term interest rates have historically been far more volatile than intermediate- and longer-term rates. Thus, return volatility (i.e., risk) of a laddered portfolio could be raised significantly due to a bias toward shorter maturities over an extended time frame.

This point is clearly illustrated in Table 1, which identifies the monthly standard deviation of yield changes along the yield curve over a number of time periods. As shown, short-maturity securities have historically exhibited a higher degree of yield (i.e., income) volatility than longer-dated securities.

The relative level of income volatility along the yield curve is also presented in the matrix distribution shown in Table 2. It shows that, since the mid-1970s, the 30-year Treasury Bond exhibited only 53 percent of the yield (i.e., income) volatility of the six-month Treasury bill.

The downward slope of income volatility from short to long maturities clearly demonstrates that laddered portfolios, biased toward shorter maturities, may actually produce much higher degrees of return variability (i.e., risk) than portfolios with an extended maturity focus.

Deceptive Appearances

The old adage that looks can be deceiving could easily be applied when evaluating laddered portfolios. The subtle differences among securities, their weighting within a laddered portfolio, and the timing of portfolio cash-flows, can produce significantly different results. For the unseasoned investor, these key points are often overlooked and unappreciated when evaluating a laddered portfolio and other active investment techniques.

To demonstrate these points, we analyzed the historical performance of three laddered portfolios over several years using only U.S. Treasury securities. They were constructed by using zero-coupon, on-the-run, and off-the-run securities individually in each portfolio. We relied solely on U.S. Treasury securities in order to eliminate the differences or risks attributable to credit quality or market liquidity. Each portfolio was then laddered in two ways:

1. On a duration-weighted basis to match the duration of an equally weighted maturity portfolio of one- to five-year U.S. Treasury strip securities, and

2. On an equal-distribution-maturity basis to replicate the conventional approach applied by most investors.

The results of our analysis are presented in Table 2.

TABLE 1.   Laddered Maturity Portfolio
Annualized Total Return Comparisons
(12/31/87 - 12/31/94)

Duration-Weighted Portfolios (1)

Period	Benchmark 3Yr U.S. Strips*	Zero Cpn.	On The Run	Off The Run	Return Range (bps.)
7 Years	8.16%	8.06%	7.42%	7.83%	64
5 Years	7.80%	7.54%	6.78%	7.18%	72
3 Years	4.45%	4.49%	4.02%	4.37%	47
1 Years	-2.02%	-1.48%	-0.54%	-1.48%	6

Characteristics

Duration	3.00Yrs	3.01Yrs	3.00Yrs
Maturity	3.00Yrs	3.67Yrs	3.74Yrs
Quality	TSY	TSY	TSY
Coupon	0.00%	7.23%	8.05%
YTM	8.12%	7.99%	8.07%

Equally Distributed Portfolios (2)

Period	Benchmark 3Yr U.S. Strips*	Zero Cpn.	On The Run	Off The Run	Return Range (bps.)
7 Years	8.16%	7.76%	6.97%	7.40%	79
5 Years	7.80%	7.20%	6.39%	6.80%	81
3 Years	4.45%	4.38%	3.81%	4.21%	57
1 Years	-2.02%	-0.66%	-0.44%	-0.16%	50

Characteristics

Duration	2.63Yrs	2.31Yrs	2.18Yrs
Maturity	2.63Yrs	2.61Yrs	2.53Yrs
Quality	TSY	TSY	TSY
Coupon	0.00%	6.00%	6.80%
YTM	7.83%	7.69%	7.74%

*Single issue holding-period return.

Notes: 1. Duration weighting based on the duration achieved through an equally weighted portfolio of zero coupon U.S. Treasury securities with maturities of one to five years. The coupon portfolios are weighted by maturity to match the duration of the strips portfolio using securities between 6 months to 7 years.

2. Equally-distributed portfolios are based on an equal 25% allocation of the portfolio to 6 month Treasury bills, 2-yr, 3-yr, and 5-yr maturity securities in each category.

3. Index values as of 12/31/94.

4. All market return data is based on Merrill Lynch taxable bond indices.

TABLE 2. Historical Relative Yield Volatilities of U.S. Treasury
Securities (1974-1994)

Mty.	6Mo.	1Yr	2Yr	3Yr	5Yr	7Yr	10Yr	30Yr*
6Mo.	1.00	0.97	0.87	0.81	0.70	0.63	0.58	0.53
1Yr		1.00	0.90	0.83	0.72	0.65	0.60	0.55
2Yr			1.00	0.92	0.80	0.73	0.67	0.61
3Yr				1.00	0.87	0.79	0.72	0.66
5Yr					1.00	0.91	0.83	0.76
7Yr						1.00	0.92	0.84
10Yr							1.00	0.92
30Yr								1.00

*17 years of yield data available

Observations

- Despite virtually identical levels of credit quality and market liquidity within each portfolio, respective returns were materially different over most of the periods reviewed.
- The range of returns between the best- and worst-performing portfolios exceeded 9 percent or more per annum in all time periods beyond one year for both groups.
- In almost all periods for both groups, the zero-coupon portfolio provided superior returns to either of the coupon-bearing portfolios.
- Off-the-run portfolios provided somewhat less-competitive gross returns compared to zeros. Interestingly, off-the-runs did have the best risk-adjusted returns of the three alternatives.
- The on-the-run portfolio achieved the least attractive performance results in both groups for almost all periods.
- The duration weighted portfolios achieved tighter performance results for all periods versus the equally distributed portfolios.

Conclusion

As identified throughout this report, there are a variety of risks and issues that must be considered when evaluating a laddered portfolio. This investment technique can be a useful approach to solving financial problems. However, like any other alternative investment discipline, there must be an objective in order to measure its success.

The methodology employed in managing a laddered portfolio must be well-studied, consistent, and disciplined. Like any other management style, the investor should identify a measurement standard by which to evaluate the performance of the laddered portfolio. This standard should reflect the risk tolerances as well as the quality and liquidity requirements of the investor.

The performance results presented in our analysis clearly demonstrate the significant return disparities and the higher volatilities that are possible with only minor portfolio adjustments in the securities held or their relative weightings. These results should be considered against the range of performance established by fixed-income managers during the last quarter of 1994. For example, a 9 to 10 percent performance differential would have taken a manager in the Mobius Group's broad fixed-income comparative universe from a first-quartile ranking to a (below median) third-quartile placement. For the discerning investor, these performance differences would be deemed unacceptable and be grounds for a management reevaluation. Unfortunately, in a conventional laddered portfolio, these types of comparisons are uncommon.

Based on our analysis, in normal market environments, the on-the-run laddered portfolios offer little or no comparative advantage versus the zero-coupon and off-the-run portfolios. This is unfortunate, because it has been our experience that most investors tend to favor on-the-run securities when constructing their laddered portfolios. The relative attractiveness of the zero-coupon portfolio is also supported by the inherently lower transaction costs that it offers due to its minimal annual cash flows versus the alternatives.

Overall, given our analysis, it is not clear that a laddered-maturity portfolio management style offers any distinct operational, return, or risk advantages over other investment techniques. Indeed, depending on one's investment objectives, a more active or defensive style could offer more suitable and/or superior returns and risk characteristics.

CHAPTER 12

Yield Curve Risk Management and Asset Allocation*

John D. Wibbelsman, CFA
Portfolio Manager
NYNEX Asset Management Company

Introduction

Over the past few decades a virtual explosion of new fixed-income securities and products have been created for bond investors. During this period much academic literature and research has been written to support and debate the use of individual fixed-income securities. At the same time, much has been overlooked about the role an entire collection of fixed-income securities plays within a *total* portfolio. More research on fixed-income portfolios, rather than on individual fixed-income securities, is needed. This chapter will focus on how a fixed-income portfolio can play a role in the management of a large institutional retirement fund.

At September 30, 1995, the total market value of the 1,000 largest U.S.-based private and public retirement benefit plans exceeded $3.1 trillion dollars. Plan sponsors invested these dollars in four major asset-classes: equity, fixed income, real estate and alternative investments. Approximately 34 percent, or $1.1 trillion, was allocated to fixed-income securities.[1] With such a large commitment to fixed-income securities, the performance of the fixed-income asset class has a major impact on the funds' overall investment results.

*The author would like to thank Bernard Hilscher of NYNEX Asset Management, Gray Smith of Arbor Trading Group, Scott Taylor of Bear Stearns, and Thomas Winters of Ryan Labs for their comments and suggestions on earlier drafts.

1. "1,000 largest funds top $3 trillion," Eighteenth annual survey of 1,000 largest employee benefits plans, p. 1, *Pension & Investments,* January 22, 1996.

To study the performance effect of the fixed-income asset class, the plan sponsor should first analyze the assets that define the investment class. In other words, Why invest in a particular type of fixed-income security in the first place? An assessment of the asset's investment merits, as well as its drawbacks, should be carefully weighed. The investor will then be able to study the behavior of the asset class as a collection of the *entire* portfolio of fixed-income securities. Finally, the plan sponsor can analyze the behavior of the asset class relative to the behavior of all other investable asset-classes.

The analysis will allow the plan sponsor to fully understand how the asset-class exposure affects the total fund. The investor will then be in a good position to maximize the contribution of the fixed-income portfolio exposure to the performance of the *total fund*. The outcome of the analysis leads to the formation of an asset-allocation plan that apportions the fund's total assets on a percentage basis. The overriding goal of the plan is to develop the optimal allocation mix to achieve the fund's investment objectives.

Fixed-Income Securities

Investors have generally invested in fixed-income securities for two key sources of return. The primary return is generated in the form of periodic coupon interest payments and is commonly referred to as current income. The interest component of the security provides a stable cash-flow stream over the life of the security, which produces a stable return over the investment horizon. The next source of return is achieved in the form of potential price appreciation, which produces a capital gain. The opportunity for a fixed-income security to produce a capital gain normally arises when interest rates decline. The two sources of return, when combined, offer attractive investment opportunities for investors, which explains their widespread use in institutional portfolios.

There are numerous risks involved in the purchase of fixed-income securities. By far, the largest risk for fixed-income securities is interest rate risk. Fluctuations in the general level of interest rates cause variability in prices of fixed-income securities prior to their maturities. Because fixed-income prices move inversely with interest rates, an increase in interest rates will produce an interim capital loss prior to the security's maturity. Overall, in historical studies of fixed-income investments, returns and risks demonstrate the potential for solid returns and moderate risk compared to other asset-classes.[2]

---

2. "Investment Dimensions 1926-1995," published by Dimensional Fund Advisors Inc.

One characteristic of any fixed-income security that dramatically affects its return-potential is the issue's term to maturity. The term measures the number of months or years that the borrower pays the periodic coupon interest and the final principal payment at redemption. In addition, the price volatility or interest rate risk of a security is closely linked to its maturity. Securities with longer maturities normally have much larger price volatilities than do shorter-term securities.

U.S. Treasury Market

The most popular type of fixed-income security is the U.S. Treasury security. As such, the largest component of the fixed-income markets is the U.S. Treasury market. Treasury securities are sold to finance the borrowing requirements of the U.S. Federal government. Because U.S. Treasury fixed-income securities are backed by the full faith and credit of the U.S. government, they are perceived to have little or no default risk.

The U.S. Department of the Treasury is responsible for the issuance of Treasury securities, which take the form of bills, notes, and bonds. Bills are generally issued with maturities up to 12 months, while notes have maturities between one and 10 years, and bonds have maturities beyond 10 years, up to 30 years in maturity. The 30-year bond is the longest U.S. Treasury security and is commonly referred to as the *long bond*. The initial issuance of Treasuries in the primary fixed-income market occurs through periodic auctions held by the U.S. Treasury. The auctions are conducted via a competitive bidding process. As of year-end 1995, there were a total of 171 Treasury bill, note, and bond issues outstanding, with a total market value of $2.1 trillion dollars.[3]

The Treasury department is assisted in the primary distribution of its securities by a network of 38 primary government dealers designated by the Federal Reserve. The primary dealers are large buyers of Treasury securities sold at the auctions. The Federal Reserve also expects the dealers to make markets in Treasury securities by buying and selling for their own accounts in the secondary market. Approximately $80 billion in Treasury security trading occurs each business day in the secondary market between primary dealers, interdealer brokers, and institutional investors (Appendix A to this chapter).[4] Primary dealers also have an obligation to assist the Federal Reserve with its open market operations, conducted through a direct Fedwire link to the trading desk of the Federal Reserve Bank of New York.

3. Lehman Brothers Treasury Index, December 31, 1995.
4. GOVPX Quarterly Treasury report, estimate for first half of 1996 average daily trading volume, June 28, 1996.

The Treasury Yield Curve

The most recently auctioned Treasury securities are known as the *currents* or *on-the-run* issues. These are the most liquid fixed-income securities available in the fixed-income markets. Issues from previous auctions that have seasoned are referred to as *off-the-run* securities.

Yields on the current Treasury auction issues are generally recognized as the benchmark yields in the U.S. fixed-income markets. Fixed income participants also use the currents to benchmark yields in the global fixed-income markets. Market participants traditionally plot the yield levels of U.S. Treasury securities versus their specific maturities, which is referred to as the U.S. Treasury yield curve. The primary use of the yield curve is to illustrate the trade-off between differences in yield and differences in terms to maturity of currents.

The most recent list of the current U.S. Treasury auction issues by maturity and their yields as of July 9, 1996, is shown in Table 1.[5]

Figure 1 plots the yield curve of the current auction issues from Table 1.

The graph is an example of an upward-sloping yield curve where investors earn a higher return for investing in longer-term maturity issues. Investors generally require a higher return due to the higher interest rate risk associated with longer-term fixed-income securities; that is, the investor needs to be compensated for accepting the greater interim price variability caused by interest rate changes that are inherent in longer-term securities. Flat and downward-sloping curves are two additional examples of yield curve environments. The most prevalent curve

TABLE 1. U.S. Treasury Yield Curve

Auction issue	Coupon rate[a]	Maturity date	Yield (%)
3-month Treasury bill	n/a	October 10, 1996	5.33%
6-month Treasury bill	n/a	January 9, 1997	5.62%
12-month Treasury bill	n/a	June 26, 1997	5.92%
2-year Treasury note	6.250%	June 30, 1998	6.37%
3-year Treasury note	6.375%	May 15, 1999	6.55%
5-year Treasury note	6.625%	June 30, 2001	6.75%
10-year Treasury note	6.875%	May 15, 2006	6.99%
30-year Treasury bond	6.000%	February 15, 2026	7.13%

a. Treasury bills do not pay an explicit coupon rate. Treasury-bill securities are issued at a discount price to their face or maturity value. Therefore, the yield on the Treasury bill reflects the difference in the purchase price and the final redemption price of the security at maturity.

---

5. Bloomberg system, July 9, 1996.

FIGURE 1.   U.S. Treasury Yield Curve on July 9, 1996

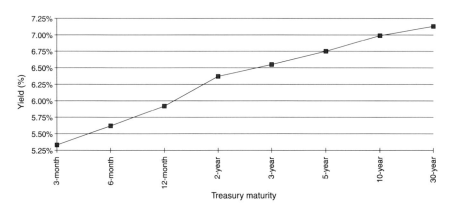

environment is the upward-sloping yield curve. While the yield curve is a useful investment tool, it is only a static snapshot of the shape of Treasury market yields. An investor who is analyzing a number of potential securities across the curve must also consider the shape of the yield curve that will prevail at the end of the expected investment horizon. Thus, the return potential of a security, relative to alternative securities on the curve, will depend on both the beginning and ending shape of the yield curve.

Fixed-Income Rates of Return

We know that investors have traditionally favored fixed-income securities for two key sources of return: the coupon return and the potential for capital gains. A third, and often overlooked source of return, is the reinvestment return. The third return is earned by reinvesting the proceeds of coupon payments at prevailing market interest rates over the investment holding period. The reinvestment return is also known as the interest-on-interest component of a security's return. The third source of return can impact a large portion of a security's total return, especially for longer-term maturities.

Fixed income market participants calculate a return measure referred to as *yield to maturity* (YTM) to quantify the expected return for securities. The measure solves for the return an investor would have to earn, given all of the investment's cash flows, to equate to the current price of the security (Appendix B to this chapter). The YTM of a security is essentially the discount rate on an investment that makes the sum of

the present value of all cash flows equal to the current price of the investment.

The yield to maturity calculation for a fixed-income security quantifies the two key sources of return for the security: interim coupon payments and the final principal redemption at maturity, given today's
market price of the security. The YTM formula also captures the security's
third source of return, the reinvestment return. The formula implicitly
assumes that all future cash-flows (from the security's coupon payments)
will be reinvested at the derived yield to maturity. While this assumption
allows for an elegant solution to the return potential of the security, it is
more convenient than realistic.

A 30-year Treasury bond will have sixty semi-annual coupon payments over its life. It is safe to assume that at each of the sixty payment
dates that the yield on the T-bond will have changed. Thus, a portion of
the realized yield, or return, from the security will depend on yields
available in the marketplace at sixty future dates when coupon payments
must be reinvested at prevailing yields. If, for example, yields consistently fall over the 30-year period of the bond's life, then the realized rate
of return for the security will be much lower than today's yield to maturity. The return will be lower because successive coupon payments will
have been reinvested at lower yields than today's yield to maturity. The
opposite is true for a scenario of rising yields over the 30-year period.[6]
The uncertainty related to changes in yield levels on the coupon dates
means an investor in coupon-paying fixed-income securities assumes
what is known as *reinvestment risk*.

Long-term securities have more coupons to invest than short-term
securities and therefore have substantially more reinvestment risk. Large
fluctuations in reinvestment rates during the investment period can have
a substantial effect on the realized total return for a security. The reinvestment risk inherent in a fixed-income security creates investment uncertainty for an investor over the *entire* investment holding period or
horizon. Prior to 1982, there was no efficient way for the market to over-
come the uncertainty of coupon reinvestment.

Zero-Coupon Securities

One form of fixed-income security that eliminates the exposure to reinvestment risk is a zero-coupon security. By definition, a zero-coupon
security does not pay any periodic coupon payments over the life of the

---

6. The examples do not include the capital gain or loss effect from interest rate changes
over the security's term to maturity.

security. Rather, the security is sold at a discounted price, which is substantially less than its maturity or face value. The return derived from holding the zero-coupon security to maturity is entirely the difference between the discount price and the final redemption price. The benefit to the investor is that the security does not have any inherent reinvestment risk. The expected return measured by the security's yield to maturity will be exactly equal to the realized return, if the security is held to maturity. Therefore, the uncertainty surrounding the reinvestment of coupon interest is eliminated with a zero-coupon security.

In 1982, a number of investment banks were the first to create widely-issued zero-coupon securities for investors. Essentially, the banks structured a series of investment trusts to separate, or unbundle, the principal and interest payments from regular Treasury securities. The banks then sold separate investments in each cash-flow payment as an individual security. For example, the bank would purchase a 30-year Treasury bond and sell a total of 61 separate zero-coupon securities that represented claims on the 60 individual coupon payments and the one final principal payment of the underlying Treasury.

Unfortunately, secondary market trading of zero-coupon securities was very low. Then in 1984 the U.S. Treasury announced it would create a program to easily separate the cash-flow payments from Treasury securities. The Treasury department launched its STRIPS (separate trading of registered interest and principal of securities) program in 1985. Under the program, each new Treasury issue of 10 years and longer duration is allowed to be stripped of its underlying cash-flow payments. Each interest and principal strip created is registered as a separate security and can be traded individually. The sensitivity between strip securities and changes in the level of interest rates is comparable to regular Treasury securities. Prices of strips and interest rates move inversely and the sensitivity of price changes increase for longer-term strips compared to short-term strip securities.

The strips created under the program are issued by the U.S. government as Treasury securities and therefore have no default risk. The Treasury added an additional innovation in 1987 when it announced that it would repackage strips in exchange for the underlying Treasury securities. With the development of its STRIPS program, the U.S. Treasury created a new and very large market for zero-coupon securities. One of the major reasons for the success of the program was the ability of investors to eliminate the reinvestment risk of regular Treasury securities. Secondary trading in strip securities increased dramatically after the program. As of February 1995, there were a total of $216 billion of outstanding principal and interest strips Treasury securities. This represented approximately 27 percent of the total $807 billion of outstanding Treasury notes and bonds eligible for the STRIPS program.[7]

Maturity-Matching and Zero-Coupon Securities

One primary feature of zero-coupon securities that is valuable to investors is the ability to structure maturity-matching investments. Treasury-strip securities are particularly useful in this regard because they allow the investor to precisely match investment payoffs (in the form of redemption proceeds) with future financial obligations. The matching of the investment maturity with the date of future payment-needs also provides certainty to the strip investor because the necessary maturity-proceeds required for the future payments can be determined on the date of the initial investment.

Because there is no reinvestment risk with the zero-coupon strip, the investor can solve directly for the present value of the required future maturity value that will fund the obligation. The present value solution determines precisely how many dollars of investment are needed today to fund the future liability. The discount rate used in the present value formula is the current market yield-to-maturity of the strip security. Held until maturity, the strip's yield to maturity today will equate to the realized return over the life of the strip. In effect, the investment's expected return is locked-in at exactly the required discount rate to fund the future obligation.

For example, assume a parent wishes to invest funds today for college tuition payments in 18 years. The parent could purchase a Treasury-strip security with 18 years remaining to maturity. Held until maturity, the realized return on the strip will be locked-in at today's yield to maturity. Eighteen years later, the proceeds received from the redemption value at maturity may then be used to pay the immediate tuition payments required by the university.

Assume the parent needs $250,000 in 18 years and the current market YTM on an 18-year Treasury-strip security is 7 percent. The parent will then purchase a Treasury strip with $250,000 face value, which will require an investment outlay today of $73,965. In 18 years, the strip can be redeemed for exactly $250,000 to fund the required tuition payments. In this example, the investment's YTM, or expected return, of 7 percent is locked-in at *exactly* the required 7 percent discount rate to fund the future obligation. The process to solve for the required investment today to

---

7. *Ryan Labs Review,* "STRIPS (the First Ten Years) February 1985–February 1995," first quarter 1995.

receive a known future value is called discounting (Appendix C to this chapter).

Because zero-coupon securities have no coupon payments and therefore no reinvestment risk, the YTMs on strips provide investors with a market-determined price for investment discount rates for a variety of maturities. The discount rates effectively price the time value of money. The YTM is the equilibrium discount rate currently demanded by investors and supplied by borrowers for a given term to maturity. Participants may then plot the Treasury-strip-curve discount rates (in similar fashion to the U.S. Treasury market yield curve) over the various available maturities. Since there are no interim coupon payments, the return on a zero-coupon security is purely the difference in the current market price and the final redemption price of the security. The yield-to-maturity measure for strips can therefore be thought of as *pure* term rates.

The discount rates embedded in the Treasury-strip term structure can be used to price or value fixed-income assets and other financial obligations (liabilities) with similar maturities. Because the term structure constantly changes, the price or value of these assets and obligations will also constantly fluctuate. The strip curve provides market participants with discount rates to measure the fluctuation in the present value of assets and liabilities. Changes in the present value over a given period of time allow an investor to measure the growth or decline in the value of assets and liabilities. Thus, the Treasury-strip curve can be used to benchmark asset and liability returns.

Long-Term versus Short-Term Investment Horizons

Many industry pundits refer to the presumption that pension funds should position their investment portfolios for the long term. However, this time horizon is often never defined. The optimal horizon will also be very different for different plans. To make matters even more challenging, the optimal investment horizon for a plan's assets will change over time as a plan matures.

Pension assets are invested over the working life of an active employee and the retirement life when the employee retires from service. Liabilities take the form of current benefit payments for retirees and accrued pension expense for active employees. The pension payment schedule for active employees and retirees is an example of a fixed-income liability. The company creates a liability for the pension fund when it promises the retiree a fixed income over the retirement life of the employee. Generally, a new company with younger employees will not have any current retiree payments and will just accrue pension expenses for its future retirees. Therefore, a young pension plan may indeed have the luxury of investing its assets for the long term. An aggressive investment strategy that is focused on high total returns with the purchase of long-term assets will be appropriate.

However, mature plans with large number of retirees often have very large current liabilities in the form of monthly benefit payments. Also, the plan will usually have large numbers of active employees who will begin to receive retiree benefit payments in the very near term. Mature plans force the sponsor to focus on the short term with at least a percentage of the plan's assets in order to fund benefit payments with cash. This characteristic of a mature plan has profound implications for the development of an appropriate asset-allocation strategy. An aggressive strategy for a mature plan that is focused solely on high-return, long-term assets may *not* be appropriate. Mature plans must determine a strategy that is able to invest over the long term to meet future liabilities and at the same time still be able to raise cash to fund the short-term liability requirements of the plan.

Plan Objectives

A typical plan sponsor must meet the following pension-fund objectives:

1. Pay existing retiree benefit payments
2. Fund active employee retiree benefits
3. Minimize fund expenses, costs, fees, etc.
4. Minimize or eliminate corporate contributions

A subtle, yet very important, conflict exists in the objectives listed above. Many corporations are loathe to take a portion of the firm's operating income to fund corporate contributions to the pension fund (objective #4). As a result, a plan sponsor may often be compelled to invest the fund in assets that offer the highest expected rates of return. Over the long term, the hope is that the assets will outperform the growth of the fund's obligations and generate a surplus for the fund. However, these assets generally require the long term in order to reach their payoff; that is, the investments may not appreciate at all for a number of years. The investments may even decline substantially in the short term. The conflict arises because objective #1 requires the immediate liquidation of the fund's assets to raise cash to meet current liabilities (retiree benefit payments). This conflict creates an inherent mismatch between the objectives of the fund, which may cause the fund to fail to meet its investment objectives.

A plan sponsor that owns only long-term assets may be forced to sell these assets at inopportune levels prior to their expected payoff.

Worse yet, the investment may be liquidated when that particular asset market is declining. In falling markets, the trading costs of inopportune liquidations can be substantial. Generating large trading costs is at odds with objective #3 from Table 2. The dilemma for plan sponsors is how to balance the conflicting objectives of the fund.

Plan Assets Relative to Liabilities

The solution to the conflict between plan objectives is to properly position the fund's assets relative to its liabilities. Each pension fund will be affected by a myriad of factors, which will be unique to that fund. The factors affect both the assets and liabilities of the fund. Specific factors that affect the plan's *assets* include asset-class expectations and realized returns, market conditions, volatility, and correlations, among others. A few factors that affect the fund's *liability* schedule include plan demographics (number and age distribution of current and future retirees), actuarial assumptions, and liquidity needs. Both the factors and their influence on the fund are not static. As the factors constantly change, then so must the positioning of the fund's assets relative to its liabilities.

A necessary requirement to properly position the fund is to be able to value *both* the fund's assets and its liabilities. Once valued, the plan sponsor will then be able to revalue the fund's assets and liabilities at a future periodic date (usually an annual valuation). In this way, the plan sponsor will be able to assess the asset growth (or decline) of the fund relative to the liability growth (or decline) of the fund. Because the liability structure of a fund is based on a series of expected cash-flows, the valuation of liabilities will be very sensitive to changes in the general level of market interest rates. The yield-to-maturity levels of the Treasury-strip curve can serve as useful discount rates to compute the fund's liability growth.

Because the distribution of fund liabilities is normally wide for mature plans, the liabilities can be valued using discount rates from maturities across the entire Treasury-strip curve, in order to match the maturities with the promised benefit-payment dates. The Financial Accounting Standards Board (FASB) that governs corporate pension fund accounting principles has stated that liabilities should be valued using high-quality zero-coupon securities whose maturities coincide with a fund's liability payment dates.[8] The highest-quality zero-coupon securities are U.S. Treasury-strip securities. The returns on strip securities (posi-

---

8. Financial Accounting Standards Board, FAS 87, Pension Liabilities, paragraphs 44 and 199, December 1985.

tive or negative) over a given investment period may also be used as an alternative investment to the fund's *asset* returns (growth or decline). In effect, Treasury-strip returns can be used as a benchmark for both asset and liability growth.

The goal of the valuation of pension liabilities using strip securities is to optimize the asset growth of the fund relative to its liability growth. Therefore, a mature pension plan with large short-term liabilities should fund those liabilities with short-term assets. Investing otherwise will lead to a mismatch between assets and liabilities. For example, if 70 percent of a fund's liabilities are considered long term, then roughly 70 percent of the fund's assets should be invested in long-term assets. The return performance of the long assets can then be compared to the growth of long liabilities. The remainder of the assets will be invested in shorter-term assets to match the short-term liability exposure of the fund. Some investors might disagree and respond by stating that the fund should invest 100 percent of the fund in long-term assets anyway. Such a strategy may not be able to avoid a corporate contribution or a major liquidation of long-term assets prior to their expected payoff levels.

Some would also argue that the fund will not be able to build up a surplus over time if it continuously invests a large portion of its assets in short-term investments to meet large short-term liability payments. However, a fund may actually build a surplus even with large short-term liabilities. The key is to measure the growth of the short-term asset relative to the growth of the short-term liability. A surplus can then be generated when the short-term asset outperforms the short-term liability. The return of the asset is compared to the return (growth) of the liability using the Treasury-strip curve. Properly measured, the short-term assets may still generate a surplus (given the fund's short-term liabilities) and minimize or eliminate the need for a corporate contribution to the fund. The failure to measure short-term liabilities, and therefore to position assets in short-term vehicles, may actually increase the probability of a contribution to meet pension liability payments. If a contribution is untenable, the fund may be forced to liquidate a portion of its long-term assets unexpectedly. The total cost to the fund of an unexpected liquidation of long-term assets will often be substantial.

Pension Fund Asset-Allocation Plan

The plan that summarizes a fund's investments across its asset classes is known as the asset-allocation plan. Normally the plan also describes the fund's strategy for meeting the specific objectives of the fund. Most investors understand that a fund's asset-allocation strategy will be the key determinant of its future rate of return. An oft-cited investment principle is that asset allocation explains 90 percent of a portfolio's rate of return. If true, this suggests that investors should spend close to 90 percent of their time in the pursuit of the optimal asset-allocation strategy.

Common industry practice indicates that plan sponsors spend a very small amount of their time on asset allocation and a relatively large amount of time dedicated to everything else but asset allocation. The mismatch between investment theory and investment practice can lead to unintended consequences that may harm the performance of the overall fund. Such a mismatch between the theoretical importance of asset allocation and actual investment practice creates the potential for *objective shortfall*; that is, an investor may struggle to attain the fund's investment goals and objectives. Not recognizing the mismatch, the investor may be hard-pressed to explain why the fund was not able to meet its objectives. By dedicating more time to the asset-allocation plan an investor may dramatically improve the fund's investment results.

The optimal asset-allocation strategy for a pension fund is the optimal percentage mix of its investable asset-classes that achieves the fund's investment objectives over time. The phrase *over time* suggests that as the plan's investment objectives change, then so must the asset-allocation mix. Therefore, a plan sponsor must take a *dynamic* approach to the management of the fund's asset-allocation plan.

Asset-Mix Drift and Rebalancings

Once an asset-allocation strategy has been developed, it must be implemented. Assume for example, that a plan sponsor chooses the following optimal Asset Mix$_t$ shown in Table 2. Furthermore, assume that one year later the investor has Asset Mix$_{t+1}$.

The differences from the optimal asset-mix occur because of different asset-class performance, cash flows, etc. For example, Asset Mix$_{t+1}$ may have come about because the U.S. equity and venture-capital asset class had returns that were significantly better than U.S. fixed-income, international equity and real-estate asset classes, all else being equal. The mix may have occurred in either a period of positive or negative rates of returns for the asset classes. The differences from the optimal asset-mix are determined by the performance of the asset classes *relative* to each other.

The over- and underweights in Table 2 are evidence of an investment mismatch between the actual asset-class weightings and the optimal asset-allocation strategy. If left uncorrected, the mismatch can lead to unpleasant surprises in the form of a performance mismatch for the fund relative to the plan's objectives.

TABLE 2. Asset-Mix Drift

Asset Class	Asset Mix$_t$ (% of Fund Investment)	Asset Mix$_{t+1}$ (% of Fund Investment)	Difference from Optimal Mix
U.S. Equity	45%	48%	+3%
U.S. Fixed Income	30%	27%	-3%
International Equity	15%	13%	-2%
Real Estate	5%	5%	0%
Venture Capital	5%	7%	+2%
Total	100%	100%	0%

Now assume that at the end of the year$_{t+1}$ the optimal asset-mix required by the strategy is unchanged from the original Asset Mix$_t$ in Table 2. In order to eliminate the asset-mix mismatch, a *rebalancing* of the asset classes should occur. In this case, the overweighted asset-classes are sold to reduce their weights back to their optimal weights. The corollary to this is that the underweighted asset-classes are purchased to increase their weights to optimal levels.

Research has shown that a disciplined approach to the rebalancing process can actually increase a fund's return by 40 to 60 basis points per year versus an asset mix that is allowed to drift. A rebalancing strategy is essentially a mean-reversion strategy. Asset classes that have performed well recently (relative to other asset-classes) are pared back to be reinvested in asset classes that have not done as well. In essence, the rebalancing process sells investments that are high (relative to the other asset-classes) and purchases investments that are low (relative to the other asset-classes). The rebalancing discipline forces the plan sponsor to, in effect, take profits and reinvest the proceeds in asset classes that offer higher expected returns.

An asset-mix strategy that is allowed to drift beyond the optimal strategy can be thought of as a momentum-based strategy. This strategy can be interpreted as an implicit bet by the plan sponsor that asset classes that have performed well recently will continue to do well. There is also an implicit bet that asset classes that have performed poorly will continue to do so. The implicit bets can be removed through the rebalancing process that removes the asset-mix mismatch.

The procedure to rebalancing the fund would be to sell the U.S. equity and venture-capital asset classes equal to 3 percent and 2 percent of the total market value of the fund. At the same time, the sale proceeds would be used to purchase U.S. fixed-income and international equity asset-classes equal to 3 percent and 2 percent of the fund's total market value. The real estate asset-class at an actual 5 percent weighting is exactly on target with its optimal 5 percent weighting and would not be rebalanced. After the rebalancing occurs, the differences from the optimal weights are all removed and the asset mix will be repositioned at the optimal levels required by the asset-allocation plan. Table 3 summarizes the process for rebalancing the fund.

Creation of In-House Plan Asset Managers

In the past decade or so, many plan sponsors have created in-house plan asset managers (INHAMs) to assist in the management of pension funds and other asset-based investment plans. One particularly useful function of an INHAM is to support the implementation of a fund's asset-allocation strategy.

Many plan sponsors still implement their asset-allocation strategy solely with external investment managers hired under contract. Typically the plan sponsor will search for firms that have expertise within a particular asset-class. For example, assume that a plan sponsor's optimal target for the fixed-income asset class is 30 percent. The beginning market value of the total fund is $1 billion. The fund, therefore, will have $300 million to invest in the fixed-income asset class. A portfolio of 10 fixed-income managers will be assembled, each with a unique investment strategy. An equal allocation to each would require a $30 million commitment for each investment manager.

This strategy may pose a number of problems though, especially for a mature pension plan with large monthly benefit payments. The challenge for the plan sponsor is to efficiently keep the optimal fixed-income exposure at 30 percent of the entire fund. However, there are many factors that tend to move the fund's exposure to an asset class away from the target. The further the fund drifts from the target, the greater the potential

TABLE 3

	Asset Mix$_t$	Change in Asset Mix$_{t+1}$	Asset Mix$_{t+1}$	Asset-Mix Rebalancing$_{t+1}$	Asset Mix$_{t+1[r]}$ after Rebalancing
U.S. Equity	45%	+3%	48%	−3%	45%
U.S. Fixed Income	30%	−3%	27%	+3%	30%
Int'l. Equity	15%	−3%	12%	+3%	15%
Real Estate	5%	0%	5%	0%	5%
Venture Capital	5%	+2%	7%	−2%	5%

mismatch between assets and liabilities. Thus, asset-mix drift can greatly affect the probability of objective shortfall.

The total value of the managers' portfolios will not stay static at the optimal 30 percent target for the fixed-income asset class. Why? The answer relates to the returns of the fund and the cash flows required in the management of the overall fund. For example, external managers may be called upon to raise cash in order to provide for benefit payments. The managers may receive additional cash inflows to invest on behalf of the fund. Managers may be fired due to a change in strategy for the asset class, poor performance, or because the investment team leaves their firm. Portfolio market values may fluctuate dramatically due to market conditions. Accordingly, the total value of the asset-class may significantly rise or decline from the 30 percent fixed-income target.

In other words, each external manager normally does not have the luxury to manage money for the fund in isolation from the operations of the total fund. Monthly benefit payments, inflows, manager terminations, and plan rebalancings can all unexpectedly increase or decrease the size of external managers' portfolios. Very large, mature pension plans with substantial monthly pension liability-payments obligations may be required to direct their external managers to undertake a few billion dollars of trading activity each year in order to invest and divest cash for the fund. All of these cash-flow activities reduce the value of the external managers' portfolios by the substantial commission and market-impact costs incurred to meet the cash-flow needs of the fund. Managers with concentrated portfolios and illiquid securities may find the large cash-flow needs of the fund particularly disruptive to the management of their portfolios.

One potential solution to the challenges associated with the cash-flow activity of the fund is to create an INHAM within the fund. The INHAM will be able to help in three specific areas related to the management of the fund: (1) to execute asset-mix rebalancings, (2) to provide for the cash flows required by the fund, and (3) to keep asset-class exposure pure.

The INHAM becomes responsible for centralizing the cash flows into and out of the external managers portfolios and across the entire spectrum of asset classes. In this way, the INHAM is able to optimize fund assets in order to meet the overall liquidity needs of the fund. The internal group creates a portfolio for each asset-class that is then used as a natural liquidity provider to the total fund. The portfolios are used to fund benefit payments and to perform asset-class realignments across the fund. Internal portfolio may especially benefit from the use of derivative positions for these activities. Exposure for an internal portfolio derived via a futures position keeps cash on hand for the fund's liquidity needs and simultaneously gains exposure to a required asset-class.

One main benefit of creating an INHAM to manage internal portfolios is achieved from a large reduction in trading activity (and therefore trading costs) that normally is handled by directives issued to external managers related to the normal cash-flow needs of the fund. The in-house provision of liquidity allows the external manager to focus on investment strategies without the normal disruptions caused by fund cash-flow activity. Internal asset management groups may also avail themselves of quantitative trading techniques in order to reduce trading costs versus external-management trading costs. These techniques may not be available to external managers who tend to trade individual securities.

Cash Positions

An example of the value added that an INHAM can provide a fund is to keep the fund's asset-class exposure pure. For example, most asset-allocation plans have a zero percentage allocation to the cash asset-class. However, mature plans may often have 5 percent or more of their assets in cash. In this case, the plan implicitly overweights the cash asset-class by 5 percent and underweights its optimal asset-mix by 5 percent. Therefore, a large mismatch between the optimal asset-allocation strategy (with 0 percent cash) and the actual asset-mix (with 5 percent cash) can exist.

The mismatch between the optimal and actual strategy can greatly increase the difficulty of achieving the plan's investment objectives. The actual investment results will not match the optimal plan's performance because the optimal asset-allocation strategy has not been strictly implemented. In addition, the plan sponsor may not be able to easily explain or recognize the performance shortfall. In this case, the objective shortfall can be attributed to the plan's actual weighting in cash holdings. The larger the cash positions of the plan, the larger the potential objective shortfall will be over time.

A portion of the cash may stem from the cash holdings of external managers hired by a fund. The managers normally hold a portion of their portfolios in cash vehicles for liquidity purposes. These holdings are often referred to as *frictional cash*. The problem is that if each manager holds 5 percent of the portfolio in cash then the entire asset-class may hold 5 percent less exposure than it should. If each external manager holds a 5 percent cash position for every asset-class, then the entire fund would be overallocated to cash by 5 percent and underallocated to its asset mix by a total of 5 percent. The impure asset-class exposure leads to a mismatch between the actual and optimal allocation. In this case, the mismatch occurs intra asset-class. This is similar to the inter asset-class mismatch that occurs from asset-mix drift.

One solution to reduce or minimize the frictional cash of the fund is to overlay the cash holdings with asset-class exposure via derivatives. For example, the INHAM can receive a summary of all external manager cash positions in the U.S. fixed-income asset class, as well as cash that is held to pay benefit payments. Assume that the cash represents 5 percent of the total fixed-income asset-class market value. Under this scenario, an internal portfolio can overlay the external cash with fixed-income futures contracts to increase the fund's asset-class exposure by 5 percent to its optimal target allocation. As managers reduce their cash position, the internal derivatives portfolio will reduce its exposure to fixed futures contracts. If managers increase their cash positions, the internal portfolio will increase its futures exposure proportionately. While short term by design, the futures positions can be continually rolled from expiring contracts into future-maturity contracts in order to keep continuous overlay exposure to the fixed-income asset class.

While there is no broad-market futures contract (like the S&P 500 futures contract) for the fixed-income asset class, a basket of individual futures contracts can be purchased to create the required fixed-income exposure. For example, the investor may purchase a mix of Eurodollar and two, five, 10, and 30-year Treasury futures contracts as a proxy for broad fixed-income market exposure across the entire maturity spectrum of the Treasury yield curve. The economics of the cash returns added to the returns of the basket of futures, over time, will equate to the expected return for the fixed-income asset class. The effect is to reposition the asset-class exposure to the optimal target allocation. The derivatives position provides some unique advantages to the fund that other investment vehicles may not offer. Through the use of futures, the plan gains the flexibility to meet cash payouts and to eliminate frictional cash, while keeping the optimal asset-allocation plan intact. This approach can reduce or eliminate the mismatch between the optimal asset-allocation strategy and the actual strategy that holds large cash positions. The outcome is an actual asset-allocation strategy that mirrors the optimal strategy. The actual performance of the fixed-income asset class that is executed will then match the performance of the optimal strategy. The benefit is a reduction in the potential for objective shortfall.

The Fixed-Income Asset Class

Over the last few decades the fixed-income market has become very large and well-diversified. The entire market is really a set of thousands of individual fixed-income securities. A fixed-income investor has an almost overwhelming choice of securities with unique features and characteristics. The challenge for the fixed-income investor is to understand how these securities behave, both individually and together as a total fixed portfolio. Investors need to understand how the return and risks of the fixed-income portfolio will affect the overall performance of the fund. In addition, investors should analyze how the fixed-income asset class performs relative to other asset-classes. A correlation study of a fund's asset classes can provide valuable information to optimize the size of each asset-class allocation. For the fixed-income asset class, one important question to consider is, "How does the fixed-income asset class perform when other asset-classes are not performing well?" If the correlation with other classes is low or negative, then the fixed-income class may be favored when other asset markets are not performing well. Finally, investors need to be able to measure the performance of the fixed-income asset class as a whole, as well as the entire fixed-income market. Until about 20 years ago, there were no convenient measures of performance for the fixed-income market.

As a response to investor needs, a few of the largest Wall Street investment houses created investment indexes to gauge the performance of the fixed-income market. Over the years, these indexes have been widely adopted by investors as proxies for the performance of the fixed-income asset class. A few of the most widely used series include indexes calculated by Lehman Brothers, Merrill Lynch, and Salomon Brothers. Correlation statistics that compare these indexes are very high, which indicates that the return behavior of the indexes are very similar. Subcomponents of the indexes are also computed to derive performance and characteristics for different subsets and sectors of the main indexes.

Plan sponsors use the historical performance of the bond indexes to guide the development of *expected* performance measures for the fixed-income asset class. Characteristics of an index such as returns, volatility and its correlation with other asset-classes may then be used as model inputs for asset-allocation-strategy decisions. Once the strategy is implemented, the actual performance of the fixed-income asset class, as well as the bond index, can then be used as feedback versus the initial, expected performance of the asset class.

The performance benchmark for a fixed-income portfolio will generally be one of the popular bond-index series. A decision as to what type of index to use will be necessary for the plan sponsor. Should the benchmark be based on a U.S. Treasury index? What about a government index that includes agency securities? The investor could also choose a government/corporate index or even an aggregate index that includes governments, corporates, and mortgage securities.

One research study documented how a government index could be replicated by purchasing an equal-weighted portfolio of the current on-the-run U.S. Treasury auction issues. Using monthly rates of return, the correlation between the equal-weighted Treasury portfolio and the Lehman Brothers Government/Corporate Index was .987 over the 1980–1988 period.[9] A portfolio that more closely aligns its maturity-sector weightings versus the government-index weightings can produce even better replication results. Another interpretation of the high correlation is that over 95 percent of the total return variation of a bond index may be explained by the return variation of the U.S. Treasury yield curve.

This finding suggests that an investor may not need to construct a portfolio that owns thousands of bonds, such as the popular indexes, in order to gain broad fixed-income exposure. Rather, investors may build a portfolio of efficient, liquid Treasury securities across the yield curve in order to replicate the required benchmark index. The investor should focus on the factors and characteristics of the benchmark, such as the interest rate risk embedded in the index that can then be replicated using the Treasury yield curve. Just as the Treasury-strip curve can be used as a benchmark of the fund's asset and liability growth, the Treasury yield curve can be used as a proxy for the performance of the fixed-income asset class, bond indexes, and the U.S. Treasury market. The ability of a well-structured index portfolio to track the performance and behavior of the designated bond index means that there will be virtually no mismatch between the plan's fixed-income asset-class benchmark and the actual performance of the internal portfolio. Decisions about active strategies used to potentially add value above a benchmark return may also be considered.

Strategy Implementation for the External Fixed-Income Portfolio

Suppose the pension manager chooses the asset-class percentages under Asset Mix$_t$ in Table 2. In this case, 30 percent of the fund, or $300 million of the $1 billion, is allocated to the fixed-income asset class. Assume in this case that the plan sponsor divided the allocation evenly, so that 10 external managers would each receive 3 percent of the total fund or $30

9. Frank K. Reilly, G. Wenchi Kao, and David J. Wright, "Alternative Bond Market Indices," *Financial Analysts Journal*, May-June 1992.

million in initial funding. The plan sponsor would then periodically meet with the investment firms to review their individual performance records.

Over time, managers that did not perform well would be fired and replaced with new managers. One of the drawbacks to this approach is that plan sponsors spend most of their time arranging meetings and discussing individual fixed-income portfolios. Rarely does the plan sponsor focus on that particular fixed-income portfolio's affect on the entire fixed-income asset class. In addition, the plan sponsor should analyze the effect that the entire fixed-income asset class is having on the performance of the overall fund.

The return of the fixed-income portfolio as a whole is affected by the returns of the individual investment managers and their percentage weights in the fixed-income asset class. In our example, we assumed that each manager's percentage weight was equal to 3 percent of the fund's total assets. Therefore, one manager would have a 10 percent (30 percent/3 percent) effect on the performance of the total fixed-income asset class, while two managers would have a 20 percent effect on the performance.

Now, however, assume an *unequal* allocation scheme where two fixed managers each received a 9 percent allocation and the other eight managers received a 1.5 percent allocation. The performance of the two large managers now becomes much more important to the fixed-income asset class as a whole. In the latter example, the two large managers affect 60 percent [(9% + 9%)/30%] of the performance of the total fixed-income asset class, versus 20 percent in the former case. If the top-two managers outperformed their eight peers, this would have a significantly positive effect on the performance of the fixed-income asset class as a whole and vice versa if the two managers underperformed their peers. The risk of underperformance from an unequal allocation scheme may lead to the potential for objective shortfall.

Unfortunately, plan sponsors do tend to let their *intra* asset-class allocations (to their investment managers) drift over time. Managers who have done well recently tend to receive new cash inflows, or they are asked less frequently for cash calls (e.g., to fund benefit payments). If the larger managers in an asset class later underperform, the plan sponsor may unexpectedly need to reallocate portfolio assets. Through an INHAM, the plan sponsor can create a periodic discipline to reallocate assets across managers in order to minimize the potential for performance shortfall. Planned, as opposed to unexpected liquidations, can minimize trading and administrative costs associated with the asset reallocation.

Conclusion

Investors need to understand the effect that a fixed-income portfolio can have on the performance of a pension fund with multiple asset-classes. The U.S. Treasury market and yield curve can provide valuable information to investors in order to help in the analysis of the fund's fixed-income asset class. The U.S. Treasury-strip curve can be used to value a fund's financial assets and liabilities and, therefore, to benchmark the performance of the fund. By properly valuing the fund's liabilities, the plan sponsor can avoid the potential for objective shortfall. Thus, the plan sponsor can position the fund's assets to maximize the probability of achieving all of the fund's objectives.

Because the asset-allocation mix will affect most of the fund's performance, plan sponsors should spend a majority of their time on the development and maintenance of the optimal asset-allocation strategy. INHAMs may be used to assist the plan sponsor in the execution of the asset-allocation strategy. Finally, the U.S. Treasury market can serve as an excellent proxy or benchmark for the measurement of the fixed-income asset class and the popular bond indexes. The basis for the development of the optimal fixed-income asset-class strategy that will contribute to the optimal asset-allocation strategy for a plan sponsor will, indeed, be the U.S. Treasury yield curve. A more advanced approach can utilize the U.S. Treasury yield curve and the U.S. Treasury-strip curve.

APPENDIX A
List of 38 Primary Dealers and Five Interdealer Brokers[10]

Primary Dealers

Aubrey G. Lanston & Co., Inc.
Barclays de Zoete Wedd Securities Incorporated
BA Securities, Inc.
Bear, Stearns & Co., Inc.
BT Securities Corporation
Chase Securities, Inc.
CIBC Wood Gundy Securities Corp.
Citicorp Securities, Inc.
CS First Boston
Daiwa Securities America, Inc.
Dean Witter Reynolds
Deutsche Morgan Grenfell
Dillon, Read & Co., Inc.
Donaldson, Lufkin & Jenrette Securities Corporation
Eastbridge Capital, Inc.
First Chicago Capital Markets, Inc.
Fuji Securities, Inc.
Goldman, Sachs & Co.
Greenwich Capital Markets, Inc.
HSBC Securities, Inc.
J.P. Morgan Securities, Inc.
Lehman Government Securities, Inc.
Liberty Brokerage, Inc.
Merrill Lynch Government Securities, Inc.
Morgan Stanley & Co. Inc.
Nations Banc Capital Markets, Inc.
Nesbitt Burns Securities, Inc.
Nikko Securities Co. International, Inc.
Nomura Securities International, Inc.
PaineWebber, Inc.
Prudential Securities, Inc.
Salomon Brothers, Inc.
Sanwa Securities (USA) Co., L.P.
SBC Capital Markets, Inc.

---

10. *1996 Committee and Staff Directory, Public Securities Association,* The Bond Market Trade Association, May 1996.

Smith Barney, Inc.
UBS Securities, Inc.
Yamaichi International (America), Inc.
Zions First National Bank

Interdealer Brokers

Cantor Fitzgerald Securities
Euro Brokers Maxcor, Inc.
EXCO RMJ Securities Corp.
Garban, L.L.C.
Hillard Farber & Co., Inc.
Liberty Brokerage, Inc.
Tullett and Tokyo Securities, Inc.

APPENDIX B
Yield-to-Maturity Formula for a
Fixed-Income Security[11]

The general formula for the YTM for a bond paying interest semiannually
is

$$P = \sum_{t=1}^{2n} \frac{C/2}{\left(1+\frac{r}{2}\right)^t} + \frac{R}{\left(1+\frac{r}{2}\right)^{2n}}$$

where

P = price of the bond
n = number of years to maturity
C = annual dollar coupon interest
r = yield to maturity
R = redemption value of bond at maturity

---

11. "Bond Yield Measures and Price Volatility Properties," Frank J. Fabozzi, p. 64, *The Handbook of Fixed Income Securities*, 2nd ed., Frank J. Fabozzi, ed. Dow Jones-Irwin, 1987.

APPENDIX C
Formula for the Computation of Present Value[12]

$$PV = FV/(1+r)^n,$$

where

PV $=$ present value
FV $=$ future value
r $\quad=$ discount rate
n $\quad=$ number of periods

12. "Bond Yield Measures and Price Volatility Properties," Frank J. Fabozzi, p. 58, *The Handbook of Fixed Income Securities,* 2nd ed., Frank J. Fabozzi, ed. Dow Jones-Irwin, 1987.

INDEX